PACKTRAINS
& AIRPLANES

I dedicate these memoirs to all the people and other animals who gave me the greatest pleasures, and the deepest sorrows.

PACKTRAINS & AIRPLANES
MEMORIES OF LONESOME LAKE

Trudy Turner

ISBN 978-0-88839-710-2

Library and Archives Canada Cataloguing in Publication

Turner, Trudy, 1929-
    Packtrains & airplanes : memories of Lonesome Lake / Trudy Turner.

    Issued also in electronic format.
    ISBN 978-0-88839-710-2

    1. Turner, Trudy, 1929–. 2. Frontier and pioneer life—British Columbia—Lonesome Lake Region. 3. Lonesome Lake Region (B.C.)—Biography.
I. Title. II. Title: Packtrains and airplanes.

FC3845.L66Z49 2011   971.1'82   C2011-901489-0

Printed in South Korea — PACOM

Editor: Theresa Laviolette
Production: Mia Hancock, Ingrid Luters
Cover Design: Ingrid Luters
All photos by author unless otherwise noted.

We acknowledge the financial support of the Government of Canada through the Canada Book Fund for our publishing activities.

Published simultaneously in Canada and the United States by
HANCOCK HOUSE PUBLISHERS LTD.
19313 Zero Avenue, Surrey, BC Canada V3S 9R9
1431 Harrison Avenue, Blaine, WA, USA 98230-5005
(604) 538-1114 Fax (604) 538-2262

www.hancockhouse.com I sales@hancockhouse.com

contents

My lovely, gentle Breezie Future.
Photo: Hans Granander

acknowledgements

I want to thank my daughter, Susan, for all the time and effort she put into organizing, suggesting changes and corrections in this book, and my late husband, Jack, for being the family photographer. I must also thank my son-in-law Tom, for his technical expertise, and both Tom and Susan for thrusting me into the high tech world of computers, which was an enormous help in preparing my manuscript.

And last, but not least, my editor, Theresa Laviolette, for her patient help and suggestions as she edited my manuscript.

Without all their help this book would never have gotten off the ground.

how this book came to be

This book got its start in life as a result of a somewhat inaccurate story in a magazine. There were several exaggerations and distortions, which I tried to correct when the magazine asked us for some pictures to go with a story they wanted to print. I pointed out in a short story of my own where they didn't have the facts quite right. They didn't use it.

That made me so annoyed that it lit a fire under my dormant desire to write, and set me on the road to another book, just to correct the record of where I lived for 60 years and record the history of Lonesome Lake for my descendants.

Once I began writing, and remembering my life, the story took on a life of its own and I ran with it as I scribbled frantically and hoped not to get run over.

If my story seems a bit disjointed in places that is because I intended it to read somewhat like my visitors ask, and I answer, questions about my life at Lonesome Lake. Those questions and answers would often remind me of other incidents, perhaps many years before. So I would go off on side trips, before returning to the original question.

introduction

I believe the oldest surviving memory I have of my life at Lonesome Lake is of the fire that turned my parents' beautiful home into a pile of ashes as Mother carried her six-month-old daughter across the creek, and my brother waded beside her, to escape the roaring flames.

I may not remember that incident directly, but carry a mental picture that formed in my memory from the shock and distress the older members of my family must have felt and expressed as they struggled to accept the reality of their loss. With winter only a few weeks away, and having lost everything, I imagine they would have discussed the devastating destruction of their home many times. The loss of their home was bad enough, but they must have been eternally thankful none of them was hurt and their horse was safe.

This story is the history of two pioneering families who developed their preemptions in the Lonesome Lake area in southwest BC. It covers over three-quarters of a century, starting in 1912.

Clearing land and growing crops with horses for power to help us went on for many years. What horses couldn't do, we did with hand tools, double-bitted axe, crosscut saw, peavey, mattocks, and the lighter carpentry tools, and determination.

Eventually, with money from many squirrel skins, I bought a two-and-a-half-horsepower outboard motor in 1947. That was the first motorized machine to come to Lonesome Lake, but not the last. Following close on its heels came an airplane in 1953. Then in 1956 a chainsaw followed, along with my husband-to-be.

prologue

When my brothers and I were growing up in our home in the remote wilderness of Lonesome Lake, airplanes and flying was a favorite topic for family discussion. We kids built and flew model planes. We flew them from high in a fir tree. Some crashed, but a few flew for some distance, then landed in the field, unbroken. In time, play would become reality. At age 24 I made my way to Vancouver Airport where I learned to fly. I bought a two-place Taylorcraft floatplane.

Flying it home to Lonesome Lake the first time, I made several mistakes. The worst one was when I missed finding Stewart Island where I wanted to get gas and innocently landed a couple of miles north of Stewart Island. There I finally looked at my map more carefully and discovered my mistake. As I thought I was only a short way from where I should have been, I elected to taxi to the correct place.

Tho I had made many approaches to the seaplane dock in the Fraser River in Vancouver, I was not prepared for the tidal current at Stewart Island. The instant I cut my power the plane began backing away from the float. As I had a full load in the passenger seat, I had to crawl across on the spreader bar to swing my propeller from the right side. When the engine started I would have to crawl back under the belly of the plane on that narrow spreader bar and then get in the plane to take control of it. In the meantime, the plane went about as it pleased. At the rate I was drifting I did not want to do that, so I paddled franticly, losing ground, or water, by the second.

In real trouble, I was mighty glad, and thankful, to see a boat come out to rescue me and tow me back to the float.

Gassed up and on my way once more, I do not believe I dared to think about how wonderful it was going to be to have an airplane actually sitting on Lonesome Lake, bringing to conclusion all our hopes and dreams for so many years. To do so could have jinxed the whole thing. I just went along quietly and tried not to draw attention to myself, and the airplane, at least not until I was home and "they" could not interfere.

Am I superstitious? I usually do not consider something good will happen until it has happened. This way of looking at life reduces the disappointment if it doesn't happen.

I flew that tiny airplane for only three or four years, but in that brief time I developed a feeling very close to love for her. After all, I put my life in her wings every time she lifted me sweetly into the air.

With CF-HEO at Lonesome Lake the trumpeter swans no longer were the largest things flying over the valley and landing on the lake. The swans' wings spanned seven feet. My wings were over five times longer, at 38 feet, wingtip to wingtip. And I could fly faster. But for grace and musical ability, they beat me wings down.

chapter 1

LONESOME LAKE

Lonesome Lake, one of six, lies in the beautiful and gentle Atnarko Valley, about 60 miles inland from Bella Coola in Southwestern British Columbia. It is the second largest on that river system. Lonesome Lake is at 1600 feet above sea level. I believe it is the deepest in the system. Charlotte Lake in the Chilcotin, at 2800 feet, is the largest of the six.

My father got his first glimpse of this beautiful six-mile-long S-shaped lake when he was on a hike into the area with a trapper in October 1912. Dad had come to Bella Coola, then traveled up the valley, passing some settlements and farms on his way. He was looking for a lake and unsettled land where he might be able to build a home and farm.

Arriving at Stillwater, he met Frank Ratcliff, later to become my uncle. He had settled at the north end of the Stillwater. Uncle Frank invited Dad in for a chat and coffee. During the visit Uncle Frank learned what Dad was looking for. Knowing about the S-shaped lake, he suggested they go take a look. Uncle Frank wanted to make a trip to that area anyway and see Hunlen Falls on the way to Turner Lake.

Turner Lake and six others lie along the length of a hanging valley 2000 feet above Lonesome Lake, parallel to and west of it. The water from those lakes creates Hunlen Falls at the outlet of Turner Lake.

Hunlen Creek begins its life in a rock-shouldered, ice-decorated valley with a two-mile-long ant-shaped lake lying between the sloping walls. On its way the tiny river meanders across extensive meadows to flow gently into Ant Lake. Leaving the lake peacefully, it soon churns down a steep crooked path to flow into another lake about 500 feet lower. After passing thru five more lakes, it glides smoothly over a rock lip to fall 1325 feet to disintegrate in a rock-bound pool in a froth of spray and jumping waves that cascade up the walls hundreds of feet, only to fall back into the pool again, accompanied by a thunderous roar that seems almost to make the rocks tremble, as a wet mist rises out of the canyon. Boiling out of the pool, it crashes and foams its way down several channels that cross the mile-and-a-half-wide delta, to lose itself in the Atnarko River, losing about 700 feet more on the way, as well as its identity.

Clambering up to where the Turner Lake chain lies, Uncle Frank and Dad admired the falls from the top of the a quarter-mile-deep chasm where the creek heads for the Atnarko River far below. They continued on the west side of Turner Lake and built a raft, of pine logs. It barely carried them to the other side. They continued east across the flat towards the edge of the Atnarko Valley where lay Lonesome Lake, named later by Dad.

As there was no trail down the mountain that disappeared practically beneath their feet, they scrambled straight down. Soon they found themselves in an area of bluffs and canyons, later to be called Hell Canyon Creek.

Safely down, they arrived on the shore of one-mile-long Big Lagoon at the head of Lonesome Lake. There they made camp. Ducks and geese flying over disturbed their slumbers most of the night, I recall them saying. In the morning they crossed the river and had a good look at the land on the east side. Liking what he saw there, Dad staked it, and then he and Uncle Frank returned to Stillwater.

Dad applied for a preemption in 1912. On receiving it, he and Uncle Frank returned to Lonesome Lake in January 1913 with about 600 pounds of supplies. At the north end of Lonesome Lake they built a sled to convey the freight across the lake on the ice.

They built a 10- by 12-foot log cabin near the south edge of the preemption. I believe it took them just three days. They didn't peel the logs in the walls, and the roof was almost flat, no ridge. A fireplace and smoke-hole served for a stove for heat and cooking. A bough bed on the floor and a drop table completed the furniture. Rather minimal, but adequate.

With a snug building for shelter, Dad began preparing materials for a real house. Some of the time his brother, Uncle Earle, helped. Trees had to be cut down, branches removed, and the bark peeled off, then sawed to length. No chain-saws then. Most of the trees would have been second growth cedars. On some areas of the preemption there should have been some pretty good stands of young cedars and firs, a forest fire having roared thru the valley 50 or 60 years earlier.

Dad's first building.

With no horses at Lonesome Lake to haul the logs to his house site, he built a track to that area from where they were and moved them on that. One of those young stands must have stood near where he built the cabin, judging from the small stumps still standing all about the building many years later.

Dad built his house close to a good creek, on level land six feet higher than the stream, called Homecreek. It was a nice, neat three-room building with a cellar under the floor to store fresh vegetables and canned food.

With his house built, Dad worked at clearing land for garden and field. As there was a fair acreage of good land growing alders, gooseberries, birches, red osier dogwood (red willow), and devil's club, he could get garden land and fields fairly fast. He soon had

15

crops growing among the stumps. They could come out later and a lot easier after a few years to decay.

He built fences to keep out bears, but they didn't pay much more attention to rail fences than they did to logjams on the river. What bears cannot crawl thru, they climb over. Returning from down the valley for mail, Dad sometimes found some of his produce had been harvested and eaten.

In 1917 Dad, having been turned down by the Canadian Army, crossed the border and joined the US Army. He wanted to be a pilot but was refused because of insufficient education. He joined the Signal Corps instead.

On his return to Lonesome Lake at the end of World War I, he picked up where he had left off in his farm development. He had planted quite a few apple trees, but with no one there to look after them, some had died over the winters. The cleared areas he had seeded were doing well anyway, with timothy growing six feet high.

For a while Dad was going to Firvale for his mail and staying overnight with the Hober family. On one of his trips down there he took notice of one of the daughters, Ethel. He invited her and her mother to come to Lonesome Lake. Accepting the invitation, they hiked with the young bachelor to his home. Ethel liked the place very much from the first time she saw it. Her mother encouraged her, telling her it was her duty to marry Dad and try to bring him back into the Seventh Day Adventist church. Grandma Hober thought he was sort of slipping away, out there by himself; and as history was to show, he continued to slip as the years passed, and took Mother with him.

While Mother and Grandma Hober were at Lonesome Lake they began to clean up the young bachelor's house, including soaking and washing the bowl he mixed his flap-jack batter in. That bowl had a thick crust of dried dough stuck to the inside of it. They soaked it and scrubbed until they had the old crusted dough all off and the bowl was nice and shiny, like a new bowl again. But now it leaked! This just goes to show people shouldn't get mixed up in things they don't understand. When they found out why the dough was dried on the bowl they must have felt rather embarrassed.

Either before or after this incident, it was Dad's turn to be embarrassed. He had made the arduous trip 30-odd miles to Firvale not only to get his mail, but also to see Ethel. When he arrived at the house only she was there. Dad asked where everybody was. On being told they were all out at the barn, milking, he rushed out there leaving Ethel alone in the house, missing completely the reason they were all out and Mother was in—so she and he could visit alone.

On one trip out for mail Dad had his horse, Dan, with him loaded with furs. Somewhere along the way a brown object came hurtling onto the trail too close for comfort. Dan, eyes bugged, reversed and raced away. Dad jumped into the jungle onto a big log lying over the swampy ground. He ran along the log, jumped off and lay down in the mud right against it. Seconds later a bruin came galloping along on the log, stepped down the same place Dad had and fled into the distance.

A short time later Dad slowly raised up, looked around, and listened. As nothing disturbed the peace and quiet of the day, he returned to the trail to look for Dan. He had gone only a short way, when who should he meet but Dan, looking for him, his pack still in place. Only his lead rope showed a bit of extra wear from having been trod on a few times on the rocky trail. Dad and Dan continued on to the Hober place.

Sitting resting in the parlor, Dad was telling the bear story when one of the Hobers looked down at Dad's leg and remarked something to the effect that there was a perfect bear track on his pant leg. Dad had just told them how he had felt the bear step on him on its way off the log.

Dad and Mother were married in 1923 in the Hober house. Mother was 19; Dad was 32. They lost no time and hurried back to Lonesome Lake to begin married life in Dad's log house.

In 1929 everything was running smoothly at the Edwards home. The family of two boys and one girl was complete. The cellar was filled for the winter; the barn was full of hay. There were only a few more spuds to harvest.

Then disaster.

The worst disaster to hit any of us who lived at Lonesome Lake happened that fall. Dad was working down in one of the fields. Johnny was sick in bed in the kitchen. I was in a crib, as I was only six months old. Stanley, the eldest, was playing outside. Ginty was tied on a long rope attached to a stump so he could graze near the house.

Johnny had asked Mother to move a curtain so he could watch her working about the kitchen. Then she took something down into the cellar. While she was down there admiring her jars and more jars of canned supplies for the coming winter, she became aware of a crackling noise. Alerted, she looked up the stairs. Shock sent her flying up those stairs into her beautiful kitchen. Flames raced up the wall! She snatched up a pail of water and flung it into the flames, not even causing them to pause. She grabbed her children and raced out the door, snatching the cashbox on the way. There was not a smidgen of hope she could save the house. She yelled to Stanley to go get Dad.

By the time Dad arrived it wasn't safe to be anywhere near the raging inferno. Ammunition stored in the house was going off, adding to the crackling and roaring of the greedy monster as it destroyed their beautiful home.

Ginty, terrified by all the noise, raced to the end of his tether, pulled the stump loose and galloped away, so then he was pursued by his anchor as well as the uproar of the burning building. The poor old horse never forgot that brief interval of terror, and for the rest of his life he was gun shy.

I believe it made an impression on me also. I do not trust fire. A nice gentle fire behaving itself in the stove makes me want to turn it down if it so much as makes the tiniest sound of getting out of control.

I seem to retain a picture in my memory of being carried across the creek in Mother's arms, as Johnny followed her. Many years later my brother told me that did happen. I do not have any memory of being carried in anyone's arms on any other occasion. Six months since birth seems pretty young for anyone to remember anything, but perhaps I could.

After the fire all five of us had to spend the winter in the tiny cabin Dad and Uncle Frank built. Thank God we had it.

Some time after the fire destroyed the house, the family began digging into the ashes to see if anything had survived that could be repaired or re-tempered. They found quite a few tools that Dad was able to re-temper to make usable again, tho not as good as new. One of those tools was a square. My husband, Jack, and I used it for a few years, but the burning had smudged the numbers so badly it was difficult to read. Dad had given me the burned one when I started my own place. It certainly was better than nothing, but eventually we bought a new one.

It is sometimes said that disasters come in threes. The second one came about two months after the fire, on a trap-tending trip to the Elbow Lake area.

As the snow was getting deep, Dad decided to bring in the small herd of several cows and a bull. He caught a gentle heifer and started off. The others—including Bruce, the six-year-old Holstein bull—followed, except for one cow and her calf. That cow was crazy and never got tame and she refused to follow, instead running off into the brush with her calf.

Not wanting to leave her out all winter, he tried to catch the bull and tie him up so he couldn't assault the tied-up cow, while Dad tried to drive the wild cow back to the herd. However, Dad could not catch Bruce unless he set his rifle down well away from the bull. The bull was scared of sticks. He set it down under a leaning tree, to keep it out of the snow. Armed only with one end of the heifer's long rope, he approached Bruce from the other side of the heifer and flipped the rope over his horns.

Instantly, the bull lunged, knocking the heifer into Dad and flinging him onto his back in the churned up snow. In a second he was on Dad's chest with his heavy head, grinding him down in the snow. With only the bull's eyelid in Dad's sight, he bit down hard.

Dad and the angry bull.

Shocked, Bruce pulled back, giving Dad a chance to bring his feet up to begin kicking the bull's face. That allowed the bull to start tossing Dad about, slamming him into trees, and getting one horn tangled in one of Dad's pack straps, then the other.

When Dad was flung against one tree he grabbed onto it and quickly slipped out of the other strap. Bruce, now blindfolded by some frozen martens keeping the sack spread over his eyes, and thinking he still held Dad on his horns, went off fighting and pummeling the pack. Dad quickly, or as quickly as he could, went and got his rifle and cured that poor bull's blindness.

Those frozen martens very likely saved Dad's life.

I believe Dad left the wild cow and her calf and went straight back to his cabin that night. The next day he made it home, as far as I can remember.

Soon after he got home to our little cabin, Mother asked him something about the bull and Dad said he had died of fatty degeneration of the heart. Even with all his injuries he still could joke. Actually, the real cause of death was lead poisoning.

I can't remember if Dad went back for the crazy cow and her calf, but he did not succeed in bringing them home. In the spring when he put his cattle back up there he did find the calf, alone. He was not terribly thin, but the cow must have starved from feeding the calf.

I hope I have remembered this story more or less accurately. I certainly heard it enough times as I was growing up.

We had to wait a few years for the third disaster. The mashing he'd received from that nasty-natured Holstein devil was to lay Dad up for a long time for any kind of hard work. Since he had already built part of a 10- by 20-foot henhouse, and had logs cut to finish it, he did so, hoping someday to build a larger house. So, we moved out of the tiny cabin and into the slightly bigger henhouse. He never did enlarge the house until after the kids had all left home and chainsaws had arrived at Lonesome Lake.

In the meantime, since there just was not room in that small henhouse for all five of us to sleep; some of us were sleeping in various outbuildings. Johnny had chosen the hay barn. I clearly remember when it fell down in the night. There was already a lot of snow on the ground when daylight drifted away, absorbed by the heavy, dense snowflakes that continued to fall. The air was filled with them.

When it came time for Johnny to go to bed, one glance out the window where the light shone on the snow showed there was a lot more than there had been at dusk. Johnny didn't want to go out there and plow thru that deep snow a hundred feet to the barn. He asked Mother if he could stay in the house. Yes, he could.

In the morning we all saw why he hadn't wanted to go to the barn. It was flat! We were shocked. My brother was surely one lucky kid. Or was it just luck? Johnny's request illustrates my belief that often we use a practical reason to justify an emotional or intuitive desire.

I was not grown up enough to be of much help rebuilding the barn, but I could help with the job of working the hay out from under the collapsed roof to feed the stock. We didn't want to remove the flattened roof sections, as then there would be no cover over the hay at all. The two sides of the roof came straight down, one resting on top of the other with a short overlap in the middle. The two eave edges had pushed out-wards as the heavily laden unsupported center came down.

When Dad rebuilt the barn, he designed the new one with a ridgepole on which the rafters rested and were nailed. The lower ends were nailed on the plates. And he put in a purline plate, supported by a long, strong post in the center of each slope of the roof. The barn was 30 feet square, and 30 feet to the ridge. This allowed enough height for a pulley-and-rope system to be installed. Then the team could sling the hay off the wagon and into the haymow. That saved much hand labor and time. Without that system, we had to pitch all the hay into the barn while the horses stood around sleeping. The team re-hitched to the wagon, we could soon be back out in the field to pick up another load.

That rebuilt roof supported many loads of snow over the nearly 70 years it stood there, until the devastating forest fire of June and July 2004 destroyed it.

The job of milking was usually Mother's, with us kids helping by bringing in the cows from their pasture twice a day. I had begged to help with milking for several years before they let me sit down and squeeze a few drops of milk out of a cow. But they were right. Getting a decent stream of milk into the pail did require some hand strength, but a lot more technique, which had to be learned. That took a bit of time. And when the poor cow became irritated by my inept fumbling and gave me a gentle push with her mighty hind leg, I would feel she didn't like me and was hurt emotionally, because she was my pet and I loved her. I didn't understand. There was a whole lot I didn't understand about cows, calves and horses in those far-off days. I like to believe I have a lot more understanding and sympathy for them now. Now when it is too late; too late for them anyway.

I remember Mother telling us about how one time when she and

Dad went out to find a cow way down on the meadows on the head of the lake. As Maybelle was several inches deep in water, they just ran the canoe under the cow and milked her there. I wonder now what they would have done had she planted one of her big two-toed hooves in the canoe. Much later I was the one who found the cow on the head of the lake and milked her there, but on dry land.

We could spend a lot of time looking for the milk cows in our large pastures, but in time I learned to watch the cows after we had finished milking. They liked to lie down for a snooze. In an hour or so they'd get up, and as they finished their cud chewing one would decide which pasture to go to, and that was usually where I would find them.

Milk Cows

Searching, searching, walking thru
Under trees and in the slough,
Look for tracks and scuffed up ground
From their bells there is no sound.

When at last I find the critters
They are standing in the river,
Chewing cuds and half asleep
Avoiding flies in water deep.

When I ask them to come out
They respond with bovine shout,
"Sure we'll come and give you milk,
And also cream as smooth as silk."

Back at barn, and milking done
They recline in lowered sun.
One rests her chin upon her hoof,
There is no need for wall or roof.

With cool of evening flies are gone,
They'll not return 'til after dawn.
With peace and quiet of the night
Cows will sleep 'til morning bright.

Then up they'll get from humus bed
And gather at the milking shed.
When the milking chore is over
They'll wander off to graze in clover.

And so the time just ambles on
From morn to night, and dusk to dawn.
Summer, winter, fall and spring
To them the time means not a thing.

I used to believe horses and cows and dogs did things just to annoy us. Now I think this idea is quite wrong. They have much more important things to occupy their minds than annoying puny humans. They are much more interested in where the food is, and where the rest of the herd is, and how safe they are. And sometimes the cow might be having a problem with her newborn calf. This happened on my place once.

We had been away on a trip somewhere one summer. On our return we passed Apple, our expecting milk cow. I noted her udder was quite large for a cow who was not due for another three weeks. We continued on to our house. We had a few things to do that evening, and we were tired and hungry.

In the morning Apple started bellowing outside the fence where we had passed her the evening before. As pregnant cows seldom call for no discernable reason, we went to investigate. Apple was alone, but as soon as we were out there she turned and headed away, looking back to see if we were coming, then continued. Her udder was much larger.

That was a tip-off. She led us to where her three-weeks-premature little calf was standing, none too steady on her tiny hooves. Apple really needed help to get that little calf to take her very important first meal. Since Apple could not get her calf fed without help, she called on us.

Apple was the granddaughter of an Ayrshire bull I had bought in 1948, hoping to improve the milk production of our cows.

Spicy came from a dairy farmer in the Fraser Valley dairy farming area. He had been shipped up the coast to Bella Coola, then was trucked to the end of the road. Dad and I brought the calf from there to Lonesome Lake.

The trail downstream of Stillwater had been slightly damaged by a large rock rumbling down a steep, smooth piece of rock-bluff where the trail builders had built a bridge (mentioned in chapter 7, It's a Challenge). The rock had removed the bridge. Fortunately, about 15 feet up the bluff there was a narrow ledge wide enough for people, and for one amiable Ayrshire calf to pick his way across carefully.

When we arrived at Stillwater with the calf we decided to take him on a small, unstable raft. He wasn't very heavy and we had the small outboard to push the raft three miles up the river—much easier than walking around the rocky east shore of that deadhead-filled body of water. As the raft was a little inadequate to support the calf, the boat had to help. We tied the bow of the boat to the stern of the raft, and then guyed it so the boat and raft became a single craft. At Lonesome Lake we built another raft to take the calf across the six-mile stretch.

Finally home with our calf, we turned him loose with the cows in the pasture. Spicy promptly gave them all pinkeye, a common disease of cattle. The resident cows had no immunity, so they had a lot of running eyes before the ailment finally died out as they gained immunity. Spicy should have been kept separated from the other cattle for a long while.

Spicy was a very smart creature and so polite. One day I was going to the pasture and he just happened to be standing beside the rail gate I would walk thru. As I approached it he tipped his head, put one horn between the rails and then swinging his head just right, opened the gate for me. He stepped back out of my way. I walked thru and thanked him. He unhooked his horn to allow the gate to swing closed. I thought it was a pretty neat trick.

Is it fair to call a part of a body a tool if it is used for a purpose it was not intended for? Are cows using tools if they use their horns to pry boards off the walls of the hay barn to get at the hay? Are they using tools if they reach curved horns thru cracks to drag out the hay? These things did not happen just once, but many times. Until we built a log wall around the barn wall, the cows would not forget that knowledge.

When I was a little brat, as opposed to a larger brat, Dad taught me a very valuable lesson. Namely, do not change your mind without a good reason. One day when he was hauling manure over to one of the fields he asked me if I wanted a ride on the wagon. As the box would be full of manure I could stand on the projecting ends of the bottom boards and grip the tailgate. However, that time I declined. He drove off. A minute after he had driven out of the corral I yelled, "Wait!" Dad just drove right on. I bellowed, "Wait!!" He didn't even look back, but kept right on across the field.

Angry, hurt, disappointed, I stumbled after the wagon. It was so far away by then that pursuit was futile. I trudged back to the barn and waited for his return. It crossed my mind that I should not have said no, and then turned around and wanted to change it. When he returned for another load he gently pointed out why he didn't wait for me. It was a lesson I never forgot, and try to live by.

There were other times when Dad did wait for me to run and catch up with the wagon. That would happen if I had gone to the house and had not noticed he was just about ready to drive to the field. I would have a long run then, but he would wait if I was running as fast as I could. Catching up, I'd scramble onto the platform and stand up as the wagon started off.

Sometimes it would be the hayrack on the wagon for hauling hay, and I was supposed to be on the wagon anyway to tramp the hay down. If I was late, then I would run up behind the wagon, grab part of the rack and swing up. If that wasn't risky enough, I'd jump off, then get back on again as the wagon lurched and bumped its way across the field. I did not play that game on the bridges; they were too rough.

Sometimes I'd get on the rear of the wagon, then work my way to the front end of the rack by going from one stake to the next on the side of the rack until I arrived at the ladder on the front end of the rack. There I stood, clinging to the ladder beside Dad, imagining I was driving.

I seem to remember that all of us except Mother rode the hayrack, clinging where we could when going out for hay. Mother preferred to walk. The three or four hayforks that rode along were safely secured, where we couldn't hurt ourselves on them.

Here is another pleasant memory I have of haying. Dad was way across the farm, mowing in Little Field, the field farthest from the barn, except the Pen. I watched from the house until I thought he was just about finished, then I ran across the mowed fields to the edge of the field he was cutting and waited there until he began unhitching the team. With the horses off the mower, I went over to where Dad was getting ready to drive them home and asked for a ride on one. Dad separated the horses, set me on Susan's soft, harnessed back and we started off. He led both horses and I sat up there, high above the ground, and thoroughly enjoyed myself. That wasn't the first time I rode a horse, of course. It was just nice with Daddy beside me, even if he was on the ground.

It was only a few years until I was mowing that field as well as the others, but I was grown up then, at least 14 years old.

After struggling with homesickness for 10 years and mostly winning, I decided in August 1999 to make a trip back to my valley. I went in with my brother as he had boats on the lakes.

We visited my old place, Arbordale, also known as Fogswamp and originally as Seven Islands, and several places on The Birches where we roamed when we were children. I was there six days. I got to see Foxi several times when he came into the house to receive food from John's hand. Foxi was a red fox who adopted my brother and stayed around for 10 years, raising several litters of pups. Foxi was tame, but his lady was less so; she never brought the pups to John's house, so their dad did it.

When I saw Foxi he was getting old and looked tired as he took the food, turned and went out the door to race across the field to where the pups were waiting. I saw two or three little light brown things running around on the collapsed roof of the mill building, about 600 feet away across the field.

In the morning shortly before we left to return to Bella Coola (Salloompt) I was out in the yard tying some plants on my pack when Foxi walked into my sight. He stopped, uncertain about me, watched for a minute, then walked around me and continued past the house. I had remained frozen in place, hoping I'd not frightened him too much. I wish I had said, "Hello Foxi." I was as unsure as he was, I guess. It was very rewarding for me anyway to have a delicate, beautiful wild animal come so close to a total stranger and not be unduly alarmed.

Foxi was not the only wild animal that had come close to me, of course. As I had been feeding trumpeter swans for many years and had been rewarded by their company and music, I was quite used to wild animals crowding around me. However, it had taken many winters of feeding those big white birds before they gained enough trust to get really close to me.

Trumpeter swans at Lonesome Lake almost define the area.

They were the only wintering birds in the area when Dad started his farm there—well, except for some little ducks and chickadees. Perhaps Dad wouldn't have even known then how important the swans would become to him during the long snowy winters of loneliness, or how important we would become to the big birds, thru the decades of our residency at Lonesome Lake.

Each fall, hearing the first call of the swans caused great excitement and joy. I, at least, went about my tasks each day with one ear permanently tuned for that first bugle. From about October 20 to sometime in November I would be rewarded, and my heart soared on the wings of swans. Tho I seldom hear the swans where I now live, one bugle still gladdens my heart and excites me. They have never bored me, and I believe I got almost as much from them as they got from me, from the feeding.

After supplying supplementary food to the Lonesome Lake trumpeter swans for 56 years, the Canadian Wildlife Service decided to terminate the feeding in 1989. That was the last winter I fed the swans. There were only about 120 birds that winter and I fed for only three weeks. It was a warm winter.

I would have been four years old when the feeding started, but by the time I was 10 or 11 Dad had given me the job and I did it for part of each winter for close to 50 years. Then it all stopped and left a hole in my life. I really missed seeing the swans each day, even though in our new home in Bella Coola there were new things to do and new opportunities to help me adjust. I still miss them.

During the 32 winters that Jack and I fed the swans we walked an impressive 13,000 miles.

When I visited Lonesome Lake in 1999 it was the last time I saw the forests and all the buildings built by my parents and Jack and myself. Oh, Lonesome Lake.

My next visit was on July 27, 2004, by helicopter four days after our beautiful valley was destroyed by wildfire. There was so much smoke choking the valley the pilot had to fly almost at treetop height to see where he was going. We landed in one of the scorched and blackened fields. We made our way to where the barn, house, implement shed, and small outbuildings had stood, being careful to check for still-burning deep holes where trees had been. There was very little left of the log house and barn. Only piles of metal roofing, bent and twisted indicated a building had ever been there—and ashes.

We soon left and flew out of the ruined, smoking valley to Anahim Lake where Susan, our daughter, drove Jack and me back to our place in the Salloompt. I did not see Arbordale, but have no reason to think it looked any better. That fire could have been stopped by BC Parks a few days after it was started on June 24 by lightning near a bluff 2000 feet above Lonesome Lake about four miles north of the head of the lake. I was told that BC Parks did not want to spend 250,000 dollars to stop it, so it was allowed to burn. In time, with no rain for the next two months or so, the fire went where it pleased. Finally out of Tweedsmuir Park and threatening the communities of Anahim Lake, Nimpo Lake and Charlotte Lake, BC Forest Service could get on it. In the end, according to the media, the cost to stop the fire's spread was over 10 MILLION DOLLARS!!

On July 30, 2005, Susan and Tom, their sons Alex and Brendan, and I chartered a flight on our local airline to go in and fly over the badly wounded valley, not so much to see what was gone, as to see what still lived, having somehow been missed by that starving monster of destruction.

The only building on either place was a new one, built in the fall of 2004 by John. Despite the shock and sorrow of having his home, his valley, utterly destroyed, my stubborn brother gathered strength enough to rebuild on his blackened charred place. A few friends helped, but not without John's driving force, aided by little Vicki, a fox who somehow survived the roaring monster. In fact she was there on the blackened ruins a few days after the fire when some

Forest Service people flew in by helicopter to check on things. She came right up to them and they shared their lunch with the courageous little fox.

My brother passed away from cancer July 16, 2007. He was 80.

In the fall of 2007 Susan and Tom went in to Lonesome Lake to check on things for the winter, and Vicki came to them and once again shared lunch.

Truly My Home

How dear to my heart is Lonesome Lake.
How dear to my heart is the valley.
How dear to my heart is the land of my birth.
It's the best place on earth.

I grew up with wild music from wolf and swan.
I grew up with beauty galore.
I grew up with values of infinite worth.
It's the best place on Earth.

The mountains and trees guard the valley from storms
And river runs sweet thru its length.
And the days I spent rambling and gathering truths
Are the best memories of youth.

I lived in that valley for sixty years,
with brief visits to cities and towns.
With husband and daughter, and lots of good water
There was no reason to wander and roam.

And with horses and cows, and a dog and a cat,
It was the only place to be truly my Home.

chapter 2

Rebel, or Breaker of Traditions

I must have been born a rebel, or at least a breaker of traditions. My two brothers were born exactly as planned. Stanley was planned to be born on September 24, 1924; my second brother was planned to come on July 7, 1927, even the month is the seventh. And they did.

When it came my turn, I was planned to come on March 29, 1929. That was my planned birthday. But as the 29th oozed along and the birthing had actually started, I apparently decided to assert myself in the matter and thought, "No, I am not going to let other people tell me when to make my appearance." So, all that was "go" was suddenly stopped! Until the 30th. Then it started up again, and I came into this world with chubby little fists clenched and plump little legs kicking, and soon yowling my displeasure at being forced through a tight, bony tunnel, then into a world of cold and bright light, a terrible situation for any poor little innocent baby. And I have been trying to change traditions ever since.

Two matters of contention between Mother and me were long hair and dresses. Sometime in my early years I observed that females had long hair and wore dresses, or at least Mother did, and all the ladies in magazines and the big Eaton's winter catalogue certainly did, and by Mother's decree, so did I when I couldn't avoid it.

Girls, it seemed, had to wear dresses or skirts and blouses; it was the custom! Mother never, ever wore pants in all her life, poor lady. And she tried to see to it I didn't, either. But why? What difference did it make? Both garments covered one's body. Pants actually did a better job than dresses and no wind could lift the hem. But I demanded pants and pointed out how much better pant legs were at keeping out mosquitoes and black flies, and how much warmer they were in winter, and better at keeping snow from getting my legs wet and cold. Looking back, I guess dresses would have been better to wear if I was going wading in the cold creeks in the cold fall time. I just rolled up my pant legs, though somehow they usually got wet anyway, and then my legs hurt at night. I guess the creeks were deeper than they should have been. At some time in my pre-teens, I decided to stop playing in the ice water and my poor legs stopped aching. I guess I'd had enough of cold water wading, and then did everything possible to avoid getting wet when it was cold.

As I grew up, I began to notice that the shorthaired males in my family could have their hair combed without a lot of complaining about their hair being pulled, like I did with my long hair. Somehow Mother never seemed to have any trouble with her really long hair. She braided it, then coiled it all up and made a nice, neat bun, which she pinned to back of her head. She told me that if I'd just let it grow really long like hers was and had it all done up that way, I wouldn't have any trouble at all. And I thought that with all the snarls that seemed to develop in my hair whenever I got sticks, hay, cones, leaves and any other debris that kids can collect rolling around in the hay pile and on the ground and climbing about in any handy trees, even the neatest of braids would surely collect that much more stuff to tangle my hair up even worse. She was the one who had to comb it all out as I was much too much of a coward to pull out the snarls myself and soon gave up. And why couldn't girls have short hair like boys were allowed to, anyway? It was the custom.

Actually, by this time, if I remember correctly, Dad had very little hair on his head, though he still had his fine red whiskers, and he never seemed to collect anything in what hair he did have. Of course, he never rolled around on the ground, or climbed trees, though he certainly had lots of chances to collect hay when throwing big fork-fuls over his head and onto the wagon when haying.

It seems like I had no sooner sworn off cold water wading when we were faced with a job that involved a lot of cold water wading. Having lost everything in the house and under it in the fire, my parents decided never to put the storage of food under the house again. Storing canned food and vegetables in a cellar under the house was a common practice back then. It was easy to get to and easy to make frost-proof, but obviously not a good idea to have all your food in one place, which could be destroyed so easily. If it had happened later in the year I don't know what they would have done for the winter. I have often thought of this.

When they rebuilt their house in a different area, they did not put a cellar under it, but dug pits well away from the house and stored the canned food and fresh vegetables in the pits. There was one for jars, one for spuds, one for parsnips, carrots, and beets, and one for carefully selected seed potatoes. All was well until a particularly wet November when it rained a lot and the creeks all rose, and the underground springs flooded the pits. There had been no sign of the springs when they dug the pits some years earlier.

So all the potatoes, carrots, etc., had to be picked up by someone standing in cold water up to his or her knees and put in buckets, so someone standing on the dry ground outside the pit could haul the filled pail up and dump it into sacks, until all the vegetables were out of the pit. Then they were taken by wheelbarrow to the house to be dried. My folks didn't know, but were afraid that if the vegetables were left wet they might rot. Knowing what I know now I think they would have been all right. The creeks did not stay up very long, and vegetables can dry themselves quite a lot. But they didn't want to take a chance and I cannot blame them.

They hauled all the jars out too, tho I can't think now why. Water would not have hurt the jars. They were sealed, of course. Guess who was down there in the water, the COLD water, filling that bucket with jars, spuds, carrots, seed spuds, etc.? Someone who can still remember how COLD her little hands and legs got. But someone large and strong had to lift the full pail out, and the only ones strong were Mother and Stanley. My memory is hazy on who else may have been in the pit filling pails, but Johnny could very well have been. I remember myself doing it because it was so bloody cold! Thinking about it 70-odd years later makes me shiver. Dad had to tend the trap line, our only income.

When the pits were dry everything went back in and we got thru the winter. The next year we selected an area on top of a higher piece of ground and dug all the pits there. To my knowledge they never flooded.

The above account reminds me of a nice spring-fed pond. When we children were young, Dad dug it for us close to the barn where springs rose for several weeks most springtime. The pond was about 15 feet long by 10 feet wide and more or less pear-shaped. The stem end pointed to where the water flowed out over a dirt and grass dam. The inlet end resembled the blossom end of the pear. The pond was about three feet at the deepest part. On three sides of the pond lay a bench of good soil. We divided up this arable land for our little gardens. I seem to remember we raised radish and lettuce, and I think some peas and corn. There was just one little problem, eight or ten little problems, actually. Chickens!

You can keep cows and horses out of the hay fields and gardens with a pole fence no higher than themselves, but hens can jump, fly and crawl. Only chicken wire six feet high will stop them, and then only if you clip the flight feathers on one wing, and sometimes half the feathers on the other wing.

We tried small poles tied to posts driven into the ground, but the more determined hens would jump over, then industriously weed and "de-bug" and "de-lettuce" and "de-plant" our gardens to their hearts' content. Of course they cultivated and fertilized the soil just fine. And they actually ate the lettuce!

I seem to remember we planted our gardens for several years, but as we could not keep those pesky hens out, we gave up and invested our energies in the big family garden, far away from where the chickens roamed.

At some age my brothers built a small cabin each, rather than just playhouses. Stanley's was set on a flat area right beside his garden by the pond, but a couple of feet higher. There was room for a trail between his garden and his cabin. This was the trail we took from the house to the cow pasture to milk the cows in the summer. Stanley's

My first cabin.

cabin was only about 30 feet from the house. When Johnny decided to build his cabin, he went a bit farther from the house, ending up about 300 feet away, right on the edge of the fir forest in the cow pasture. There he made a really neat little log cabin on a level spot. As best as I can recall, Johnny was about 11 when he made his cabin and Stanley was probably around the same age when he made his.

These bedroom cabins would seem to suggest my brothers didn't want to be too near each other, but I don't think that was the reason at all. I think each one was seeking individuality, or they were pretending to be pioneers. And when I decided to build a log cabin for myself, I selected a spot even farther from the house, about 400 feet. I, however, was already an adult when I made my cabin.

As we were always so pleased when any visitors came, I don't believe the placing of our cabins meant anything except a personal choice. We were always happy to see visitors, except once.

That was when the policeman came to see if the kids were being properly cared for or not educated. He made himself unwelcome immediately that he arrived at our house, accompanied by our Uncle Earle as guide. Dad met them out in the yard. Once being invited into the house, the officer met Mother, who happened to be sweeping the floor, quite an ordinary chore in any household. The policeman insultingly asked as he passed through the door, "Are you working?" She ignored the question and invited him on into her house.

My brothers made a fool out of the policeman by beating him at cribbage and several other bits of knowledge. Then something happened that all of us considered amusing, but I am sure he didn't. Uncle Earle was playing with a rifle cartridge one evening. He was squeezing it with a pair of pliers, turning it around and squeezing it some more. Finally, Mother asked him if he thought what he was doing was safe. After a bit of thought, Uncle Earle said he'd just turn around here, then. That move had the cartridge aiming at the policeman. We all kept our amusement to ourselves.

Since the child welfare people didn't take us away from our home and parents, I assume they decided to take a chance that we were going to get some kind of education. After all, it wasn't us Lonesome Lakers who were playing with the rifle shell.

This incident reminds me of the unpleasant midnight visit Jack and I had from the RCMP many years later, just because we hadn't answered our local phone system for a day or two. I am still scared. They came in the dark of night and woke us up. Jack went out to see what whoever was there wanted. Bright lights were flashed all around, and there was a lot of loud talk, then Jack told me I had better come out so the cops could see that I was alive. They kept their bright lights shining right into our eyes all the time they were verbally intimidating us. Finally, they decided no serious crime had been committed, even if we hadn't used the phone for a day or two, and left. I suppose it could have been worse. They could have taken our baby away. That was what I was scared might happen, but it didn't. Come to think of it, I don't actually recall seeing any RCMP identification, but why would anyone else be in there, claiming to be police?

chapter 3

FRUIT

For the first few years of my childhood all the fruit we had was canned tomatoes and boxes of dried prunes, raisins, dates and some figs, all carried to Lonesome Lake on packhorses. We also had various wild fruits, raspberries, gooseberries, hawthorn berries and squashberries. We had apple trees, but they take a few years to begin bearing. Also, the common varieties could not take our climate, except yellow transparent, and even it needed protection from the cold north wind. In time Dad bought several varieties of apples from a Manitoba nursery and they could take our robust climate. And in time we were raising large, good flavored apples, and even some hardy and tasty small pears. Some of the pear trees are bearing there yet in spite of the 2004 forest fire and the bears.

Dad also obtained red currants and black currants. He must have really liked red currants. He planted two patches of them. The larger one was 100 feet long and 15 feet wide, with three rows of bushes. So we had lots of fruit, at least lots of red currants, oh yes, lots of them, oh God, yes there were! And they all had to be picked! Every one, and they had to be stemmed. Then Mother made them into juice, jelly, or just canned fruit for winter. The juice we would dilute about two parts water to one part currant juice, add some (a lot) of sugar and stir it up in a jar, for a delicious cooling drink on a hot day.

We also had tame black currants, which made jam. They were quite sour. The wild gooseberries and hawthorns were made into jam or canned as fruit. The squashberry, commonly called high bush cranberry, was used for jam. Altho it is extremely sour, with sugar added, then cooked up for jam or jelly, it can't be beat for flavor. Even after we got lots of other tame fruit, we continued to harvest the squashberries. They grow among fallen trees and other obstructions, along tangled, brushy creek banks.

The hawthorn berries weren't bad as fruit, but it was difficult to pick them, as they grew among alder trees and devil's club canes, and they had thorns. As the hawthorn trees were 15 feet or so tall, and bore their fruit near the top, it was necessary to walk up on logs that lay at different heights among the hawthorns to reach the purple fruit. As the logs we had to walk up on to get the berries were usually covered with branches and knots, one had to be careful not to fall off and spill all the fruit. And we certainly didn't want to fall into the devil's clubs, great robust plants with poisonous thorns on their thick stems, and on the underside of their maple-leaf-shaped leaves, a foot across. They also favored the moist, rich soil. The hawthorns, as their name suggests, had real thorns, spikes more like, all over their stems, and an inch long! At least the currants didn't have any thorns.

Eventually we had tame gooseberries, but in the meantime wild ones did well enough, once we got them picked. And they had very effective thorns, tho much shorter than those on the hawthorn trees. Except for the gooseberry thorns, the next most unpleasant thing about them was where they grew. They seemed to prefer to grow among logs and brush, scattered all over the cow pasture where land clearing had begun but was not finished. So we had to travel a long way around and about to find them. Long after we began getting "civilized" fruit from tame plants, tho still thorny, the gooseberry bushes finally were liberated from the logs; but we didn't want them then.

Years later, on my own place, we had to go miles, wade across rivers to small islands, carrying our daughter on Jack's back in her carrying chair while we picked the wild fruit. Later, we too got tame bushes, from my parents. Life was easier then.

To return to the red currants for a bit, picking them was done by the whole family not just by me, tho at the time I felt I had to do the whole job.

Even before we could begin picking the red currants, someone had to get on their knees and hand pull all the blue grass that grew luxuriantly among and thru the heavily laden currant canes, or we couldn't even get in amongst the bushes. And one of us at least usually got cuts on her fingers from the fine barbs that are on the edges of grass leaves.

We had huge pails, which had to be filled with the tiny, sour, beautiful ruby-red fruit. The bushes were huge too, towering over my head as I sat on a stool in front of them, holding the pail between my knees much as if I were milking a cow, as I picked each raceme. If the berries were stripped off the racemes out in the currant patch, it took forever to fill a pail, and all that time we had to sit out there in the heat and bugs. So it was better to pick the whole raceme, and then stem them in the cool of the house. And the pails filled faster too. And if a person—guess who—wanted to fill her pail really quickly, a few leaves added and then of course covered with more fruit, filled the pail more quickly still. Only one problem with that innovative strategy was she just had to go back out to the berry patch and pick more berries than she would have had to pick in the first place. She did not try that again.

Years later I got even with those currant bushes, tho. One day Dad asked me to dig out about half of the patch. We didn't need them, and he wanted the bushes out of the field so he could run the mower right around the patch. I was happy to do this. We never needed all the currants that grew on those bushes.

When people ask questions that seem to indicate they think we were living a subsistence life off the land, I can only detail how impossible that would be, unless they mean growing our food as compared to buying it all at the grocery store, which I assume they don't mean. Ultimately everyone lives off the land. I think they believe we just went out in the woods and ate whatever we could find lying around. This could never be a choice in the Lonesome Lake area. Except for some half-rotten, spawned-out salmon lying along the river bank—in season, very short—and mushrooms of dubious edibility, wild fruit, also in season, very short, and the tender bottom inch or so of large sedge that grows in swampy areas, there is precious little that one could harvest without tools and equipment of some kind to clear land and grow crops, and also produce milk, butter and beef.

RED CURRANTS: THEY ALL HAD TO BE PICKED

The dreaded red currant patch.

Back to those red currants again, they didn't have thorns. No, they had something worse. Wasps! Too often they harbored yellow jackets, hot little short-tempered yellow and black insects that seemed to prefer to build their gray globular paper nests six to eight inches in diameter hanging on the currant canes, hidden among the branches and fruit. Usually the first we would know of their presence was when a sharp pain, much like a devil's club thorn jab, sent us quickly out of the berry patch, leaving stool and berry pail behind. They could be retrieved on a cool morning when the little stingers would be asleep in their warm nest. We could then sneak in quietly, grab the pail and stool and run for our lives. As yellow jacket nests grow rapidly, we would not always find them while pulling out the blue grass, necessary before berry picking could begin. When the nests are small the bugs don't come out to sting, but over three inches, they will surely attack.

chapter 4

BIG SPRUCE & NOON TREE

Looking back down the long road of my life, sometimes rock-paved, often flower-strewn under glorious sunsets and sunrises, and occasionally watered by tears of sadness or joy, I see the answers to several questions, none of which I had ever asked. I am asking them now.

Why on earth did my parents continue to live at Lonesome Lake, so far from any help should they need it? Why did they willingly engage in a lifestyle that involved such a strenuous existence? Where did Mother find the strength to endure the stress of never knowing if her husband would return from each and every trip he made away from the farm?

I think we all simply did what others were doing in that period of pioneering and just didn't question the risks. Even to consider risks would have somehow reduced the feeling of power and victory over self. Being dependent entirely on oneself can make one very careful and aware of one's surroundings, and pay close attention to everything that goes on around oneself and be very observant. None of us would have hiked the many miles of trails wearing Walkmans crammed into our ears, or even wearing bells on our packs. In fact, we would tie up the bells on the cows and horses when we were taking them anywhere, so we could listen automatically for any sounds that were of interest to us. You can't do that very well with any overpowering noise clanging in your ears.

Judging from the amount of hand labor I did clearing my own property and helping at clearing on my parents' place, I seem to recall that a lot of The Birches was clothed with small willows, alders, red willows, gooseberry bushes, and robust devil's clubs, spiny but easy to grub out as they have weak roots and grow on damp, rich soil. These areas Dad would have tackled first as one can just dig these plants out easily with mattocks, then use a pitchfork to pile the thorny things up for burning. Maybe it was not such a strenuous existence after all.

A lot of what he cleared for garden and hay had extensive areas of those good soil-building plants. Sometimes, places where devil's club grows it is so wet that it needs draining, especially if there is a lot of snow melting and raising the various underground springs. So he had to dig drain ditches, but the soil was worth it.

Most of the land by the river was natural meadow with only the odd alder or willow growing there, often on a hummock, which made clearing quite easy. Then, in time, the hummocks could be reduced enough to let the horse-drawn mower get over. Of course, in the cutting and digging that had to be done to remove the tree or trees much of the hummock would have been already reduced a lot. The soil was good, but being low and close to the river only meadow grass could grow there. But it didn't need planting. Farther away from the river there was good land under mostly cedar and paper birch with some highland willow and a bit of red alder, which was good for timothy and clover.

Where the forest was dominantly birch and cedar, I seem to recall Dad cut the trees down and piled and burnt the branches, keeping any logs that were of use for firewood or building materials and putting them aside for the future. Then he could plant tame grass among the stumps and in a few years they came out easily with the stump-puller and his horse to wind up the cable, lifting it out slowly but surely.

Dad had tried blasting the stumps out with stumping powder to start with, like people down the valley did. However, there was one big problem with the blasting. The soil on and around the stumps, and small stump parts, were flung far and wide, so they all had to be gathered up and returned to the stump holes, and never quite filled them. I remember mowing one field many years later and coping with the mower suddenly dropping one wheel into an unseen hole, with an accompanying lurch to that side and an unpleasant slam to the horse on the same side. No wonder Topsy didn't like mowing.

Pulling the stumps let most of the soil fall back into the stump holes. As he didn't have a mowing machine for several years, and had to cut his hay with a hand scythe, these scattered stumps would not have mattered much, anyway.

For garden and orchard Dad would have cleared the easy-to-clear areas where gooseberries and red willows (actually red osier dogwood) grew. After removing these shallow rooted shrubs the soft soil would have been dug up almost enough for planting. As there would have been some wild grass growing on open ground between the bushes, that ground would need digging up before planting garden crops or tame grass.

Most of the trees on The Birches were on the small side, four inches to a foot in diameter, except for some large cottonwoods, which stood on a square of rocky ground near the barn, and some larger Douglas firs on higher, drier areas. But two trees towered over all the others for a number of years. They grew about a hundred feet apart.

The fir, known as the Noon Tree, clutched a rocky ridge with its roots, its six-foot-diameter trunk taking up most of the top of the narrow ridge, leaving barely enough room for a wagon to squeeze past with a load of hay on board. On one side of the ridge there was a swamp. On the other side runs a sweet and shallow cold creek. This tree was 120 feet tall in the early 1950s.

The other tall and large tree was a Sitka spruce, about seven feet in diameter. It was anchored firmly on the bank of one of the many creeks that headed for the river 200 yards away, near the west side of the property. This tree was called the Big Spruce, for obvious reasons. No other trees of any species within a mile were larger. It ruled alone.

One year, probably in the 1930s, a brush pile too close to the big tree was doing a fine job of reducing a large heap of branches to ashes when a wind started up. Altho some of us were there, with the brush pile on fire and a rising wind there was nothing we could do to quiet down the flames, and the wind carried it to the pitchy bark of the spruce. With a roar like a jet breaking the sound barrier, the fire streaked to the top of the heavily branched tree in seconds. We were scared! With the fire over a hundred feet in the air the potential for spreading was great.

The ruined monarch stood there for years, its gradually loosening burned and blackened bark providing sleeping quarters for many little brown bats thru the cold and snowy winters. I think it was while Mother, Stan and I were in the Bella Coola area visiting our relatives and anyone else we chose to that the great old tree, fire-killed but still bracing up against the north winds, was brought down with a muted thud, landing on a couple of fences and finally falling on a rich, black bed of soft muck soil, driving some of its broken branches deep into the ground. It was a sad ending for a brave tree.

Once on the ground it was an easy matter for me to measure its length. Before it fell, it had stood 140 feet tall. If the fire hadn't killed it, it might very well have been standing there until 2004, when the disastrous wildfire raged thru the valley. Thank God the Noon Tree survived that fire, which destroyed my home, my valley.

chapter 5

HAPPY RETURN

Ransacking my memory for interesting bits of trivia, I see many times where Mother must have been worried about Dad out there alone in the cold and snow of winter. Some of the worst hazards were the foot-logs he had to use to cross the river.

Those foot-logs were large trees felled over the river, which was some 40 to 50 feet wide. The logs were often icy or covered with deep snow. If icy, they could be sanded, if sand was available. If the logs had deep snow on them, it would all have to be kicked off; a rather delicate operation, performed while standing on one leg as the other kicked the snow off the log. Five or six feet below the log was the riverbed, filled with large irregular boulders, over and around which splashed and tumbled the Atnarko River.

If the rocky bed of the Atnarko was not hazard enough, there were the large leg-hold traps, set on the log close to a flimsy fence of a few camouflaging tree branches, so anchored to help obstruct the view of a potential victim. A pole laid across the foot-log was to make the wolf or cougar step over it and into the trap. An unlucky wolf or cougar so caught would almost always fall off the log and hang by its caught leg, to die in agony as shock and cold took their toll on the suffering, innocent animal. If Dad were to step accidentally in one of those sets, he would have fared no better. Dad always made light of the risk, so Mother never realized the actual hazard the large "double-springed" steel traps with sharp teeth presented. I knew, as

I had negotiated the sets more than once and did not like them, but tried hard not to appear a coward.

Thinking back on those traps, I believe it was just plain dumb to set such hazards on a foot-log, usually icy, in the hope of catching one or two wolves or cougars. I have to admit they were quite successful, until the wolves learned to wade the river and avoid the logs.

My dear parents seemed to have had some feelings of sorrow for the small creatures on whose lives they made their living, but I know they not only didn't waste any sympathy on the coyotes, wolves and cougars because they killed and ate deer, but rejoiced when one more "deer killer" put his foot in it. They tried hard to train us children to hate the large predators, and to have no thoughts as to how they suffered just as much as the small creatures. In time, and with Jack's help, I recognized that fact.

It was a great moment of relief and joy when one of us spotted the tiny light from Dad's "bug" coming slowly thru the trees at the edge of the clearing, as he walked along a large log over a tangle of other logs and brush. Seeing the light we shouted, "Daddy's home!" If Dad was returning in subzero temperatures we kids continued to watch as he neared the house. When he stepped up on the porch we could hear him crunch across it to the door, the snow squeaking a welcome with every step. When we heard him prop his snowshoes against the wall that was our signal to fling open the thick door for him to enter the warm room.

Struggling out of his snow-covered, ice-encrusted pack, he'd trudge to the stool beside the stove and sink down on it with a tired and thankful sigh. And the kids would bombard him with questions, which just couldn't wait for answers. But they had to wait. Poor cold Dad could not answer us, or drink the hot cocoa Mother had ready for him, or even kiss her. There'd be a curtain of icicles joining his mustache to his beard. He wanted to untie his shoelaces, kick off his shoes and stretch out his tired legs and rest his feet on the warm rug. He couldn't until the heat from the stove thawed the frozen snowballs clinging to the laces and knots. Sometimes he'd fall asleep there on his stool before the ice melted, he was so tired.

As Dad warmed he would take off his coat and let the heat from the stove warm his back; his shirt steamed like a hot kettle. Finally the icicles would melt enough that he could pull them off his whiskers to drink. He was very thirsty, not having been able to drink all day because of the icy fence over his mouth. I recall that he drank several cups of hot cocoa. Mother would have prepared a large pot full.

I can't remember the many times Dad returned from a trap trip or mail trip when he wasn't snow covered and ice encrusted, but there had to have been many more of them than there were when it was really cold. The cold spells were infrequent, but memorable.

Mother seldom let on to the children that she was worried, unless Dad was late getting back. However, I now believe she was always worried. In my own life I was in the same position as Mother was. However, I had two big advantages that she did not. I had backup. There were Mother and Dad to render assistance had Jack not returned, and I had only one child. In the early days Mother had three children, none of whom could be left alone, nor could she have taken them with her if she had wanted to go to see why Dad had not come home.

Now I remember, once—sometime after Stanley and Johnny were both off on their own, leaving just Mother and me at home— when Dad was late getting back. Mother felt he was late enough that someone should go and investigate. We fixed the cattle up with hay, leaving them out of the barn so they could get water. We took off to find out if Dad was injured or maybe needed help with the animals that were still out on fall pasture.

Fortunately, Dad was safe. I think he had some trouble getting the horses or cows across the river, or something like that. Of course we had already thought of that possibility, but he seemed to be too late for even that problem. Anyway, no harm done and Mother had a nice trip away from the house.

Mother almost never went far from the house, tho she must have wanted to quite often. I feel now that too frequently we get so caught up in our daily chores that we forget to just walk out the door and go do something not related to work, chores, house, meals, or whatever, to look at things outdoors and forget about everything for a few hours, or even days, to enjoy the freedom of not doing a single darn essential thing.

For as long as Mother was at Lonesome Lake, I can't think of more than a very few times that she went on any hikes away from her kitchen just to explore and relax out in nature. Perhaps she never felt compelled to go hiking, but I think she simply felt she had to be in the kitchen all the time or she would be wasting time. I really don't know. But I do wonder why she didn't ever want to get out at least once in a while. All the other members of the family had outdoor jobs and interests. I am sure Mother must have sometimes wanted to go out, too.

chapter 6

BACKWARDS TOPSY

Topsy was a very determined horse. She had several notions about how a horse ought to behave, none of them conducive to getting the job, our job that is, done. One of her more memorable notions was that I couldn't get her to leave the farm with a rider on her back, even with another horse. She would go willingly to the "shakepile," where I often took the horses to water them. Then one day I decided to go for a short ride beyond the creek. Topsy said no, she could see no reason to go in that direction. She had had her drink, so the next obvious step was to return to the barn, preferably at a fast canter.

Back at the barn, I told Dad that Topsy refused to go beyond the creek, so what should I do? He advised me not to whip her, as she might buck. He didn't tell me what to do.

Well, I certainly didn't want her to buck. I had heard a lot about one of his packhorses who seemed to delight in bucking his pack off just because it rattled a bit. He would then spread it far and wide. No one seemed to know too much about Old Blue's history. I believe now that Old Blue could have had a very traumatic experience that had involved a rattling pack, and the horse was just plain scared.

Anyway with no knowledge as to whether or not it would work, I decided to try and see if I could persuade her to go in reverse gear. She could, and would, reverse just dandy. That was all she would do, if she moved any amount. She stepped backwards. She gave me the idea of backing her; she shouldn't have been surprised if I used it. She was a very smart horse, too. I tried not to push her too far. I thought she might rear if I did, and I didn't need that either.

So the next time I wanted to ride beyond the creek, likely the next day, she quite determinedly refused. I simply turned her about and asked her to back up. She did, for a few steps, until she realized she was still leaving the barn. Then she began resisting. I turned her and asked her again to go in forward, and again she backed. So, another turn around and again a request to back up. She went farther that time. Her ears were twitching forwards and backwards as if she was trying to figure out a way to get back to the barn. Had I known then what I know now, I would have stopped her when she was going backwards away from the barn and taken her home as a reward for doing what I had asked, to go backwards. Every positive action requires a reward to let the horse, or any other animal, know that was what you wanted, even if it was only one step in the right direction. I didn't do that because I did not know.

Day by day Topsy and I moved farther and farther from the barn, but still in reverse, until we were a mile from home. I gave her frequent opportunities to walk away from the creek in forward gear, but she still refused. Then one day she went forward, in the right direction. But would I stop then? Oh no. I had to be sure she was going to keep on going in the correct direction, the right way around, before I took her home. However, even with that one mistake that I made, she did learn and never again refused to leave home, in forward gear. In fact her willingness to leave home allowed me to make a 14-mile ride on her.

It was in the winter. Lonesome Lake was frozen over from one end to the other with good ice, nearly two feet thick. The day was warm, and I wanted to go down the lake with the horses to meet Dad on his return from his February mail trip and assist him home.

With Topsy and one saddled horse I left the barn. Seeing two horses leave, the other two decided to come along on whatever adventure Topsy and I were about to have. On bareback Topsy, and leading my saddled horse, the others following, we set off on the trail along the hillside to where I could get on the lake ice, nicely covered with a layer of compacted snow.

We walked down the lake, everybody trusting my judgment on the safety of the ice. In early February the ice would be as safe as it would ever get that winter or any winter. About the only danger spots would be pressure ridges, clearly defined by their shoved-up shape running across the lake, and spring holes, always located just off Double Bay where several small holes get melted thru the ice by narrow ascending streams of spring water. This part of the lake bottom is 12 to 15 feet below the ice, and one can look down and see the lake bottom completely clear of weeds. Not enough light penetrates to allow any crop to grow. The sides of these holes are vertical, and one can let an axe down and then bring the bit up until it catches under the edge of the ice and so measure the thickness of it. Eighteen inches is about average, I think, having done this during several winters.

As we walked down the lake, the sun rose and before long the ice began to sing, as the surface warmed marginally. The horses didn't like the noise the ice made. It cracked and boomed, and one crack ran off across the ice right near us. That was too much.

The strung-out pack of horses, weighing perhaps 5000 pounds, no weight at all for 18 inches of hard ice to support, all began crowding together in a defensive group, making sure all would fall thru if the ice would let them—clearly showing, to me at least, horses do not have any instinctive way to avoid weak ice except simply by not going on it.

Horses do not automatically trust ice in the fall when it first forms on lakes and rivers, but once they find out some is safe they seem to think it all is. Except to get feed, they don't walk on lake ice, even when they know the trail around the lake is a lot harder to walk over than just hiking on the ice. They will take the trail on terra firma. They know it won't break.

They will learn that ice can be safe, but they ascertain that in one or two ways. They start by eating grass along riverbanks where shallow water allows it to freeze thick ice. As they graze along the bank, they gradually, step by step, work themselves out on the ice. In time, finding the ice will hold them along that shore, they then start walking all over the frozen river, even along vertical banks where the water is 10 feet deep and the ice could be of dubious strength. They can't know this. Sometimes they fall thru and cannot get out.

Even I, with my "superior intelligence," almost fell in one winter when I was trying to find the horses, who were walking on ice they shouldn't have, to take them home. The only reason I didn't lose my life was because, unknown to me, a log was lying under the ice about a foot down. The log saved me, but it had also caused the ice to be thin over it, allowing me to get a wet foot; a horse would have fallen in and died.

The other way horses check the safety of the ice is to follow our judgment. As the example above shows, we can make mistakes too. I knew there was a fair current in the river in that place. A horse would not have known of the current, and the significance of it as relating to the safety of the ice.

Now I'd better back track here and catch up those crowding horses out there on Lonesome Lake. We paused there for a bit.

We were close to a rocky point, which ran out into the lake just beneath the ice a few feet. Even so, I really didn't like it very much myself, but still considered the ice safe. Nobody fell thru, so we started again for the north end of the lake, keeping an eye open for any signs of unsafe ice. One sign of a coming hole is a faint shadow on the snow, seen in the distance ahead. With the sun up any dip that would indicate a coming hole would be visible to me, up on the horse. Even quite thick ice can have small holes from those narrow ascending columns of spring water when it is not down around zero Fahrenheit or lower. They would not be dangerous to a human, but a horse could step thru one and break a leg. They could not fall thru, but a broken leg would be just as bad, or maybe worse. Therefore we tended to be careful, always.

One result—an unpleasant result—of being careful got me kicked on the right ankle one winter. Susan and I were riding our horses, Rocket and Cloud, down the Big Lagoon ice to feed the trumpeter swans. Susan was ahead, on Rocket; I followed on Cloud. We sped down the mile-long lagoon. As I could see no reason to stay behind Susan and have to squint against the snow flying off Rocket's hooves, I decided to come up beside Rocket. Also, I'd be better able to watch for shadows on the ice. Rocket responded to this action by twitching her butt left a fraction and aimed a kick at Cloud. She didn't even break stride. Cloud didn't get kicked; I did. Rocket had not had a lot of riding, and not with another horse beside her and both at a canter. I should have gone farther to Rocket's left. She felt Cloud was crowding her, a no-no in horse society. Rocket was boss. Susan never felt Rocket do anything. She cantered on down the ice. I told her I had been kicked, and we changed places and ran on to the end of the lagoon. Finally, there, the nerves in my ankle began to wake up.

We tied our horses about 500 feet from where we fed the swans. Then we walked along the short hillside grade, fed the birds, and returned to the horses. I was glad of a horse to get home on, as by then my ankle nerves were fully awake and outraged. The two-and-a-half-mile ride home was uneventful.

As the day slowly turned into evening, my nerves were profoundly outraged. With my boot off, I was standing by the cook stove, sort of leaning on the warming shelf, as my abused right ankle and foot kept stepping around, and I began gnawing on the top of the warming shelf. The darn thing hurt.

In a few days a whole palette of fancy colors decorated my injury. I wore a big soft cloth "boot" for several weeks, but continued to ride down and feed the swans. I had several offers of help, but as I could do the job I felt I was going darn well to do it. Tho I will have to admit, when it was Jack's day to feed swans, I sort of was glad of it.

Back to the ride down Lonesome Lake now. When I arrived at the north end of the lake there was no sign of Dad. There was nothing for me to do but ride home again. It was getting late, and I had seven miles to ride to get home. I wanted to get off the ice before it got too dark. We all turned around and headed back up the ice.

I seem to remember getting off Topsy's back only once, at the north end of the lake, and I was very tired. The monotonous, never varying walking on a dead level surface is far more tiring than a 14-mile ride along a trail would have been. I imagine Topsy was glad to get off the ice, too. She was hungry. They all were.

I have digressed far enough for this chapter; well, almost.

The training of Topsy reminds me of another horse I was riding, or trying to ride, who didn't want to leave home in forward gear. No one could make him, I was told. Could I? Maybe.

He was a pretty brown and white tobiano paint gelding named Shorty. He was owned by a couple in the lower Fraser Valley I was staying with when I was learning to fly an airplane.

Shorty exhibited the same problem Topsy had about leaving the barn, and I tried the same remedy, with a similar result. About the only thing different was that Shorty and I had to back along a public highway with vehicles passing us all the time.

One driver, curious, stopped to ask me why my horse was going backwards. I told him backwards was the only gear my horse had, and I was hoping he would find his forward gear somewhere on the road. The fellow laughed and drove on.

It only took two miles of backing for Shorty to finally find his forward gear, and once he found it he didn't seem to lose it again. After that he would go anywhere with anyone. Once he found that missing gear we went for long pleasant rides all over the country, always accompanied by busy vehicles. He was a nice horse, and quite comfortable on the shoulder of any busy highway.

We walked, trotted and cantered. We wore out his iron shoes on the gravel alongside the pavement. Then his hooves got worn down too much and his feet were getting tender. I had to stop riding on the roads. I had no extra money for horseshoes. I had to buy an AIRPLANE! I could, however, ride Shorty on grass without hurting him. And he was an excellent puller from his saddle. He had been a roping horse.

My host and hostess, the Hatches, owned a large farm on which was an old stanchion barn where cattle had been housed. They wanted to renovate the building, renew the floor, and use the barn to raise sub-yearling steers in. Before they could renew the floor all the old timbers had to be removed, the drains replaced, then new floor laid. Where Shorty and I came into this project was he could, and did, haul all the timbers outside. I rode him and they tied a strong rope to the timber to be hauled. I wrapped my end of the rope around the saddle horn, asked Shorty to walk out of the barn. The crappy old timbers went along right smartly.

It was only when whatever Shorty was hauling ran out in front of him that he stopped—suddenly. Anything that happened to be between that rope and the saddle horn tended to get mangled a bit. I know. I was there.

My host and hostess were trying to move five or six steers from the barn, thru the yard and on to another field. They decided Shorty, with me aboard, could do the job one steer at a time and keep them out of the garden also. Steers that came along behind were no problem. One fellow decided to precede the horse to the new field, however. That was when I found out that Shorty not only could pull, but also would do his best to stop the steer from running away. There would not have been a problem if I had paid more attention to my fragile fingers. Caught between the horn and the rope, with the 500-pound steer pulling one way and Shorty resisting with his 1000 pounds, my thumb took a beating—or squeezing. I said an awful word, but Shorty would not let up on the steer, or my poor crushed thumb. I was not used to roping horses. I quickly unwrapped the rope. My thumb survived the insult.

I remarked that it wasn't much of an injury, and Johnny Hatch responded with something like, "It didn't sound like it."

Well, I couldn't fly a plane for a few days, but it did, in time, recover, only to get broken more severely decades later by a misstep on a mossy rock slope that had looked dry. It wasn't. However it healed up from that and is still able to hold a pen.

Now back to Topsy.

Topsy was sometimes mean to other animals but never to us, and she was stubborn, or perhaps not schooled as well in some things as she might have been if Dad had had more knowledge about ways to teach the more uncooperative horses. Anyway, it seemed her stubbornness was exceeded only by her jealousy. One could not pet another horse without Topsy becoming angry, not at you, but at the other horse. One couldn't even catch another horse but Topsy had to shove herself in and insist on getting caught first. The reason for catching the horses was to do a day of hard work. But Topsy didn't mind hard work at all. Perhaps she enjoyed the attention, and it put her in the center of things.

She worked hard carrying heavy, cumbersome objects on her back over rough and rocky trails for several hours each day for weeks. The other horses did too, but they weren't jealous of anybody, or stubborn. The other horses were a gelding, Ginty, and a mare, Susan.

Topsy worked hard at hauling logs. One day I had Topsy and her four-year-old son, Rommy, hitched to a load of logs, and they were hiking right along. Surging up a slight slope the logs hit a strong root. There was a healthy CRACK. Both horses almost went on their noses, corrected themselves, and stopped. Both over-worked singletrees were suddenly in two pieces each. It was the first time either Dad or I had broken both singletrees and at the same instant. We were very proud of the team for this accomplishment, I especially. It was sort of my team, you see, and they hadn't been working as well as Dad's team, Susan and her son Prince, had been. The broken singletrees were not a calamity. They were made of maple wood and could be easily replaced.

Topsy was a pretty good, if sometimes erratic, puller. Some of the things she had to help pull were wagonloads of manure for the garden or fields, and one time, sand. Dad had her and Susan, a really good puller, hitched to a heavy, very heavy, load of sand, which was stalled in a soft place on the road. They had tried several times to move it, but didn't seem able to keep it moving out of the soft place. Dad walked around them, pulled at the harness and did something to the wagon, then asked them to try again. That time they kept it moving and took it onto harder ground before Dad stopped them to take a breather. They had worked hard, and it was their finest moment. The load really was too heavy for those two small mares. We all were mighty proud of those two little mares that day. Dad never hit them. He just asked, and they really gave their all.

It probably helped, too, that Dad made them think he had lightened the load, so they tried harder, believing they could pull it. Horses soon learn that if their load gets stopped by a stump or rock, and you shift it off the obstruction, they can then move it. That encourages them to try it again after you have done anything to it.

I have to wonder what it is in the horse, dog, cow and elephant families that causes or allows them to become slaves, companions, or partners to humans. And in the example of dogs and horses, to seem to be happy and cheerful about the situation, often considering their human overlords as friends, and important enough to them that dogs, at least, will put themselves at risk to protect their human boss. I don't really think dogs are thinking about the dinner bowl when they race out to confront a grizzly bear that seems to have its eye on the dog's "god." And I don't believe the dog is answering the natural instinct to chase things, but is in fact trying to protect the pack leader.

The foregoing thoughts remind me of one horse that I had, raised

59

from a foal, born at Lonesome Lake. She learned to be ridden just past two. Her name was Bess, big, beautiful and black and white.

When Jack and I sold our farm at Lonesome Lake and moved farther down the valley, we brought with us the four horses and three cattle, mentioned elsewhere. A few years later I was riding Bess on a ride with two other people on an old logging road up the Salloompt Valley. A teacher was riding the lead horse. I came behind her, and a teenager rode behind on a somewhat nervous gelding. We had crossed a wooden logging bridge and were ascending a fair grade on a curve as we went uphill.

Suddenly I heard a noise behind me and looked back to see the teenager's horse turned around and appearing to be heading back down the road as his rider was falling down his left side, somehow entangled in his reins. The horse lost his cool and broke into a bucking, kicking run down the road. The rider was now hanging head down and flopping like a rag doll when they disappeared from my view as they rounded the turn. Afraid I might scare the horse more and cause him to go off the road and plunge down a steep embankment into a mess of rocks and trees below, I just followed along. When we got around the turn far enough, I saw the young girl lying unmoving on her back on the road, and the horse nowhere in sight. The youngster was groaning and screaming in pain. By then the schoolteacher arrived where the injured girl lay.

As the teacher probably knew more about helping injured people than I did, I offered to ride back down the road and phone for an ambulance; I had a phone near the start of the logging road. I was scared the injured youngster could die there where she lay. Bess was quite nervous; she seemed to pick up on the urgency and was pretty "hyper." She stood rock solid to help me get back in the saddle from a large stone by the side of the road. Then we took off.

Crossing the bridge carefully, Bess lit all four "after-burners" as she began the two-mile run to my place. She ignored the hard road surface and just ran. At one point, without breaking stride, she performed a flying lead change.

At about halfway to my place there was a house where I could use a phone. I rode into the yard, dismounted, and was immediately invited to leave by two large and defensive dogs. Acceding to their demands, I remounted my hot and sweating mare, shot out the driveway and continued to my own place.

Leaving Bess tied to a tree by my door, I phoned for an ambulance. Once it was on the way, I unsaddled my tired horse and turned her loose to walk herself and have a roll while I waited on the road for the ambulance so I could guide them to the injured teenager. The ambulance people strapped the girl securely on a stretcher, loaded her into the vehicle and took off for the hospital, about 20 miles away.

When the horse who had caused the injury ran home into my daughter Susan's yard, without his rider, she went looking to see what he had done with her. Susan knew we had been intending to ride up the Salloompt logging road. So that's where she went. I got a ride back to my place with her.

When I checked on Bess, she seemed none the worse for wear. The next day, tho, and for about a week, her legs were really stiff. She was very careful walking down hill, even groaning a bit. Bess was not inclined to do a lot of unnecessary work that she could see no reason for. That she made that fast two-mile run on that hard logging road, for no reason that would help her in any way that I can see, makes me believe she exerted herself to help my friend. She must have known the young girl was in trouble from the noises she was making. I think she picked up on the emergency and she did her best.

The teenager recovered from the injuries she received that day and still has horses in her life.

chapter 7

It's a Challenge

Many things can challenge us in our lives. Challenges can add zip and spice to life and make the juices flow. Some challenges are simply not worth answering. Those one would just walk away from and seek something else to make their lives worthwhile.

When my father traveled up the Bella Coola–Atnarko Valley, seeking a lake and free land nearby that could be preempted and developed into a farm, he passed many developing farms along the way. The ones farthest from the growing village of Bella Coola, set at the head of North Bentinck Arm, were arranged along the grassy banks of Stillwater about 60 miles inland.

At the north end of Stillwater lay a beautiful big meadow, lightly treed with willows, alders and a few cottonwoods along the riverside of it. Very little clearing was required before hay was being harvested. My Uncle Frank Ratcliff had preempted this 160-acre lot.

Farther upstream, Uncle Frank's half-brother took up a long slim lot. It was also lightly treed, and easy to clear and harvest hay from.

At the south end of the Stillwater is a large area, much of it gently sloping up to the base of the mountain on the east side of the valley. There another Ratcliff, Uncle Johnny, staked his 160-acre preemption. Most of this property is the alluvial fan from a good creek tumbling down the mountain. And this one was partly lightly treed with willow and alder and some birch. Uncle Johnny cleared a long strip along the river and planted tame grass and clover on it. It is all reforested now, but the tame grass and clover still are there.

All three of those settlers were young bachelors with lots of ambition. However, the challenge of developing farms seems to have been more than they really wanted to spend their lives at. They seem to have begun questioning what they were doing there, each with no family. What was their future? One by one they drifted away, leaving the Lonesome Lakers with fewer neighbors and more lonely.

They didn't know it then, but if they had stayed until 1936 they would have found out the real reason they packed up and left. Goat Creek, which charges into the Atnarko River just downstream of Stillwater, and in fact created the gently flowing three-mile section of river, went on a rampage. Three days of very heavy rain swelled that volatile creek and it carried enough debris to dam the Atnarko, flooding all the nice meadows along its length, creating a lovely "lakescape." They had left in time.

My father's property at Lonesome Lake was flooded also. However Hunlen Creek couldn't keep the dam it threw across the river at the outlet of the lake in place. With help from Dad and his shovel and wheelbarrow, Atnarko River wore most of the dam away, thus bringing the lake level to almost to where it had been before the flood.

This reminds me of the night all five of us spent in the rowboat, tied to a fir snag anchored almost upright, about a hundred feet from shore. We all had gone down the lake to work on the dam at the outlet. Not wanting to row all that six miles back home only to row the six miles down the lake again, the folks decided to camp there. It seemed like we might be safer from bears way out in the lake than we would be camped on shore on a bear trail. As I recall the night was warm and almost calm, with only the occasional gentle rocking of the boat. It was a very pleasant sleep, tho the boat was a bit crowded with five of us bedded down in it.

The first white settlers at Stillwater would have been faced with some serious trail building. If no horse trail already existed from Atnarko settlement to Stillwater, they would have had to build one. I don't remember, and seem unable to find out. I know there was a trail to Stillwater. I don't know when it was put in or who did it.

As there is considerable talus, some diving directly into the swiftly flowing Atnarko River, the trail builders graded out a possible, but rocky, route for packhorses, often going high up the talus slope where the boulders were smaller. If this was not practical, they built a log bridge across the river. Then another log bridge would return the trail to the same side. But given the propensity of rivers to remodel their banks frequently, often the bridges would be left high and dry as the river ran off in another channel and chuckled.

Just past the Hotnarko–Atnarko junction the trail builders put a high, long, fairly durable log bridge across the Atnarko River where it all was in one channel. It stayed in for many years. Then high water in the summer of 1948 lifted off the stringers but left the piers standing there, to be carried away later. Upstream of the long bridge, the river was in several channels, each one being bridged. However, those bridges were not of much use as the river channels would move and forget to take their bridges with them.

Finally the trail builders got the message and abandoned the whole bridge idea. They rolled rocks, filled large holes between the rocks until they had a rough trail, steep but passable, over the large granite bluffs that had caused the builders to bridge the river to begin with, except for one place. A short stretch of sloping bluff plunged straight into the river 50 feet below. There was not much of a way over or around it. After scratching their heads for a while, they decided to try one more bridge. At least the river was unlikely to mess this one up.

On the upstream side of this little bluff was a gently sloping sand and gravel strip running down to the river. It was quite feasible to dig out a level place to rest the end of the bridge on. At the other side of the bluff was a nice level area about five feet wide that ran along the edge of the bluff they wanted to bridge. The other end of the bridge would rest on that. It was a good sturdy bridge, about four feet wide and probably 20 feet long, and had a stout rail on the outside.

That bridge stayed there many years, but in the spring of 1948, when the frost was going out of the ground, a large boulder was loosened above the bridge and came tumbling down the bluff, heading for the river, and took the bridge along. Once again the trail was out.

Twenty or so feet above where the bridge had been there was a narrow ledge that people could squeeze past, but it couldn't be used by horses. As we needed to have a usable trail to bring in our own supplies and feed for the trumpeter swans, Dad and I—Dad pounding as I turned the drill—put in a two-foot-wide blasted out rock cut in late summer of 1948. Due to alterations the flood of 1948 performed on the trail between Atnarko and Stillwater, there were several places we had to make new trail. That was very usual, and normal for any valley with side hills and a river running thru. The river only wanted to take back what already belonged to it, its bed. Before the 1936 flood, people and horses could travel up and down Stillwater on the dry meadows, crossing the river to get from one side to the other, usually by swimming the horses behind the boat.

On the east side of Stillwater, opposite Uncle Frank's cabin at the north end, there is a rather formidable one-third mile of talus. Huge minivan-sized blocks of granite lay in an unstable jumble along the lakeshore. It was not an encouraging sight to trail builders, and a bit too much of a challenge. They chose to work out a rough trail in the much finer material up close to the overhanging bluffs that had spawned the talus. On that side of Stillwater there were many such places, but with a bit—or a lot—of hard work and time there was then a usable trail. Many small rocks had to be carried in one's hands to fill any holes between the larger rocks so a horse would not step in it and injure a leg or foot. My horses did not like that rugged trail, and given a choice, after learning how much nicer raft travel was, were mighty glad to go on our raft when we moved down the valley.

At one place on this trail there is a bluff that runs right down to the edge of the water and there was not much of any way over it, as it also ran far up the mountain. So Dad simply carried, or threw, rocks into the water until he had a trail bed perhaps 15 feet long under the broken bottom of the bluff. I believe my brother Johnny helped with this job.

Many years later when I was bringing in a mare I had bought in the spring of 1951, I had to use that piece of trail and it was hidden under four feet of water, and where it lay exactly was difficult to discern thru the murky water. The rock fill was plenty wide enough when the water was low, but this time it was high. If the horse went too close to the bluff, she could step off the edge of the fill where the rocks were large, jagged and sunk in the mud. If she stepped off on the outside, she'd be in a deep and muddy mess of water and coarse rocks. I did not want to wade neck-deep in cold springtime water, and felt that as the mare was somewhat taller than I, she should carry me across. I jumped onto her back and asked her to enter the water. She carefully walked in, trusting me to guide her. Together we crossed the rock fill safely.

I had ridden this young horse only twice before, not really a long enough time for her to learn that she could trust me. She must have had a naturally trusting nature. Later events were to prove she did have a very trusting nature.

I don't know where the trail between Lonesome Lake and Stillwater went to begin with. I only know where it is now. However, I believe from some evidence of the remains of old broken bridges, and from what I was told many years ago, that it must have been on the east side of the river from Uncle Johnny's place to about half the way to Lonesome Lake. Most of the way it would have followed close to the river for the trap line. The terrain in that area is quite suitable for a trail.

For the rest of the distance to Lonesome Lake, on the east side of the river there are many steep cliffy sections where no one would want to build a trail. And they didn't. They crossed the several river channels on bridges. And as below Stillwater, the Atnarko River showed its usual contempt for man's puny attempts to boss the river around. It removed the bridges or buried them in logjams.

Once again admitting defeat, the trail was put on the west side of the valley, where it should have been put in the first place. Many tons of supplies have been carried over that trail on the backs of horses, and humans, during the many years since it was built.

The trail between Lonesome Lake and Stillwater leaves the foot of Lonesome Lake on the rocky Hunlen Creek delta. After crossing any number of channels, some large, some small, some dry, some roaring with foaming tumbling water that rolls huge boulders down the channel, the trail continues thru a thin forest of cedar, cottonwood and fir, all growing from between the boulders of the creek bed. Then it enters an area of moss-covered rocks. It is still rocky, but much older and the moss has been able to cover most of the ground and rocks. The creek has not used this part of its delta for many years. The forest is much denser, with larger trees, but still very rocky.

At the end of the first mile north of Lonesome Lake the trail comes out on a bench where one can look over the Atnarko River where it has spread itself in various channels from one side of the valley to the other. Cottonwoods are about all that grows on that rocky terrain, with very few cedars and birches.

For perhaps 500 feet the trail carries on along the top of the 20-foot-high almost vertical bank, then descends gently to the level of the river. Here the trail enters a dense forest of tall trees and moist ground, with a cold, delicious little creek rambling along close to the western wall of the valley. The dark, cool forest is dominantly cedar with a sprinkling of cottonwood, a flake of spruce and a pinch of fir, for about another mile. Sometimes in June this area is home to clouds of very hungry mosquitoes. One should carry a small cedar branch to whip around one's head and over one's back, in constant motion, to discourage the ravenous hoards. Of course if you are wearing a heavy pack, at least some of those enterprising little bloodsuckers will be able to sneak under the edge of your pack and get a fill of your blood. There is very little you can do about that, and they love your sweaty smell, too.

Leaving the dense forest, the trail winds out into the open. Soon it climbs up and runs along on an easy grade some 20 feet above the river, for 500 feet or so, then continues on thru the woods for a ways to once again follow the riverbank for perhaps three-quarters of a mile. On this section of the trail it wanders between many large boulders lying at the foot of talus. To build this part, the trail builders had to move many of those rocks to make a trailbed, then fill holes to make it safe for horses. The trail finally stops at the original preemption cabin that Uncle Johnny Ratcliff built in the early 1900s.

There is no trail except a very rough game trail the rest of the way to the north end of Stillwater, on the west side. The game trail is atrocious, fit only for bears and mountain goats. Humans can hike on that route, but I am very sure no one would enjoy it.

The trail into Stillwater from downstream may have been built before the Ratcliffs came in there. I don't have any information on this. There is sign of First Nations people having lived in the area. There are peeled standing cedars and dugout canoes on all the lakes. So they may have had some trails already built, at least good enough for humans. I have even considered the possibility that over a hundred years ago the river could have been all on the other side of the valley, and no very extensive trail building would have been required by anyone. The Indian dugout canoes were still usable in my day. There was one on Stillwater, one on Lonesome Lake; I rode in both of them several times in the 1940s.

Speaking of former occupancy of the Atnarko Valley by first colonizers, there was, before the 2004 fire destroyed it, quite a bit of evidence of early people living in the area, if not for whole years, at least for shorter periods of time. Aside from the dugout canoes on the lakes, we found two deadfalls, large enough possibly to catch foxes, on Arbordale. Also a salmon drying rack and quite a few standing peeled six-inch to 10-inch cedars. Someone had cut the bark eight or 10 feet above the ground and stripped it off. I assume they used it for walls or roofing on some sort of shelter. This would have been done around late 1800s or early 1900s. There were First Nations people trapping in the valley when Dad preempted there. In a few years they stopped coming down from the Chilcotin country. I think they may have found a better source of income in the Chilcotin. Fur prices fell pretty low there for several years.

There was also a six-foot-long depression in one of the areas we cleared for field, which we thought possibly could be an Indian grave. It was about two feet wide and formed a hollow some six inches deep. Believing it could be a grave, we never dug into it.

chapter 8

LOSE & LEARN

One might think tender young calves and big-bellied old milk cows, and especially fat yearlings, ranging around in dense, high grass growing everywhere along the cut banks of a river would be most attractive to a hungry predator, and very easy to catch. That was the situation where Jack and I and my parents ranged our spare cattle each year from early April to November or December, depending on how much snow there was on the feed. Surprisingly, we lost very few to animal attacks. One cow came home with three or four neat holes punched in one ear, but otherwise unhurt. She obviously had been using her beautiful Ayrshire horns effectively and survived. There were also several animals which had shortened tails and survived.

When Dad first began "civilizing" the Lonesome Lake area, he brought in a few goats. He wanted to raise Angora goats. I don't remember how long he had them, but it seems like it was not very long. On one trip to town for mail, Dad left his goats in a small corral made of tall boards forming a tight wall, but on his return the boards had been ripped off, the goats eaten, and whatever remained was buried under a big pile of grass sod and mud. He never tried goats again. He learned the hard way that such small animals can't defend themselves, and short of a solid log wall and a good roof, they cannot be protected from bears.

With the hazards of a lot of windfall, steep riverbanks and a whirlpool one place in the river near The Birches, Dad lost a cow, and one or two others had shortened tails, and one lost a rump roast, but survived. These animals were ranging in a rather poor area of windfall and steep banks. The one cow that drowned in the whirlpool likely went into the river to escape the wolves, because she was trapped by piles of downed timber on the steep bank. It was not a natural place for a cow animal to go if she wasn't being pushed.

Later, Dad started taking his cattle 10 miles south to the Elbow Lake area where there was lots of good grass and little windfall. Just swamps and miles of vertical mud banks on each side of the river, tho along the length of the quiet, meandering stream were many places where cows could easily cross. In the Elbow Lake area there were fewer hazards, and fewer losses.

Another factor that may have made a difference was the education of wolves by the leg-hold steel trap. Wolves became very wary of any hint of iron, and as the cows wore bells we think that was a deterrent to attempted predation. Also, we tried to have the calves born at home and that helped. Furthermore, our cattle all kept their horns.

Jack and I did have a hornless cow, Cindy, attacked by something. She had an injury on her hind fetlock, which greatly interfered with walking, and some other cuts and gouges on her rump and elsewhere. Also, we had three head out on range, all hornless. Somehow, they survived the attack. Ordinarily, we would not have put three hornless cattle, one of which was a yearling, out on range by themselves. My people had horned cattle that they thought they'd be putting out in a few days. Something happened that they couldn't get their cows out for a month, so our three helpless cattle didn't have that extra help. Yet they did stand off the predator.

Cindy was a cow we bought from down the valley, as we were completely out of milk cows, our one cow having failed to conceive. Our milking cow was the only one we had and we had no heifer to take her place. To have milk we had no choice but to get a new cow, so we bought Cindy.

Cindy was a story in herself. She had not been trained to lead, but she had been dehorned. Not a help for leading, but perhaps safer

71

to handle if one is not going to train the heifer all her required education to make a milk cow that can be caught, led and handled. She and I had some real old battles. She tried to smash me with her hornless, hard head when I did anything near her head. She hated me, and I seemed unable not to return the compliment. She was so different from the cattle I had known all my life until I met her. She was a very small Ayrshire, brown and white.

Her former owner trucked her to the bottom of the hill. Then, Jack, Susan, Skye (my border collie) and I were on our own. That was the first time Cindy had been in a halter, and she was determined to carry both me and Jack off through the down timber and rock bluffs, or at least wear out the seats of our pants on the gravel road. She was not over 800 pounds, but completely lacking in knowledge. In time, she came to the conclusion she could not drag an anchor weighing only 340 pounds, just as stubborn, and she gave up.

Then she had to learn to follow us. That took less time to catch onto and then we were on our way. In camp, I milked her into a small tin pail and we boiled the milk over the campfire. It was horrible!—partly from her being so scared and tired, and partly from the scorching of the pot by the campfire. And smoky. Even a dog would not have eaten it. I threw it out and hoped the next batch would be better. It was. In fact, she produced very good rich, creamy milk and butter, eventually.

I realize now that Cindy must have been totally confused and bewildered. That was probably the first time in her life that she found herself away from home, with complete strangers, and not even one of her herd with her. Also, even though she was comfortable standing in a stanchion, she had never gone anywhere with the stanchion leading her. The stuff we were trying to teach her should have been taught when she was a young calf, to make it easy for her to learn.

She also had to learn to have her right hind leg restrained so she couldn't plant her hoof in the milk pail. Where we got her from, the farmer had some kind of anti-kicking device, which we couldn't duplicate, and I, "nose-in-the-air," simply didn't believe one could merely tie a snug figure eight around both legs just above the heel joint and have it prevent kicking.

When I moved down the valley, the barn I had for my cows was too weak to tie a cow's leg to anything, so I was forced to try the figure-eight tie, and lo and behold, it worked. Because the cow can only pull against herself, she can't hurt herself, and she soon learns it is better just to stand still.

Cindy and I fought for months, more about the tying than the milking. Then she and I had a couple of months of peace, while waiting for her to calve in January. Cows need at least six weeks rest between calves. Two months is better.

Finally, the great day arrived. I was checking her one last time before I went to bed. I had to go in her stall and she attacked me. I hit her on the nose with my flashlight and departed quickly, slamming the door. When I didn't return to the house for some time, Jack came to see what was going on. We stood outside her stall and waited. I assumed from her actions she was close to calving and wanted to stay in case of any trouble. I have seen many calves get born and have never considered the event as anything but a miracle.

Cindy wouldn't even allow us to take a step without protest. She stood as far away as the stall allowed and glowered at us. Soon she got down to the business at hand, but continued to treat Jack and me as if we were salivating wolves. She never lay down, as a cow normally does to calve, but stood through the entire process. Then, when her beautiful black and white, half Holstein, half Ayrshire heifer was on the ground, she roared at us and made charges right to the gate, then stormed back to her snuffling wet calf to take a few hasty licks at the shivering little thing. As there was no way we were going to enter her stall, we left them for the night and went to bed.

In the morning her temper had not improved, but the calf had got herself up and nursed. We left them until turn-out time, for drinking and exercise, then we caught Cindy from across the stall and secured her firmly. All the time before we tied her she had kept the calf carefully between herself and the far wall. Tied up, she had to allow us into her stall, tho she roared and snorted valiantly to save her calf.

In with the calf, we found her tame and friendly, coming right up to us, ready to have her neck scratched and petted. She was the sweetest, smartest and friendliest calf I had ever seen. We named her Valerian. Showing Cindy we were not going to hurt her baby, I took her out and put her in the stanchion to milk. And she had a lot, even after the calf had taken a good lot herself. Cindy had fits, but did not hold up her milk. We were trying to prove to the wild-acting cow that we wouldn't hurt her little one. I considered her to be a crazy animal. In time I was to learn she was actually quite sweet, but had been abused.

I am not accusing the farmer of abuse, but from the transformation that eventually came over the cow I have to believe one of the people handling the animals had used a chain to discipline her. She so feared even a light dog chain rattling near her it sent her into flight. The owner had about 20 head of dairy cows and calves and had help running his dairy herd. He was a very gentle person, and a very good friend of many people in the valley, including us Lonesome Lakers.

Slowly thru the months she became tamer as we struggled over the milking. She found out we were the important link between her and her precious Valerian every feeding time, for it was me who led the hungry calf to her twice a day for her milk. I took her away too, but Cindy didn't mind after the calf was fed.

Then one day she actually gave me the "please groom me" signal as she stood comfortably before me, head stretched down, asking me to "lick" her neck, a grooming ritual cattle who are friends frequently engage in. Dominance does not matter. It is a bonding act between cattle that helps to hold a herd together. To be invited to join the herd in this manner I always considered an honor. I was a fellow cow, in their view.

Valerian was named for a sweet mountain flower, because she was just such a sweet little creature. She liked to wrap herself around us and get as close as possible, pressing against us as she walked around our legs. She was an extremely sensitive animal and easy to hurt emotionally, if I wasn't careful. If I spoke a harsh word to her she would turn her head away in submission. Thinking I was not pleased with her, it seemed like. And she turned out to be an excellent milk cow.

Susan trained her to be ridden, and often went to the pasture for her and her mother to bring them to the barn for milking. Susan would sling a rope over Valerian's horns, halter Cindy, jump onto the young cow, and bring the two in, much as if they were horses. Unfortunately no one took a picture.

It was when Cindy had her second calf at Arbordale that her transformation was complete. I had put her in a small corral rather than in the barn, as it was summer and I preferred to have my cows calve outside if the weather was good.

Still a bit wary after the way she had acted with her other calf, I stayed out of her corral until the calf was born. As she seemed much calmer this time I finally risked going in with her, watching for any signs of defense. There were none. She was licking the little wet calf, and barely glanced at me as I stood just inside the open gate. Open in case I had to beat a hasty retreat. I did not want to go where I was not wanted. New mothers can be very protective. I know. I have been there. And I have been shown the "eye" of defense even by some very tame, well-socialized cows, and backed off to give them their space.

Cindy did not appear concerned; I calmly moved closer until I was right beside her, and she just continued to do her cleaning job. Finally I reached down and touched her baby, lifted one hind leg to ascertain the gender. Male. He would be named Juno, for June. I had wanted another heifer, as this calf was a three-quarter Ayrshire. The sire was one-half Hereford, and one half Ayrshire. I really liked the

Ayrshire cattle and their good milk. Anyway we have to accept what we get. Someone else is in charge, not us. After this calf came along, the milking job went a lot smoother. In time Cindy was in calf again by the same "half and half" bull. This one was also due in June or July.

We had made a trip to the summer range, about 10 or 12 miles south of Lonesome Lake, to get Cindy and the team for haying. The horses were easy enough to find. Finding the cattle took longer. When we did find them, Cindy was not with them. We had to search for her for about an hour. Jack found her alone, about half a mile from the others. She had an injured hind hoof. Perhaps she couldn't keep up with the others and may have been hiding.

Cindy limped slowly to me, across a small muddy creek. I haltered her, then looked her over to see the damage, why she was limping. Her left hind foot had been chewed and was swollen up. Also there were several other gouges and cuts on her. If she had been a lot closer to home, we probably could have been able to treat her and save her calf. As she was 15 miles from home, and the 15 miles involved walking over a trail filled with logs and rocks, and she could not lift her injured leg over any obstacle on the trail, she would have to drag it over, making a very long and painful trip home. The misery to her did not seem worth it. As always in these cases, we have to make a decision without being able to ask the victim how she feels.

I put her down there and we left her there, a small crumpled heap in a muddy ditch. And her calf died with her. A sad end to a brave little cow who, in the end, had won my love and admiration, and now, finally, understanding.

Now on a happier note, I will go back to 1936, in November, when there were several major alterations to creeks and lakes from Stillwater to Tenas Lake, three miles south of Lonesome Lake. Two of Dad's horses, Topsy and Susan, had to save themselves on a mountainside without very much to eat, at Stillwater. More on these horses later in this chapter, near the end.

Sometime in November 1936, rain poured down hard for three days. The creeks up and down the valley all rose. The creek that comes in at the north end of Tenas Lake, normally quite small and meek, imagined itself a violent river as it rampaged thru the forest, gathering rocks, gravel, small trees and brush. This stuff it carried to the outlet of the lake. Forced right across the Atnarko River where it slips quietly out of Tenas Lake, a dam was soon built up. Tenas Lake rose. The creek carried more dam material, so the lake rose some more. And the creek responded with rocks and brush. Eventually Atnarko won, began eating at the dam. In a short time its level was down some, but higher than it had been before the flood.

The trumpeter swans lost some lakebed feeding area, but the extensive sedge meadows at the head of the lake, being flooded, afforded some feed for the birds. The "slough-grass," sedge root mass now being under water and softened, could be gathered more easily by the swans.

A similar event happened at the outlet of Lonesome Lake, but on a much larger scale. Hunlen Creek is forever getting tired of old channels across its one-and-a-half-mile wide alluvial fan of rocks and boulders and seeks new routes to the Atnarko River. To build those channels the streams can carry a vast cargo of rocks, sand, boulders, logs and, often, whole trees. If the new channels happen to enter the Atnarko at the outlet of the lake where the outflow is relatively slow, the dam builds up. The lake rises and so on just as with Tenas Lake with the resultant rise of the lake, then an eventual washout of the dam. The lake gets a new higher level, and drowned meadows at the head, and water too deep for the swans to feed in. However, to partly compensate, the flooded sedge meadows become feeding areas until ice forms over the new wetlands.

The shallow areas in the head of the lake always freeze very early, but a slight current helps the ice to melt with any warm-up after it has been very cold, something like minus 10 degrees Fahrenheit or lower.

Stillwater, with a creek much wilder than lake-strewn Hunlen Creek, is subject to more frequent flooding. Goat Creek, the one that creates Stillwater, is violent and can carry a good load of remodeled creek channel to dam and raise the lake more readily than Hunlen Creek does Lonesome Lake.

In the 1965 flood Stillwater rose eight feet before cutting out by the awesome weight of water impounded in the four miles of new lake. That year, however, when Stillwater cut out it removed some of the older dam and left the lake lower by half a foot or so than it had been for years. In the flood of 1936, it did not go back down to its former level, but remained four feet higher, flooding all the meadow areas with two to four feet of water, creating some new feeding areas for the trumpeter swans.

Stillwater was the best place for the swans to feed and rest. Only a few could find food in open heads of the other lakes on the Atnarko. The next best area for the trumpeter swans was Lonesome Lake. When Dad began the swan feeding, he chose to feed them at Stillwater because that was where most of the swans were. The reason for feeding at Lonesome Lake was they could be fed every day instead of infrequently, just when he made mail trips. Of course they were better fed with everyday feeding and made out better. Even with the feeding, the swans continued to visit every piece of open water that supplied food for them any time it was open, all up and down the entire river system from Bella Coola to Knot Lake. Some swans even fed on the lower Kleena Kleene in the early spring.

None of the above areas were available when it got cold and stayed cold for weeks on end, as could happen any time during the winter. Minus 30 degrees Fahrenheit was not uncommon any winter.

When the trumpeter swan feeding began in the early thirties there were only 32 birds barely surviving in the Lonesome Lake and

Stillwater area. With the help of feed, the tiny flock slowly increased. By 1952, there were 94 birds in February. By 1972 there were over 400. That was their highest point. The next year they had begun declining, year by year. In 1988 there were only 120 coming to be fed, and only for about a month when the weather was the coldest for that winter. I assume they spread back into areas they had been shot out of in the late 1800s and early 1900s. Then that misguided persecution of the big birds was made illegal, and the swans eventually learned they could go back to their old wintering areas, more or less safely.

I believe quite a few of "our flock" were adding themselves to flocks elsewhere where there was feed for them. Also, we had a number of milder winters, so more areas of wild feed were available to them, not being frozen over for long periods of time.

I had better get back to those two mares, marooned on a barren mountainside, but safe from the flood. They were Topsy and Susan.

At the end of horse packing in the fall of 1936 Dad left Topsy and Susan at the Stillwater. I have no memory of why, and it really doesn't matter. He brought Ginty home. The mares were fenced so they couldn't follow the old horse. Then it rained. The river rose. The mares were on low meadow along the river, with no place to go to reach high ground. Some of the hazards they could have had to cope with would have been floating logs from beaver logging operations in the meadows. Other problems were beaver ditches across the narrow strip of land where the mares would have been feeding. Beavers dig extensive canals to float their winter supplies along from where they cut them to their houses.

The only place the mares could escape to was right across the deep river, a steep mountainside difficult but not impossible for them to climb. After swimming a couple hundred feet across the muddy, log-strewn current, they were safe from the water. But not from starvation. On the fir-clad hillside there was little to eat except dead leaves and moss.

Dad went down to find them as soon as the water dropped enough for him to travel. It took him a while. But he finally found them. I seem to remember they found him, actually. Needless to say there was great rejoicing both at the house and in Ginty's corral when he returned with those smart, courageous little mares. I am not sure, but I have some dim recollection he took one of the boys with him. He certainly could have used a hand getting them from where they were back to the trail after the flood.

chapter 9

MOTHER

Thinking back on my childhood, the impression I carry is that my parent's ship of marriage was powered by Dad as the engine, but Mother was the rudder. She kept the ship on an even keel and going in the right direction as the engine pushed it forward into the gales and calm weather. As the rudder, Mother seldom got angry and never seemed upset or discouraged.

She was a kind, warm, loving person. The only animals she didn't like at all were wolves, coyotes and cougars, the large predators. Perhaps they offended her sense of gentleness. I don't think she stopped to realize the large predators weren't deliberately causing pain to the deer they were programmed to catch and eat, but were merely making their living in the manner the Lord designed them to.

Mother's cows were her family after Dad left home in 1965. He had sold the farm and had given Mother all the cattle. Then he flew off to begin an entirely new life. He took up commercial fishing near Prince Rupert. Mother stayed at The Birches, and Stanley, my older brother, retired from his job in Ocean Falls and came to live at Lonesome Lake and help her with the cattle. They lived there for about 10 years more, then moved all the cows to Bella Coola.

Mother loved those cows and treated them like children, almost. She and Stanley bought, and had flown in to Lonesome Lake, fancy commercial feeds for the cattle. I think just because they liked it. They certainly didn't need it with all the good grass on their own place, and on the same summer range where Dad had pastured the excess stock each summer, and also where Jack and I ran our spare animals, about 10 miles south of Lonesome Lake. There were acres of good quality feed and they bècame fat and happy.

They also took along a young dog Susan had tried to train, but had given up on and had finally given her to her grandmother. For a short time Mother had two dogs to look after, but then I guess Candy's life came to an end and she had just Flapdoodle. I called her Flapdoodle, as she was always in a flap about something. That was not Susan's name for her, though; she had named the dog Lady.

As Flappie was not a neuter, it wasn't long until puppies began arriving and an interesting lot they were. Some large, some small, one yellow shorthaired and large, one large and longhaired and blackish-grayish. Flap herself was a collie-cross, about 40 pounds. Some of her varied pups were closer to 60 or 70 pounds. Flap was born to a tiny reddish animal, maybe 10 to 15 pounds. Her father was a huge wolf-colored longhair, 70 to 80 pounds. What a variety there can be in dogs. Then Mother had lots of dogs. I believe they managed to find homes for all the pups, or they may have kept one. I really don't remember or if I ever knew.

I really don't know if Mother never needed any kind of challenge to keep her interested in everything, or perhaps life itself was all the challenge she wanted or needed.

For years when money was really short she sewed all our clothes. Sewing was her art. She took a lot of care to make all her seams right. If a seam turned out crooked, she'd rip it out and do it over. More than once I held the cloth while she cut each wrong stitch with a razor blade, until she got past the crooked part, then back to the sewing machine it went. Next time the seam came out right and it could stay.

Mother seemed to have lived her life in the shadow of the rest of the family. She was always there, but almost invisible, gently doing her many and varied tasks. For all the years after their house burnt she had to cope with a house only 10 feet wide and 20 feet long. The cooking range, table, and her bed took up a good lot of that space. Then there would be five stools made of blocks of firewood to sit on in place of chairs. They would come later, much later. Also in the house were a sewing machine and an ironing board. The kitchen area was large enough if they had made more cupboards. Nothing about that house encouraged efficient use of the space that was available.

I don't know why we didn't either build rooms onto the building, or else make an entire new bigger house. Dad did make two additions after I left home; there were just the two of them living there. I guess it helped that by then he had a chainsaw, which did make a difference. Perhaps Dad was just too tired to face building again what they had lost in the fire.

Maybe Dad was not so much physically tired as mentally tired. It requires a lot of gathering of energy to get one's body and mind geared up to do a big building project, especially with only hand tools for the job. And when one gets older, that energy becomes harder and harder to find. He may also have had some parts of his body that never healed properly from the punishment that bull gave him, which we never heard about. Dad was never a complainer.

My parents were very honest people and tried to teach us as children the same idea. I like to think they succeeded pretty well. They both were quite self-effacing and didn't seem to want to take credit for anything, even when they deserved it. They just took life in stride.

My parents seemed not to know how to express the emotions they must often have felt, and tried to deny the fact they were sad or were in a sorrowful mood by acting cheerful and outwardly not upset, even when I am sure their hearts must have been aching. They didn't want to upset the children or show themselves as weak, I believe. I do not know. The matter was never discussed. Maybe no one had emotions in those long gone days.

Both my parents were on the short side. Dad was an inch or so shorter than Mother. She, I seem to remember, was about five feet, five inches tall. I used to be five feet, three inches. Now I am only something under five feet, because I can't stand up straight any more.

My two brothers, however, attained a decent height, but my daughter, whose father was five feet 11 inches, is only an inch taller than I used to be. But you should see her two sons. They are tall and slim handsome guys, over six feet. Good for reaching things high over my head, such as picking apples, etc. On the other hand, those tall guys can, and do, put things so far above my reach that I have to get up on something high to retrieve them. Also tall people are forever hitting their heads on things I can walk under quite safely.

So there is something to be said for both tall and short. Neither is better than the other. A person's true worth should never be assessed on his or her physical dimensions, but by his or her heart, to which height and girth are not related.

Mother and Dad were both avid readers, as were we children. Mother read to us a lot when we were young. Even when we were older, we loved it when either parent would read stories out of *Saturday Evening Post,* especially about Bullwinkle and Tugboat Annie whose tugboats were *Salamander* and *Narcissus,* respectively.

I loved my parents dearly and still miss them. And they spanked us. I am sure we deserved it—usually, anyway. However, I believe the sad, disappointed look on my Mother's face when I did something wrong or bad was a far more effective form of punishment than the spanks. Physical punishment can make one resentful, and inclined to question their love, or how could they hit you and hurt you that way? But when their faces show how hurt and sad they are because you did something you weren't supposed to, that makes you feel bad—that you hurt your parents.

I remember Mother spanking me for eating forbidden green apples. She told me they would make me sick. I thought if they made me sick that should have been punishment enough. But perhaps it was the principle. I had been ordered not to eat them, so I disobeyed when I ate one. Very bad. It could have been important, such as an order not to go near the river.

I never ate another green apple, however. But not because I was spanked. Green apples simply aren't fit to eat raw. They are much better cooked, with lots of sugar added, and cream. The green apple didn't make me sick either.

Dad passed away in 1977 at 86 years old.

Mother lived to be 75 and passed away on November 22, 1979.

chapter 10

MÉLANGE

Play can be anything that gives one pleasure. One of my earliest memories of playing goes back to when I was old enough to keep up with my brothers, and they were kind enough to suffer the presence of a sometimes complaining little sister as we all three rambled thru the woods. Studying nature, we had a lot of fun just hiking about, looking at everything and anything that caught our interest. Rocks, squirrel nests and caches, birds, creeks, waterfalls, all kinds of interesting stuff.

As far as worrying about being eaten by wild animals went, we were probably the wildest animals out there. Anything else would have run and hidden in holes, with their paws over their eyes and ears. We made a lot of noise as we went about our exploring.

Our parents invested in scientific books on trees, plants, birds, fish, mushrooms, ferns, rocks, insects, snakes, toads, frogs, spiders, insect-eating insects, animal-eating plants, and mammals. With the good books as guides we learned the proper names of many of the creatures out there in our 160-acre playground.

With our farm chores finished and the night's wood in, I could then take my little sled, in near darkness, and go across the field, covered with a foot or so of soft snow, to a bank I could ride my sled down, for perhaps 20 feet. Hauling the sled back to the top of the bank, I would take another run down until my hands, despite the warm mittens, just got too cold to stay out any longer.

We had a much better slide quite a way from the house, where we three went with our sleds to slide down a long way, perhaps a couple hundred feet. With a good "sled-way" worn in the snow, we could ride down at a pretty fast clip. As there were few trees on the hillside, we didn't need to do much steering, but we could steer and stop. We kneeled on the sled deck and could use the other foot as a brake or to power the sled. It was lots of fun!

Visitors to our home, The Birches, were rare in the 1930s, and when they did come it was always on foot. That was soon to change.

It happened when the family was standing out in the front yard. A new sound seeped into the valley. New to all of us except Dad. He had heard similar noises in the First World War in Europe, so he instantly knew what it was. An AIRPLANE! The rest of us knew of such exotic things from reading books and magazines, but we had never heard one before. We were all wildly excited, the three kids yelling, laughing, talking all at once as we raced around the yard in our joy and anticipation. Even Mother was excited.

The plane came over the mountain on the west side of the valley, slowly losing altitude. It circled the farm several times, continuing to descend, then headed for the lake and out of sight behind the tall trees by the barn. Assuming it would land on the lake, Dad raced to the river, about 300 yards from the house to where the boat was kept, and hurriedly rowed to the lake. The plane was sitting quietly on the water. The people on the plane were very glad to see him.

They explained the situation and begged him to guide them to One Eye Lake in the Chilcotin country. Dad told them where it was and showed them on their map. But the pilot said they'd been flying around in the rain for three days and had been unable to find the lake. Couldn't he just guide them there, please? Dad explained he had hay out that had to be put in the barn soon, as the rain also had been interfering with our haying. They begged and Dad relented, but explained he would have to go tell the family what he would be doing. Back at the plane, they took off for One Eye Lake. Dad had at last had a ride in an airplane. He was very happy when he returned to the house, lucky man. I had to wait a while for my first ride, but it came.

The second plane to land on Lonesome Lake gave me my first and only plane ride until I took flying lessons in Vancouver in April 1953. That plane was a two-place Aeronca, piloted by Cliff Taylor. As Dad was away with the boat that day, Mother and I were the only ones at home. I, being younger and not bothered by a more or less constant backache, raced down the trail to the main lake to where the plane was tied up in a sheltered bay.

Two people were standing around, looking as if they had no idea of how to hike from where they were to our farm, a distance of perhaps a mile and a half, on an obvious trail thru the open pine woods. They had come in to see Dad. As he was away with the boat, the people had to walk to the farm.

A few days later the pilot asked me if I would like a plane ride. He wanted to move CF-DNC to the Big Lagoon. I happily accepted his offer. He and I hiked down to the bay where the floatplane was tied up. We were soon in the air and floating magically over Lonesome Lake, looking down on what I had been able to see only from lake level before.

It was just a short flight, but how delightful! He landed on the one-mile-long lagoon, shallow and muddy along the grassy shore where he wanted to leave the plane. We had to wade to shore through the knee-deep, slimy mud and water, but I had had a ride in an airplane! I knew then that I really did want to become a pilot.

In my young years I was not a very avid student and really wasn't all that interested in the subjects I had to study. Then one day Dad told me if I were to be a pilot I would have to get a bit more education than I had to date. That set a fire under my ambition and I started to study in earnest.

In a few days the plane flew away, leaving the valley silent and lonely once more.

As the years passed, more planes flew over and the very odd one actually landed. Then as more planes came to look, or maybe just going on about their own business, they seemed to increase in number, enjoying the beauty of the area so much that there were times when the droning of planes passing over the valley almost resembled Granville Street at rush hour. Things changed in the summer of 1953. A little two-place Taylorcraft, CF-HEO, descended onto Lonesome Lake to stay and the silence of the valley was broken for good. And with the airplane there, so also went the loneliness.

Taking a second look back, I guess the real silence had already been at least wounded, even if not broken, by the arrival of my two-and-a-half-horsepower Johnson Seahorse outboard motor in 1947.

Skins of squirrels provided the money for the outboard. I had thought the best use for that resource would be something to ease the wearing work of rowing the six miles across Lonesome Lake, often against a strong wind. A short time later someone gave Dad a five-horse outboard. Then we could have a motor on Stillwater as well as Lonesome Lake without having to carry the Seahorse, 30 pounds, between the two lakes. Things were looking up. "Mod cons" were arriving in dizzying rapidity. Next came a chainsaw in 1956, brought in by Jack, then my future husband. Oh glory! More silence breaking when that machine split the air with its music.

Of course the Lonesome Lake area was never really silent of the sounds that are almost always around us. There is hardly a time or place where there are no sounds at all in nature. The silence I am referring to here is the absence of sounds of others of my own species, a little of which I want quite badly and enjoy, but too much of which I can't stand. For an example, where I now live, in a fairly rural area, there are some of the most irritating machines I have ever had the misfortune to have to endure. ATVs!

Not constantly, but too often, ATVs roar up and down at warp speed on the highway too near my house. They set my mind and teeth on edge and louse up my concentration when I am trying to write this memoir. I live right under the flight path to and from the airport, but the helicopters and airplanes don't make as much noise as those awful ATVs, and of course I don't mind the flying things at all.

Telemarketers bug me also. I think they all should take lessons in manners. They are invading my home and causing me to run—ha, I can hardly walk—on canes to the phone. Then when I do get there, they hang up after only three rings. Heck, a person sound in wind and limb can't even dry their hands if they are in the dishpan, then get to the phone in three rings. And they never phone back so I can know who needs to talk to me. Caller ID doesn't help either, because I still have to get to the phone.

There was one airplane I did not like the sound of. I was 30 feet above the ground, at the top of my barn, checking some hay, when a plane came sweeping past almost on my level, between my building and a wall of trees about 60 feet away. I was trapped up there for a moment, as I felt pretty scared he would hit my barn, he was so close. He missed the barn, but it was a crazy thing to do. This was at Arbordale.

Now I am going to mention some real noise in nature—trumpeter swans singing in a massed orchestral performance. Massed indeed when there were about 400 of them.

When I used to feed a large flock of trumpeter swans at Lonesome Lake, they were fed their grain at the north end of Big Lagoon. When the swans waiting at the feed place saw me walking across the ice, some of them would fly up, land near me, tuck their feet up in their feathers and wait. Soon my faithful companion Skye, a black and white border collie, and I passed them. In a bit they would take off, fly past us, then land again. Sometimes they would try to walk with us, but would soon fall behind. As I take a two-and-a-half foot stride, and the swans, even hurrying, can manage only six or eight inches, it is easy to see who will win the race, walking. So then they must fly again.

When they followed close behind us, Skye stayed as near to me as possible, glancing worriedly over her shoulder at the huge swans coming along behind her. They were not frightened of the little dog, but she wasn't too sure about them. I have never observed the swans showing the slightest fear of the border collie, and I never allowed her to do anything to frighten the big birds either.

When we neared the feed place the whole flock would be following right along, all around us, on each side, behind, while the ones in front would part so Skye and I could walk thru the crowd to reach the grain shed set a short way back from the shore. As we all walked along on the ice, the swans hurried to stay with me, trotting along, gabbling, getting more excited as we neared the grain shed. They reminded me of a friendly group of elderly ladies walking in the park, talking and gabbling away. I often thought about this as the entire group with Skye and me in the center moved sedately along on the ice to the shore.

There the swans stopped. Skye and I went on to the feed shed, about 25 feet from the shore. That was when the noise or music level went thru the roof. And they weren't all yelling. Looking over the flock, only about half the bills were open, the rest were silent.

At the feed shed I filled bags with 200 pounds of grain, then began carrying it down to the ice. I set my bag down and began broadcasting the feed, at about two pounds to a pan full. Often I had to be careful not to hit a swan head that was reaching up five feet to snatch grain out of the air. I also had to take care not to bump an impatient cygnet trying to grab an early feed, with no competition, out of the bag. Skye stayed in the shed.

As more grain was spread on the ice, usually in long rows to make counting more accurate, the volume of swan trumpeting would diminish to only a few low mutters, sometimes uttered thru a mouthful of grain. The quiet was in great contrast to the level of noise a few minutes earlier.

Returning to the grain shed one last time, I checked the grain boxes were all covered and my sacks secured. Then with Skye once more with me I'd head for home, unless the sun was shining and there was no wind. In which case I often stayed a while and watched the birds as Skye lay on the ice beside me. That scene is one of my most treasured memories of Lonesome Lake.

One other thing I am now reminded of is running Guenevere on the firm snow-covered Big Lagoon ice. The horse-safe length of the lagoon is just short of a mile. One day when I fed the swans, I rode her down and ran her across the ice. As the snow was well bonded to the ice, she had excellent traction. On the way home I looked at my watch as we started up the ice. I asked for an all-out run. She gave it. As she was bareback, I simply bent down on her withers and neck to keep out of her slipstream, some, and enjoyed the ride. She could run. She quickly ate up the mile. Seventy-six seconds my watch said when we arrived at the south end. That seems too short a time for a mile, even for a real racehorse, but it is probably not quite a mile across the lagoon.

Arriving home, I told my horse-crazy daughter about the marvelous run and she wanted to try it too. The next day I left Guenevere at home for Susan and walked down to feed the swans. Returning up the ice, I looked towards the south end of the lagoon. I saw a most beautiful sight. A dark object burst around a point on the lake shore, preceded, almost, by a plume of silvery-white gold, the sun shining thru the snow cloud thrown into the air as Guenevere hit her stride coming around that point. It was movingly beautiful, and the clear picture hangs in my memory.

Most winters the ice was not good enough for horses to run on, either because of being full of spring holes, or bare, or covered with too much snow, and flooded by the weight of snow could be unsafe. In the case of too much snow, we often used the trail around the lagoon and did not use the ice.

One winter the snow fell and fell until there was 52 inches of it lying on the ground, too deep to plow thru for us and too soft to snowshoe on. We used the horses to go to the "swannery," two and a half miles from home. As it was snowing constantly for three days, the trail had to be broken out each day, and the snow was almost up to the horse's back.

The swans also were having a bit of trouble in the deep snow, being unable to take off easily due to their feet sinking too deep and their wing tips hitting the snow as they began their take-off run. They could get off, but they certainly had to work at it.

With the deep snow almost hiding the horses, the swans were not too sure what we were as we rode along the shore, almost buried in the snow. All they could see was the top of the horse and her rider. Some struggled into the air, had a better look from that height, decided we were the feeder after all and landed again.

Another winter the ice was bare and sound, and Jack and I were using a bicycle to cross the mile-long lagoon. Much faster than on our own feet or horse feet. The swans did not worry about the two-wheeled contraption either.

It has been reported, incorrectly, that we who lived at Lonesome Lake were all recluses and never were away from the lake. Of course this was not a very well researched article, and far from the facts.

Mother made trips down the valley, usually in June, to visit her sisters and other relatives and friends. She and I made one such trip when I was nine.

When we made trips down the valley, we usually tried to go with the mailman. He came to Atnarko every two weeks, summer and winter. I believe he used horses from where the road ended, sometimes as far away as 15 miles from Atnarko. He would leave his truck at the end of the road, wherever it ended. Meeting him at Atnarko, Mother and I hiked down the trail with the mailman to where his truck was parked at the end of the road. Someone returned the horses to their home and we took off down the valley with the mailman.

The red truck took us down the valley to the home of the mail-man, Ole Nygaard. Mother was in the cab; I was in the truck box with another young girl. I was the younger girl and believed I had to stay with the truck in order to get home. Ole and Mother disembarked, but I held fast to the idea that I couldn't leave the truck or I'd never get home. The other young lady pleaded with me; Mother almost ordered me to get out. Finally a young man had to haul me off that red truck. I was not going to leave it. It would seem like I was more imprinted on home than on my mother. Wherever mother is should be home. But maybe it was not that at all. Maybe I was bonded to that beautiful red truck, and didn't want to leave it, not for any reason.

I believe we had supper at Ole's home, then were driven to the home of Aunt Laura and Uncle Frank and my three cousins. I don't remember making a fuss about staying there.

We stayed at Uncle Frank and Aunt Laura's place for a few days. I learned to play with my younger cousins, and a few other things. I hadn't been near anyone about my own age except my brothers since I was three. Now I was six years older, and probably had an attitude, in fact I am quite sure I did. One thing I do remember about that trip was we all picked gooseberries, great tubs full of them, as bad as those confounded currants that I picked at home.

Then we went to Ocean Falls with Uncle John McHardy and his brother, Hugh, on their two gill-netters. Mother needed tooth repairs. I don't know what the others needed, but there were a lot of people on the two boats. My aunts, Ruth McHardy and Laura Ratcliff, were among the group of people on the boats. For a while they had the two boats lashed together, but I think at some point the sea became rough and angry and they separated them.

In Ocean Falls we went to a theatre. Before the movie they showed a newscast of the burning and crash of the Hindenburg. Quite shocking for the kids, and maybe for some of the grown-ups also. I remember how the people were falling out of the burning craft as it crumpled, smoking and falling to earth on the people who had jumped or fallen to the ground. Then it lay there and continued to shrink as it flamed and smoked.

No other memory of Ocean Falls remains in my brain from that trip except the awful smell of the pulp for making paper. It permeated the air. And it rained buckets.

Since we went to Ocean Falls on those gill-netters, I presume we returned to Bella Coola on them also. We were away about two weeks, to coordinate with the mailman on his regular mail runs to Atnarko. I presume Dad met us there, tho I really can't recall.

There must have been a trip or two to Bella Coola in between the one when I was nine and the one in 1948 made during the flood, which I will recount now.

The Atnarko River was way over its banks when Mother, Stanley and I left The Birches for Bella Coola. There was no trouble getting to the north end of the lake. There the problems began. Hunlen Creek was in several channels across its boulder bar and should not have been too difficult to cross. But it was high from all the late-melting snow on the surrounding above-timberline areas all pouring their water into the creek. It had been very hot for several days and that had caused the rise. The snow should have melted earlier, then the high water would have been a lower high water.

We were able to wade across some small channels and found logs on some of the larger ones, until we came to the really big one and no log. And not many trees close to it to fall either. I was carrying my Seahorse outboard, Mother had a good pack and Stanley had a pack and a crosscut saw. One of us had an axe. We finally found a tree that could be felled over the largest channel, after scrambling a long way up the boulder bed of the creek's delta. With the tree across the creek we were on our way again.

The rest of the way down the valley was uneventful until we had hiked a mile or so past Hotnarko. Then we found the river, brown with soil, raging over where the trail should have been. The Atnarko

River had returned to the northeast side of the valley, which it had left many years earlier. Long enough for some fair-sized trees to grow up in the old abandoned channels. Now it was back.

We had to clamber way up on coarse rocks, over small bluffs, and then back down again when the boulder scrambling became too tough. The going was slow, painfully slow. I think we dragged into Atnarko at one or two in the morning, cold, wet and very tired. We stopped at the home of our friend Bert. Mother, being braver than Stan or I, knocked on the door, waking the poor man up at an ungodly hour, apologizing profusely. She asked him if he could put up "three drowned rats" for the rest of the night. Certainly he could, and he served us hot drinks all around. Bert was a very good friend.

The next morning we learned the Young Creek bridge was out. We could go no farther until a bridge of some sort was built. Two or three days later one was put over that large creek. At that time we didn't know if any other bridges had been washed out or simply abandoned by the creeks crossing the highway farther down the valley. I do not remember any more setbacks on that trip.

There was a lot of repair work to be done to the trail later that year, tho most of the sections where the water over the trail seemed to be so deep when we made that trip out had been abandoned, and the river had gone back to the other side of the valley, fortunately.

chapter 11

FLYING CANS

Before leaving Lonesome Lake most of my horse training efforts were less than satisfactory to me. One horse, however, did seem finally to figure out what I wanted her to do. She was Cloud, a washy buckskin. Beautiful little mare.

We had brought her to Lonesome Lake from the Chilcotin country when she was about 16 months old, tame and halter trained. At a little over two we trained her to do a bit of light harness work and started riding her and she did a bit of light packing. Then one day we wanted her to carry four empty five-gallon cans a mile and a half to the Big Lagoon from our place, Arbordale.

We had her tied to a long rope stretched between a dense willow bush and a tall stump. She was standing quietly, quite unsuspecting of her pack as Jack and I tied the first two cans on her saddle. Then we put the second two on. Before we could get them tied something happened. I think she may have blinked. I really can't remember. Maybe she took a step or stamped at a fly. Anyway, one of the loose cans slid off, making a tinny noise when it fell on a rock. Cloud took the other three off, violently, and quickly. As the cans were flying around, the flailing hooves somehow avoiding them, the lid came off one can and flew at her. She struck it with a front hoof sending it into a new flight path under her nose. She stomped on it. She was fighting for her life, from her perspective. Poor little scared pony. Finally, with the cans all "killed," or at least huddling submissively on the ground, she relaxed a bit, and looked around as if asking, "What was that all about?" Jack and I just stood back and laughed. Cloud needed some more education.

She got it.

After she had settled down enough, I took her to our log-walled bull corral with eight-foot-high snake fence construction, about 25 feet in diameter. It was closed by a strong pole gate as high as the walls. Tying her in it, I fastened sacks of small rattling cans to her and the saddle, one on each side, and one under her neck. From outside the corral I untied her. She walked away, sniffing the ground. Then she shook herself.

The cans rattled. She rose into the air. Bucking, she spun in a tight circle until she fell to the ground. She lay there for a minute or so while her brain unwound. Then she rose and began bucking some more. This time she raced around close to the log wall, still trying to get the cans off her back. They clung fast. Finally, she just stood in the middle of the corral and panted. She had done a lot of hard work in a very short time.

As I wanted her to walk around and feel and hear the cans, I asked her to move. She didn't want to. The cans didn't rattle if she stood still, so the lesson was don't move. Well, a packhorse can't do her work standing still. I had to encourage her to move around so she could see the rattle of cans didn't hurt her. I didn't want to go in that small corral with her, so I enticed her over to the fence and put a rope on her. Then I could rattle her cans from outside the fence. She had her head high but she didn't buck any more, just stepped around uneasily.

When I felt it was reasonably safe for me to enter the corral with that pale cyclone I went in, and with her rope around a fence pole I made her cans rattle while keeping close to her. She didn't like it, but in time she seemed to get the message that the noise would not kill her, nor would the cans fall off. I loosened her cinch, gave her some hay and a drink, then left her for the night.

By morning she was a lot more comfortable with the cans. So, to get some more action I tied a sack of cans on a long rope to her saddle. Then from outside her pen I asked her to move.

When she walked off slowly the sack started to follow. She went faster. The bag came after her faster. She cantered. The bag kept right up! Soon she was flying around inside that old corral, chased by the everlastingly persistent bag of rattling cans. There was no way to outrun them. At last she stopped, sides heaving, and took stock. The cans had stopped, too! When she stopped, the cans stopped. When she moved, the can bag moved, but it never tried to get any closer to her. This at last seemed to occur to her She finally caught on that she was in control of the bag of cans. Then they were no longer a threat to her. So far, so good.

It seems a bit strange that she was so scared of the bag of cans chasing her. She had been hauling the wagon, sled and poles for several years and had not worried about them.

Finally I could rattle her cans all I wanted and she just stood there, loose in the corral, and paid no more attention to the thing she was dragging around. It was time to advance to teaching her that cans could fall off her and not hurt her.

That step proved to take a lot longer, tho her response was not quite as violent as it was to the rattles. Almost every day for two months over winter I spent a half hour or so with Cloud in our big calving stall in the barn, letting five-gallon cans fall off her saddle. I had to see to it they never hit her feet and hurt her. There were days when it seemed we made no progress at all, and even went backwards. But I persisted. After one particularly trying day I went to the house, where Jack was cooking lunch, and sat down, tired and pretty discouraged. He asked me how it went. I told him she wasn't improving very much. Then he asked why I kept on with such a seemingly hopeless case. Close to tears, I said, "Hope dies hard." I just couldn't quit. I hoped, perhaps the next day she would get it. And in time she did.

I had two five-gallon cans that I could tie securely to the saddle that I packed her with, and I took her with me on my days to feed swans—Jack fed the swans for three days of each week and I fed them for four days—hoping she would not do anything stupid on the section of narrow trail that ran along about 15 feet above the river.

I was riding the definitely "boss" mare, and that may have helped

Cloud feel less frightened. She never did do anything dangerous or stupid. I may have been stupid, but she wasn't by then.

Finally I just tied the cans by one end and let them flop and dangle from the saddle and she accepted that.

The final test came when I had to carry a weak cygnet home to try to keep it alive with extra feed. It required both my hands to hold the young swan on Guenevere's withers, leaving no hand to lead Cloud with; she was on her own and she got an "A." Guenevere got an "A" also as, along with me, I was asking her to accept a live bird with seven feet of wing and three feet of neck on her back. She walked along as if she just had a bunch of any inanimate stuff on her.

Cloud's final test came sometime later when we packed her with a narrow pack to take along a narrower trail. There she showed she had real talent as a packhorse. Where the trail was so narrow that she would have to rub trees on both sides of her, she chose to bend the smaller tree and not touch the larger one on her other side. I don't know how she figured this out as she hadn't done much real packing. She had been ridden a lot, but we usually tried to protect our knees and let the horse take the best path for her feet.

Trying to make a workhorse out of Cloud, however, was a dismal failure for me, and her.

She was willing enough to pull but was frightened by the load, which she felt she was not equal to. She pranced and fidgeted and fussed. Working with lazy, larger Lucky, also known as Lucky Debonair elsewhere in these memoirs, she never settled down until we made the load easier for her with a brake to help ease the load down a steep slope. Before we rigged the brake, she would look back at me where I stood in the wagon and her frightened little face told me just how much she dreaded the descent of that steep slope. The brake helped, but she was still in distress.

In the end she and I lost it all. She was nice to ride, her disposition was excellent, and she had become a very talented packhorse. However there was no way we could sell a horse from Lonesome Lake, so far from any market. There were many horses much closer to any market than we were. And one must keep their animal numbers in line with the feed available. With Cloud's filly, Tempest, and another filly, Bess, feed was too close to critical.

When we left Lonesome Lake we took the horses and cows with us. I gave Tempest and Star to Susan. She sold Tempest to someone who sold her to someone else. That person made a really nice gymkhana horse out of Tempest. She is 24 years old now and I think she is still running the events in gymkhana. I kept Bess for myself.

When you have two animals of different species together, they sometimes can get their messages mixed up. One does not quite understand the other.

The year we left Lonesome Lake we had a young bull, Parsimony, in one field and Tempest in an adjoining field. As they seemed lonely in separate fields, I thought to put them together. That was a mistake. Cattle and horses do not necessarily talk the same language. At least not as far as love goes.

The young bull approached the mare, then went around behind her, had a couple of sniffs, then decided that as she was standing quietly and not moving away—even tho she didn't smell quite right— she was inviting him to act like a bull should act around a friendly, really friendly, cow. He proceeded to try to do his programmed part. Tempest, not quite knowing how a mare should respond to such a cross-species attempt at reproduction, simply stood there, assuring Parsimony that he really was on the right track. After a couple more futile attempts to honor Tempest, she suddenly became furious as it finally sank in just what that unmannerly cad was trying to do. Parsimony was not acting like an amorous well-mannered stallion at all. In outrage, she turned on him and chased him around the field; around and around they went. Parsimony was panting and desperate. Finally he sought refuge down in the waterhole, a fenced-in corner of the field where stock could drink and not escape from the field.

Tempest did not follow him into the waterhole, but paraded back and forth on top of the bank to keep him there. He didn't want to come out anyway. By then it must have percolated thru his bull head that he had made a major mistake in his innocent assumption that Tempest was a good substitute for a cow. He stood on the far side of the waterhole and rested. He was tired. As Parsimony didn't seem to want to leave the waterhole, Tempest gave up her guard duty and trotted off to the other side of the field. He stayed in the waterhole. When Tempest stopped running, I caught her and put her in the field Parsimony had been in and peace once more reigned.

This next account will illustrate a situation where a cow and a horse communicated quite well, but sex was not involved, just food.

My barn in Bella Coola was built with a 20- by 20-foot section for storing hay, and a 16- by 20-foot part for two cows and a horse, all under one roof. On the east side of the barn is a pasture and a door on that side of the barn that would allow animals to enter the barn. My horse, Bess, and my cow, Marcy, were sharing that pasture, as Bess was good with the cow and would not run her.

One evening when it came time to put the two animals in for the night, both were at the door waiting for me. There was a small problem, tho. Bess was standing right outside the door, facing a large stump. Marcy was a little way from Bess. Marcy had to go in first, as Bess lived next to the door and took up all the space there. Marcy wouldn't crowd between the stump and Bess, violating her space. It was an impasse.

I just stood in the doorway to see how they would solve the problem. The cow couldn't come in until the horse moved. The horse knew the cow had to come in first, but she didn't want to move away from the door. I waited, curious.

Bess finally solved the problem. She turned her head to the right, in Marcy's direction, opening the "gate" for the cow. Instantly smart Marcy walked thru and into the barn, followed by the intelligent mare, or should I say the cooperative mare? Those two knew how to solve their problem peacefully.

chapter 12

STAR

Altho when I began training horses to work in harness, in my late teens, they performed remarkably well, later on I seemed unable to get the new replacement horses to understand what I wanted and they became frustrated, dithering, uncooperative fools. We blamed it on the possibility that the horses we were buying and bringing in to Lonesome Lake were too old for me to train.

I had been suspicious that I was the problem rather than the horses. I felt that I was somehow training them in a manner that did not help them to understand what I wanted. What I was doing wrong I had no idea then, and still do not know. I had no trouble training all of those horses that didn't work properly to be ridden and packed, which they did well.

Anyway, if we got a stallion and bred our three mares we might be able to raise the foals in the proper way. Perhaps they would then work satisfactorily in harness. With this idea in mind, we caught a flight to Nimpo Lake. There we met a horse rancher to whom we had already written about a yearling he would be willing to sell.

He drove us in his horse-hauling truck many rough miles towards his ranch down on the Dean River. At one point he left the truck and used his tractor and wagon to go the last few miles on a very narrow rocky, wet, muddy road to his home.

The next day he went out on saddle horse and found his horses wandering somewhere in an endless pine and meadow forest and drove them in to the ranch. When he brought the bunch of horses, including the yearling, he ran them all into a loading chute, with the yearling at the last end.

Jack and I looked him over and didn't really think much of him. He was droopy looking and maybe sick. There was another yearling there that looked a lot more awake. He was an Appaloosa. We chose him.

While he was still in the loading chute I put a halter on him, then we backed him out and began halter training. He was quite nervous and didn't want to be touched. Well, he hadn't had too much handling. However he did like his neck to be scratched.

In a little while we had him leading around in the corral. Finally I felt he was good enough to leave until the following day. We would do more training before we set off for home. Before turning him loose for the night we wanted to take him a short way to where he could get a drink. To get out of the corral the Appy had a bit of a tantrum before he would step over some poles lying on the ground. The tantrum involved standing on his hind legs, sort of falling over the poles, picking himself up, then rearing again. In time he did get over the poles and down to the water, which he didn't want anyway.

That exhibition made us look at the droopy black colt again. Maybe the Appy was too much awake. I was looking for a calm workhorse type stud. We put the Appy back in the loading chute. Then I began working on the black.

As there was only about a half hour before dark, I didn't think I would accomplish much. Surprisingly, within 15 minutes the black was following the rope around the small corral. He seemed either very amiable or too sick to care. He had spent a lot of the time I was training on the Appy lying down sleeping.

The next morning we gave the black colt more leading practice and he did fine. As our host wanted to do some branding and a couple of castrations before he drove us to Nimpo Lake airstrip, I led the colt, later named Star, around and tied him some distance from the other horses, then went away to see how anxious he would get.

He didn't seem very worried. Then I took him near the upsetting branding and that didn't bother him.

Then there were the two young stallions to castrate. Jack and I thought we should watch, as we would have to geld our colt after we had the foals we wanted to raise. So we watched and tried to learn and remember the procedure. Four years later we were faced with the job. The results were less than satisfactory. That was one time I really wished we lived where we could get a vet.

As we had to hike a few miles to where the truck was, we started off on the trail with Star. He had no problem leaving his home. Eventually we arrived at the truck. We did not know when our host, Woody, would catch up. We took Star to a small meadow just off the trail where he could catch up on some breakfast. He seemed eager to eat, so perhaps he wasn't sick.

When Woody arrived we heaved the colt into the truck and were soon on our rough way to Nimpo Lake airstrip. Jack and I rode in the back of the truck just to keep an eye on our horse in case he needed some help for any reason. The road was rough and Star was soon braced on all four legs to meet each hole and bump. Woody drove fast and Jack and I had to brace also. It was a rough ride.

At last at the airstrip Woody backed up to a hill of dirt bulldozed off the runway. I asked Star to step down about eight inches, but his legs were so stiff from that hour or so of bracing he more fell than stepped down, slightly hurting one front leg. I walked him for a while until he seemed to be moving more comfortably. There was nothing there for Star to eat. We just tied him to a tree for the night. We had our supper and then we fell into a hard bed. Jack had set up our tent while I was walking Star.

In the morning we set off for home, a four-day hike involving a lot of windfall, steep mountainsides, small creeks, and some small rock bluffs where we had to build some rocky trail to get safely past. Finally we reached the valley floor on a good game trail. I thought, "Thank you, games," as we took the last steps onto level ground at last.

We were soon home. We turned the tame young horse loose in a fenced pasture, then went to the house. Soon we were met by our lonesome lady cats, eager to find out where we had been, but no wiser as we could not tell them. They were glad to see us home.

In time Star fathered three nice fillies, all made darker than their mothers, even Bess, tho she kept her tobiano paint pattern.

I must switch gears now and go way back in time.

Way back in Lonesome Lake history, before airplanes, before outboards, people had to row the boat on Lonesome Lake—to go anywhere or haul freight—from one end of the lake to the other. Freight moving was done in the fall before freeze-up.

One fall Stanley was helping Dad with the fall packing of supplies for the winter. Dad had all the freight at the north end of the lake. Stanley was to load the boat and row it home while Dad took the horses around the lake on the trail. Dad left before Stanley did and he got home before Stanley did. When Stanley hadn't arrived by the time Dad got home our parents began to worry, especially as a south wind had come up.

Sometime late at night, maybe in early morning, he arrived, cold, wet and possibly ashamed. He should not have been ashamed. He was young and had very little experience handling boats in strong winds. To be able to bring even himself home he must have done his best at the effort he put out. He lost some of the freight in shallow water, but we were so very glad that our brother, and son, was home safe that the freight was only an inconvenience. He could have tied up behind the point and waited for the wind to drop, but he wanted to get the load home and not worry our parents, so he attempted to go around the point into the howling wind. He upset, but was able to right the boat again somehow and pick up some items that floated. Later, when the wind did diminish he struggled the rest of the way, about four miles, with only one oar. The other one had been lost in the upset in the dark.

By using a leg-hold trap fastened to the end of a pole, Dad was able to retrieve many of the items from the rocky bottom of the lake. Thankfully our loss was not great. Even if no one else learned anything from that accident, I surely did.

Stanley left home at the age of 17. A year or two later, after trying several jobs, he wound up at Ocean Falls where he worked in the mill for years. And he took night school, eventually becoming the head electrician at the plant. In the 1970s Stanley moved to his property at the south end of Stillwater, where he lived until December 2000. At birth age of 76—true age 77—Stan passed away at his little cabin, sheltered by a canopy of large cedars and firs, his preferred surroundings. The cause of death was unknown but presumed to be natural.

Years later I attempted to row that same boat to the north end of the lake. When I passed the Narrows, a vicious, nasty, cold wind picked up wickedly. I was going down to help Dad home so he would not have to slog around the lake on the trail. The wind was stronger than I was—tho not much colder—by the time I admitted defeat and scuttled for home. It was so cold ice rings were forming on my oars as I dipped them repeatedly into the cold water. It was November and the lake froze up soon after.

That boat, called "the boat," there being no other to confuse it with for many years, was constructed with whipsawed lumber. I think Uncle Earle helped Dad in the sawpit and in construction.

Writing about that cold, windy incident reminds me of another incident on Lonesome Lake many years later. Tho not very cold, it was potentially dangerous.

Susan had left home to seek her own life and had met the man of her dreams. They decided to live together and get married. Several years later she came home with us on a short visit to her old home and show it to her child, Brendan. We picked up our mail where Susan and Tom were living and on this occasion she decided to come back with us.

On reaching the north end of Lonesome Lake we found a lively south wind rolling whitecaps down the lake. Susan, with a child at heel, didn't like it at all. I was not too keen myself on going up the lake that evening. Jack, who had practically grown up on the sea, was not too concerned when we set off up the lake. However the farther we went the bigger the waves got and the more worried the mother of that precious child became. She begged her dad to go ashore. As the shoreline there was not a very good place to land, we kept on until there was a shallow bay and a handy log to land the boat on; then we went ashore.

With the outboard removed and lugged ashore we hauled the boat up on the log and tied it up for the night. Unfortunately we didn't have much in the way of camping equipment, as we hadn't known when we left home that Susan wanted to come back with us. Anyway, we got thru the night with Susan, baby Brendan and me using the one blanket we did have. Poor Jack found a dry log to try to sleep under. It was not a very comfortable night, but a lot better than what we could have had. We found out how much better the next morning.

With the morning came the calm. We launched the boat, clamped the 10-horsepower Mercury to the transom and were soon humming up the lake, making good time, fairly planning on the smooth surface of the water.

Then it happened! The outboard fell off its mount.

Susan was right. I don't know how she knew. Mother's intuition? Maybe.

We didn't lose the motor as it was chained to the boat, but we had to row home.

Had we kept on into the gale the evening before we would have lost our power farther up the lake and could have had a lot of trouble getting to shore, on a far worse coastline.

One can't trust mechanical things too much. That is why we always had oars on our boats. In the old days of rowing, it was not uncommon for us to go ashore and wait for the wind to abate.

Often when we arrived at the lake a wild wind would be rolling "white horses" onto the beach near the outlet. Before outboards, we would wait until evening when the wind usually went down. But with the motor, if one could get away from shore it didn't matter so much. We didn't have to row, and as long as the motor stayed on the boat and continued to run we could make a safe run home. That time with Susan and her son we would not have made it up the lake.

On one other trip Jack and I set off in the boat at the outlet, with me rowing away from the shore to water deep enough for the motor. This was normal procedure there. Due to a slight change in the currents near the actual underwater dam that causes the lake, we were suddenly in water that was stronger than I. With my best effort pulling on the oars we were drifting down towards the break over.

I quietly said to Jack, "Better start the motor."

Four words, before destruction on the rocks below the break over, where the river churns and tumbles down a narrow rocky channel with a steep rocky bank on one side and a boulder bed shoreline from Hunlen Creek plunging into the river on the other side. I was scared, but very calm.

Fortunately, the outboard roared into life. The boat stopped drifting. Nevertheless, I continued to ply my oars strongly 'til the motor drove the boat so fast that I could no longer catch the water. Then I could rest. That day there was no wind that I can remember.

I can remember some trips up that lake before we had outboards tho, when we would start off in a nice handy north wind. Going with the wind, we made good time until we rounded Bluff Point. There the wind would be blowing crossways and had the surface of the lake confused and jumping in every direction. Within minutes the south wind overwhelmed the north wind and we found ourselves fighting a strong wind in opposition to us.

We could go back down the lake and find shelter behind Bluff Point. But if the wind was not too strong, and we were far enough across to the east shore to gain shelter from Lighthouse Point, we would just keep rowing. Due to the "zigzags" in Lonesome Lake, there are many places on both shores where one can usually find decent shelter.

Waves can get pretty impressive on that lake, with a six-mile clear run. The direction change between Bluff Point and Lighthouse Point occurs as a result of a large weather system on the outer coast sending a wind directly up Knight Inlet, making a south wind, locally, to meet a north wind from Bella Coola, where there would be a local west wind. The valley determines the local wind direction, of course.

When there is a true north wind on Lonesome Lake it flows down various side valleys from the Chilcotin country and it is cold; in winter, very cold. Especially in Bella Coola Valley.

At Lonesome Lake true north winds do not blow for very many days, even as the temperature falls and falls to 46 degrees Fahrenheit below zero. The one time in my life it got that cold there was no wind, thank God.

Lonesome Lake seems to be in a wind shadow. Cold air from the Chilcotin Plateau tends to flow towards Bella Coola, while other parts of the cold mass of air flow south to the coast, missing Lonesome Lake, most of the time.

Some time, probably in the thirties, Dad was asked by the Department of Fisheries and Oceans to build a small row boat for Tenas Lake, and another one like it for Rainbow Lake.

Dad began work right away. He had to split straight-grained cedar planks out of a big cedar log. The next step was to hand plane it down to an even thickness for the bottom and side planks. All dressing of homemade lumber had to be done by hand tools. Dad made very well designed boats with that lumber and they did not leak.

He built the one for Tenas Lake first. The family helped to carry it down to the river. There Dad and one other of us could ride in the little boat as Dad rowed it up the river to where it became too fast to row in. Then the rider got out and we all but Dad had to travel on shore as we moved the boat to Tenas Lake.

Later the boat for Rainbow Lake was built and moved in a like manner to Tenas Lake. Then the Fisheries inspector helped to move the craft on to Rainbow Lake.

chapter 13

WANDERING BOATS

Some people seem to think it is all right to take someone else's boat, use it, and leave it on another lake or at the wrong end of the lake they found it on. They never seem to think about why there is a boat on the lake, or that the owner might want to use it sometimes. And what is worse, they too often don't bother to tie it up when they leave, or they tie it in a bad place and the wind destroys it on sharp rocks. They never think about not doing to others what they wouldn't want done to them. Boats were stolen—and lost down the river—on the Stillwater also.

Anyway, sometime in the 1950s the boat on Rainbow Lake was stolen and left on Elbow Lake, upstream of Rainbow Lake and at the upstream end, not of much use to people going up the valley.

Dad had a bear hunter to guide that year and he needed that boat on Rainbow Lake. As it was gone, and he didn't know where it was, we used Thuja, my mare, to travois the boat from Tenas Lake to Rainbow Lake. Tenas Lake is only one mile long; Rainbow is about four miles long, so we left the boat there.

After that the Rainbow Lake boat was found on Elbow Lake. We left it there. Soon after that the proper Rainbow Lake boat vanished again. Dad and I went all the way to the knot of Knot Lake looking for it.

At the knot, just a narrow narrows with some current, we built a raft to cross to the other side, then paddled all the way back to the north end of that large lake, searching every bay and beach on the way. We couldn't find the boat. I seem to recall we had to go ashore several times because of wind.

Then we searched the east shore of Elbow Lake, and Rainbow Lake, by walking along the shore. That was a nasty hike as the going on that side is mostly talus slopes and rock bluffs. No boat.

Sometime years later the boat mysteriously was back at the south end of Elbow Lake. Very strange.

The sale of Arbordale was accompanied by a mix of emotions. Excitement at the thought of something new. A new place. New things to do. Who knew how things would work out? Could I even live out there in the big world? Would I regret moving away from the place where I had spent my entire 60 years? And 35 of those had been at Arbordale. I didn't know. Something drove me to try. Maybe it was the lack of challenges; maybe it was a lack of new things to do.

The other side of the mix was a feeling of betrayal. Betrayal of a generous friend who had given me support, heat, food, a roof over my head, and Jack and Susan, and much pleasure and entertainment. I would be giving this all up for something new.

The actual selling was traumatic. As the decision had been made, I had to tell my "no" side pretty sternly that my "yes" side had to be boss. There'd be no waffling. The time for that was long past. It was much like, but somewhat milder than, what I went thru every time we decided to slaughter one of the stock. Waffling only makes it worse. Once the decision is made one is better off simply getting on with it. There has to be a very strong reason to call it off and then have the whole thing to go thru again. That was one thing I hoped to avoid, for the most part. Hopefully I'd be able to sell at least some of my animals and not have to kill them.

Sadness and excitement pretty well filled the time in about equal amounts as we packed up the stuff we wanted to take with us. Over the eight or 10 months after we sold Arbordale we moved all the stuff down to the lake. We would be leaving forever. We had almost all of our stuff flown out. Most of it went to Nimpo Lake.

When we left, we had three cattle and four horses. The horses we let carry stuff down as they were going anyway, and some of it we needed on the way. We took the horses first.

As our big freight raft had been shortened by invading mushroom pickers, we had room for only two horses on it. Therefore we took them just past the worst section of the trail around Lonesome Lake. I led them the rest of the way, on the better part, still rough enough for some. We left the horses in the care of my brother, Stanley, who lived at Stillwater then.

Next day we started with the cattle. It was towards evening when we began loading the cows onto the raft. We had the old cow, Clari, her long yearling heifer, Dribbles, and her current year's calf, Sprinkle, to try to get on that bunch of logs floating way off shore.

Clari took one look at the narrow ramp we had for her to walk across to the raft and determinedly said "NO!" As she was much heavier than Jack and myself, there was no way we could force her to walk out on the ramp. Pounding on her only caused her to try to fall off the ramp, proving the whole thing was quite unsafe. But sometimes a gentle hint will work where brute strength won't.

We could move her young calf. Sprinkle didn't exactly like the ramp, but was somewhat willing at least to try it. She walked on. Then Clari had to go to protect her baby. As Clari was the heavy one, she had to be at the stern of the raft. We had to get Sprinkle past her mother, as she had to be last. Dribbles was quite eager to get on by then, as she didn't want to be left behind.

We only got a couple of miles down the lake that evening. We camped at the Narrows. The cattle had some grass we had left there for them. They were all tied to trees for the night. By morning their attitude to the raft had improved. The poor trusting things believed the raft would take them home. Instead, it took them farther away.

Where we had landed at the Narrows, the cows had to step off into a foot or more of water. There was no way we could ask Clari to step back up on the raft without injuring her udder on the log ends. We carried enough rocks to make a causeway about 18 inches wide and four feet long, almost up to the tops of the raft logs. Clari was a bit unsure, but walked on anyway, hoping to go home. The cows rode the raft all the way to the north end of the lake. They then hiked down the trail to Stillwater.

We spent the next day at Stillwater. The day after, we got an early start down the river with the cattle riding the Stillwater raft. At the north end of Stillwater we left Clari's calf tied, to anchor the cow there. We brought the raft back up the lake to where the trail was badly damaged by rock falls. There we tied it up.

The horses were still at Stanley's place. I took them on the trail as far as the raft, while Jack took the boat down, using my little two-and-a-half horsepower Seahorse for power.

When we arrived at the raft the four horses were darn glad to see it. They hadn't liked the Lonesome Lake raft at all. They had never been on a raft before. Two were born at Arbordale and the other two had come in over the mountain. They didn't like rocky trails very much and finally wanted to ride on the raft. They so much wanted to get on the raft we had trouble making them wait their turn to board.

Then at the landing place at the north end of Stillwater, a new problem presented herself: homesick old Clari. When the raft, loaded with four horses, neared the shore, Clari waded out in over belly deep water and tried to board the raft, hoping it would take her home. I had to beat her off with my poling pole. We couldn't have 1200 pounds more on the raft. She waded sadly back to dry land. We landed the raft and unloaded the horses. We camped there for the night.

The horses were Star, our former stallion; his two daughters, Bess and Tempest; and a mare Susan had found and brought to Lonesome

Lake in the hope she would work better than Guenevere did. She did, but in time she, too, became difficult. It was me, not the horses. I didn't know then what I was doing wrong, and I still haven't a clue. She was Nugget.

Nugget was a good packer, nice to ride, easy to catch, but she had only one sound leg and hoof. There was something wrong with the other three, a different fault in each one. Those faults didn't bother her much, but I didn't think she would be of much use to herself or anyone else when she got old. I didn't want to sell her, as I was afraid she would wind up starving some cold winter or be shipped to a slaughterhouse. I didn't want either thing to happen to any of my animals.

Two days later we were at the bottom of the hill with all our stock. Susan soon met us there with a large stock hauling truck. She took the three cattle to her place and put them in my corral there. The next day saw the horses at the property Susan, Tom, and I shared. It was September 15. The move was completed.

The cows were footsore and Clari was more homesick than ever. The horses seemed quite happy with the new place and new horses to get acquainted with.

In a day or two Susan drove Jack and me to Nimpo Lake. There he loaded all his stuff onto a truck and trailer, then we said a long goodbye and he was driven away with some friends, the people who had bought all our farm equipment. Jack wanted to try living alone on the south coast, as he missed it very much for all the time we were living at Lonesome Lake, having spent a lot of his life in that area until he met me.

Susan and I returned to our place, Glengarry, in the valley. She had a truckload of my stuff also. Not too long after that it finally sank in that I would not be going back to Arbordale to live again. And Jack was gone to the south coast. Would I ever see him again? Then it was my turn to feel the pangs of homesickness.

Clari's sadness at leaving her valley, her home, seemed to lessen fairly fast, bawling her distress only for a few months. I didn't bawl mine, but just endured and tried to alleviate it to some extent by weaving poems to express what I was missing.

I Miss My Home

I miss the lakes and river, and the climate, foul or fair,
I miss the winter sunshine, and soft perfumed air.
I'd like to go and see again my dear old Arbordale,
I'd like to go and hike once more that long and rocky trail.

I'd like to go and set up camp and spend a night once more
With breeze as soft as aspen fluff
And waves lapping on the shore
I'd like to hear a swan, a loon
And watch the swallows soar
I'd like to see a hummingbird
And hear a grizzly roar
I'd like to smell the pondweed
And watch its long leaves sway
In the gently flowing river
As it ambles on its way.

In a few years, and with Jack back in my life, the homesickness subsided, but still lingers a bit. A short move to where I live now helped a little. Also there is a tiny bit of Lonesome Lake-like vegetation and landforms here. This comforts me some.

I lived on my new property about half a mile from Glengarry, in the house I built there in 1992, until the disaster of losing my beloved Breezie Future in May 2005. I weathered that loss by having Susan bring me a miniature horse. I named her Sorrow. She was not enough to keep me on an even keel, as lovable, sweet and cheeky as she is. By the fall of 2005 I fell into a deep depression. To not allow things of that sort to rule me, I sought a cure. I needed something to do. A change of living quarters occurred to me. Moving anywhere from this area was not practical, for several reasons. Unknown forces were pushing me.

Finally I decided simply to renovate my barn into a woodshed in the hay section, leaving room for a stall for little Sorrow, and make the stable part, 16 by 20 feet, into living quarters. The idea opened a wide window of opportunity. Suddenly I was buoyed up and eager to get started. I also hoped to get a better water source and maybe have indoor plumbing. The old outhouse was getting harder to get to in deep snow as my arthritic hips continued to limit my walking ability.

As fall turned to winter, I nagged and pushed for someone to come and dig me another well. Hopefully one that would produce a good supply of water thru the dry summers. Some wells in this Salloompt sand and gravel bed do run low in summer, but most do produce some water. My first well has never gone dry in nearly 18 years that I have been living here. When it went low I could still get a bit of water with the old bucket on a long rope.

As soon as I got a truck, when I was 65, I began hauling water from Glengarry to my place for my garden. That worked fine for as long as I could drive. Arthritic hips eventually took that away from me too, in January 2007.

Before I went too far in plans for renovation of my barn, I consulted with a couple of real carpenters on the practicality of such a venture. One thought there was no reason why it would not work, but if I hired a carpenter it would cost more than building a whole new house because of all the fiddly stuff that would have to be done. That assessment seemed fair enough to me. Fiddly stuff takes time.

The other carpenter said flat out that the building could not be made habitable, period. I asked him what problems would cause it to be not habitable. The answer was, "It just can't." I thought to myself, wouldn't that depend on what one meant by "habitable"? Anyway that was a challenge. Now I had two good reasons to renovate. The die was cast.

In late rainy, warm January my well diggers finally arrived. Things were looking up, or rather down, deep in the rocky ground, about 18 feet. There was water. Also huge boulders, as big as truck wheels, lying cemented in the bottom of the hole. They could go no deeper. There should have been a layer of clay, but there wasn't. Would there be water in this new well in August?

They installed a 2000-dollar plastic well casing, 20 feet long and three feet in diameter. In a short time muddy water rose to be three feet deep. We set up my pump and tried to pump out the dirty water. Eventually we got it going. So, I had a nice new well and there was no rust in the water. In a couple of months I found out if there would be water in it in August. There was no water in it in March, only a wet mud pan in the bottom. Water rises in it in the early winter. Water also rises in my old well in October, and gets higher as winter drags along. With summer it slowly drops, depending on how much it rains.

With a producing well dug, I went at my renovation with energy, hammer and nail bar. A lot of removal of mangers, stanchions, walls and ceiling had to be done. Most of the old floor planks, well perfumed by nearly 18 years of animal liquid, and not so liquid, products had to be hauled out and stacked for future use elsewhere. I did this by hand. They were all still sound, but they stank. Most of the floor sills I could use, but I had to get some new ones.

I dug out a good layer of rich soil that was under the floor, by shovel. All the good soil thus salvaged later made beautiful tomatoes and spuds. It was a lot of handwork throwing it all out of the barn, but worth it if only for garden. I had to have space under the new floor. Most of the dirt had accumulated by falling thru the cracks by the trampling of the cows and horses.

As the stable part has three log walls connected to the post and beam hay section, there was no wall between the mangers and the hay. I had to put a frame wall on that side. I also had to plumb up the log walls with two-by-six salvaged lumber, so the plywood sheets could go on more or less vertical. Jack helped me with the plywood. I could no longer handle the four-by-eight sheets. After we cut them to size, I could put most of them up alone. Jack was not feeling too healthy. He had something wrong that the doctors could not discover what it was, so I didn't want to let him work too hard.

With running water from my old well, and hydro hooked up, a stove for heat, and cooking facilities operational, I moved into my 'uninhabitable' snug little house, 16 by 20 feet, in May 2007. And I have indoor plumbing, for as long as my old well produces enough water.

With the possibility of deep snow combined with a power outage or other problems, I converted Sorrow's stall into an indoor outhouse after I gave her to a family with children who just love her and are driving her in a buggy. Last fall they gave me a ride with her, in her buggy.

Well, the renovation and move served their purpose. They killed the depression and I have several other benefits. A smaller house to heat. And I am right on my driveway so I can have a vehicle right at my door. At the lower house my driveway is three feet higher than the house, and 20 feet away. One downside to my move is anyone visiting me has to walk a lot farther to reach me, and people bringing supplies to me must lug the stuff that much farther. Tom and Susan usually do this. It is a good thing they are young.

With all the benefits of living where there are more people, and having had a chance to do horse stuff with other people, and had 16 years to enjoy the company of a very loving and intelligent little dog, I still miss my old home. When I sold the place to BC Parks, I hoped they would wait until Jack and I passed away to destroy our buildings. I never asked them for this favor, as I thought they would laugh at me. I just hoped for the best. As history was to show, when opportunity arrived, they couldn't wait. The buildings are all gone, due to the fire that could have been stopped.

I close my eyes and picture the house and barns and sheds
The garden, fields and orchard
And the river in its bed
But now its desolation all burned and grey as lead
Most every tree and animal all charred...
And gone and dead.

chapter 14

Dogs & Insects

How do dogs really feel about us? Do they look on us as fellow pack members, or something godlike? Can dogs feel thankful for what small, or otherwise, comforts, food and companionship we give them? A tiny incident occurred once again this morning, as it has been happening for a while now.

I feed Liesel twice a day. During each feed she starts to eat, then lifts her head after only a few licks at her meal and softly touches my hand, then eats some more. Soon she reaches up again and gives me that soft touch with her nose. It started me wondering just what she is saying.

I never had this kind of communication from Liesel or any other of my dogs before. But looking back, I never gave them a chance, either. I thought they'd prefer I put the food down, then leave so they could eat in peace. The only reason I have begun staying around after giving Liesel her dish is to be sure she is going to eat. Her appetite has become rather fickle at times and she seems to want me to urge her to eat. But then wolves eat together on a large prey. So perhaps they don't want to eat alone.

Considering how some humans treat dogs, it is hard to understand what they see in us that they are so forgiving of our faults and so appreciative of whatever we give them. We can beat them, leave them all alone and helpless for hours, sometimes days, at a time, yet on our return they are so glad to see us they wag with joy, leap around in a frenzy of excitement, and race in circles of exuberance. They seem to forget we have left them at home alone while we have had an interesting day of discovery and companionship. They hold no grudge for our seeming bad manners, from a pack animal's viewpoint. Pack animals are born together, live together and hunt together.

The obvious sad disappointment a dog shows when she stands at the gate and watches you get in your truck and drive away without taking her, for no reason she can see, is hard to take, especially as you can't explain the reason to her. As soon as all hope for a trip to anywhere has died, she turns, ears down, walks slowly away to go to her own little log house to nurse her disappointment.

We can hurt a dog horribly, physically or emotionally, and she will run away. Soon she will return to the person who hurt her and come up asking forgiveness for something she didn't know she had done, that you wouldn't like. She hopes that with her apology you won't hurt her again.

I am ashamed, and deeply sorry for some things I have done to dogs in the name of "training." I have now learned a better means of communication when it is too late for the dogs that I had during my life, and even for Liesel, except for the last half of her lifetime. I have tried to make up for the abuse I heaped on my dogs, trying to train them, by trying to be better and more forgiving to Liesel. I cannot help the others.

Do insects learn? Yes, I think so. Not only learn, but also transmit information to one another, especially social insects, such as bees and ants. It is already known that when honeybee scouts return from a good source of honey they can tell others, by a special dance performed in the hive, where it is. They can let the other bees know how far away the food source is and in what direction from the hive. So it would not be wondered at that ants seem able to tell others when a good source of food becomes unavailable.

When we lived at Lonesome Lake we had a feeder for the humming birds. It was hung high above the cats, from a wire hooked to a beam eight feet above the ground. It did not take the little red ants long to find their way up a post, across the beam and down the wire to the feeder. As long as only an ant or two were stealing the sugar syrup, we let them be, but when they began arriving in hoards, something had to be done. Also the little hummers were afraid to stick their bills in among those red biters.

I partially filled a shallow pan with water and hung it under the feeder, and set the actual feed supply container on an island in the center of the pan, then sat back to see what would happen. The birds didn't mind the change a bit. So what would the ants do when they got to the water?

The ants came as usual, up the post, across the beam and down the wire—to the pan of water. Their feelers working overtime, they ran down to the water, then back up on the rim, one after another, agitated feelers searching for a dry route to the syrup-filled feeder, just 15 ant lengths away across that ocean. Around the rim of the pan they ran, checking, checking. There was no way across to the syrup and they were not going to swim. Finally they all gave up for that day.

Bright and early the next day the hopeful little ants were back, but not as numerous as the day before. Two or three days passed. No more ants came that summer. The next year no ants came. For as long as we lived there afterwards, the ants never returned. It would seem the ants had passed the information on that the food was no longer available.

Some might argue with me, but I believe they did pass on the information that they could no longer find food in the humming bird's feeder. I would call that learning.

Flies seem capable of learning by observing others getting caught. When Liesel was young and agile she could snap flies out of the air over her head, but they quickly learned that when she woke up, they had better fly just a bit higher than they had been when the dog was sleeping. The flies continued to zoom about my kitchen, but stayed several feet above the floor instead of going right down to the level of the sleeping dog. Their buzzing awakened her and when she stood up, up went the flies, above her reach.

I know spiders are not insects, but as they are small and share my house, or I share theirs; I will include them here. I have found them very interesting, and they do no harm, unlike flies. They don't bite, or tramp about on my food and dishes, carrying all manner of yucky stuff on their feet. Spiders used to bite me once in a while, and I killed them whenever I got a chance. Then I changed my attitude and didn't kill any more of them. They have not bitten me since. I really do not know why.

Several families of spiders of various sizes build webs along the sides of my window right beside my bed. I can lie there and watch the little predators working on their nets, or catching and eating their breakfast, and once in a while, make love, spider style. She doesn't always eat him afterwards. I watched two long skinny arachnids interacting in what appeared to be a sexual encounter. In time they separated. One stayed on the web where they had been, while the other moved off a short way and rested on another strand of web.

Now I quite admire spiders and some very fancy web construction. The ones I have the most to do with are those that get in my sink. If I let the sides of the sink get dirty enough, they can crawl up the vertical part of the wall, but I seldom let it get that dirty, even tho I am not the world's most fussy housekeeper.

What "my" spiders learned, some anyway, was to use a ladder (string) dangled into the sink and resting on the bottom. It was tied to one of the taps to keep it in place. I put the escape string in place in the evening when there were three spiders in the sink. Next morning all were up and away, the first time they all got out on their own. Before then I'd had to remove them before using my sink.

Very rarely some spiders can escape by climbing as far up the wall as they can, then they spin a web bridge across the corner. Next they climb onto that to spin another bridge higher, and so on until they reach the top and crawl out to go on their way.

Once in a while a really stupid spider finds her way into my sink and does not use my ladder, and continues to try to scale a wall which she keeps falling back down from when she gets up to where it is vertical.

Now for the learning. When a spider has been in the sink overnight, I begin educating her. I can herd her to the bottom of the ladder by just carefully touching her legs on the side away from the ladder. She tears off around the bottom of the sink, acting much like a scared wild cow. So I get in front of her again and tap the sink. She continues to press forward, as I give ground so as not to injure her in a collision. Soon she stops. I move my hand towards her and tap the sink. She turns and races off the other way. I tell her to stop and again plant my hand in front of her. This time she stops. I tell her what a nice smart spider she is, then ask her again to go the other way. This time she turns sooner and doesn't dash off so fast or run so far. I praise her again, then ask her to head for the ladder once more. On this run I can stop her at the bottom of the ladder. She still doesn't start up, but runs off. I turn her back and halt her at the ladder again. She waits there that time and I very gently encourage her to start up the ladder. She doesn't understand and runs off again, stopping when she sees my hand in her way. I herd her back to the ladder, stop her there, praise her, then try to get her to start up the string. This time she does begin climbing.

She is almost to the top when she tries to finish the trip by short-cutting over to the slippery top of the sink wall—and plummets all the way to the bottom.

So we start again. Back at the bottom of the ladder she goes almost without help up the string. This time she stays on the ladder until she is right out of the sink. She clings to a scrap of plastic bag and rests there for a while, then hikes off on a mission of her own. So can insects and spiders learn?

Update on Liesel

Liesel is gone. She passed away at 5:30 on June 14, 2009. She sleeps close to my lower house in one of my unused old gardens. She never walked on that garden. It is now just a grass patch where my strawberries have been overwhelmed by blue grass and raspberries.

Now I am dogless once more, and lonely again. There is nothing to feed every day, or to talk to, even if she could not hear me. And nothing to pet and stroke, as she lifted her head to push up against my hand.

I hope to get another little dog, but may not find what I want. I miss her so much.

I now have that new little puppy. She arrived at the end of July 2009. She is a border collie and I call her Magi, for Magic. When she was a little over a year old she seemed lonely and bored so I decided to try to find a companion for her. An Aussie puppy, whom I named Dove, came to live with us. They play with each other, wrestle and chase and are lots of entertainment for me.

chapter 15

Pets

Growing up on The Birches, we had lots of large pets and few small ones. Cows and horses served for the most part, but I wanted something small and furry and that would not be of culinary interest, so I could at last let it have my heart. Finally I was allowed a female kitten. I named her Amy. More on Amy later.

There had been baby hares before the kitten. Dad often found young varying hares in the course of land clearing or other such activities. Peter was my very first small pet.

Dad built a nice big pen for him with a nest box and two rooms. The entry was on the top of the pen thru a lift-up door of chicken wire, as was the rest of the pen. As Peter was very young when he was caught, he didn't mind the pen, and it was his home and sanctuary.

One night he got loose somehow and disappeared. I was devastated. We didn't know how we would ever find him again. Having lived only in the safety of that pen, how would he survive on his own?

Sometime later we happened to look out to the cage and there was a white rabbit sitting in Peter's pen. The door was still open. Someone had missed closing the door in the first place, allowing him to escape and return. It certainly was Peter. He was glad to see us and expected to be fed, even though while he was outside his home he must have passed lots of good bunny food.

Deciduous twigs and bark was the food of choice for winter, with some carrots for dessert. Clover, grass, fresh garden produce and leaves were choice summer rations. Oh, and apples.

That little bunny was tame enough that I could crawl into his pen and he would come up and sit on my lap. I don't remember actually holding him. I have no memory of what happened to him.

I had several more baby bunnies in my youth, but none of them lived very long. One young one I had in one of our live traps, described elsewhere, hung up high above the floor and away from anything close that a weasel could jump from. Or so I thought. In the morning my bunny was dead and partly eaten. I hated that weasel. I didn't realize just how determined weasels could be. I do now. And they are extremely strong. They can lift and carry in their teeth something outweighing them probably by three times.

I still seem to have had a baby hare in a pen for a lot of my early years. One year each of the kids had one. Those were caesarian bunnies. Stanley had been trapping the too-numerous nuisances that had been harvesting peas and carrots without permission. One morning when he checked his traps, there was a very pregnant female in one. He dispatched her and laid her down on a handy rock. Soon he noticed activity in her body. He opened her up and took out a small litter of full term baby bunnies. They immediately began breathing. He scooped them up in his hands and carried them to the house. They were still wet, of course.

Mother got towels and cleaned the tiny things up until their fur was dry and fluffy. Hares are born fully furred, eyes open and ready to run. Those little guys were ready to eat anyway. There were three of them, one for each of us.

Feeding the little things was not the easiest task. They were about the size of mice. We warmed cow's milk, stuck the corner of a small cloth in the milk and held it to the "pup's" mouth. The little guy didn't like that. Of course not. It wouldn't feel or taste right to the baby. Baby mammals seem to be born knowing what their milk tastes and smells like. In time, hunger and persistence on our part, or rather on Mother's part mostly, convinced them at least to try some. We may have added a bit of sugar. I do not remember. They did survive and grow and were very tame. Humans were the only "mother" they knew. They never saw their own.

In not too long they were drinking out of saucers, snuffling, as they didn't seem to be able to get the warm milk into their mouths without sticking their noses in too, then come up for air, snorting and spraying milk everywhere. Finished feeding, they would then need a good face washing. That over, they would cuddle up and go to sleep. It wasn't long until they were ready for fresh greens. They loved clover.

Those baby bunnies got me in trouble once. It was something about one of the milk cows. Sometimes my beloved parents were a bit late getting up in the morning and getting the milking done. So as not to wake them up too early, I decided just to take a pan out to the field and harvest a bit fresh from the source. I knew one should not partially milk a cow and not finish the job, but my bunny was hungry and I didn't know when they would get up.

I have found out that the worst that seems to happen if a cow is milked only a little is she can't give her milk down a second time until a certain amount of time has passed, for the lactating machinery to cycle thru its natural programming. Certainly only partially milking a cow won't always harm her either. It can in the right situation.

My first cat was Amy. I can't remember how long I had her. She died, we thought at the time, from eating some cooked beets, but I don't know. It could have been, I suppose. In case it was the beets, I have never fed either cats or dogs chunks of beets again. I always mashed them thoroughly. After all cats and dogs are meat eaters, not vegetarians. Mashing the vegetables will do no harm.

My next cat I named Feely, for feline. She lived a long life, somewhere around 15 or 16 years. Then Dizzy Six came to Lonesome Lake to be my pet. Why Dizzy Six? She had a purr like a DC Six airplane, affectionately referred to as a Dizzy Six. All three of those cats were dark striped gray short hairs with white trim, nice and neat.

Sometime while Dizzy was still living, Mother decided she needed a cat. She selected a longhaired yellow Persian type female. All the cats we brought to Lonesome Lake were females. We didn't want to raise kittens. There were plenty to replace any losses we might have, just a few miles down the valley. And we would have no problems with stinky old tomcats.

Mother's cat was named Psyche. I don't remember why, or even if that was the name Mother gave her. She was very beautiful and as proud of herself as a cat can ever be. But lazy, as only a cat can ever be.

Psyche preferred to sit on a soft cushion, or on a warm lap, and purr and purr as her human stroked her lovely long fur. And of course she grew lots of lovely yellow fur balls. She had to be groomed, often.

Dad had built Mother a really nice birch bench to sit on, and varnished it, bringing out a beautiful golden yellow finish. Psyche liked to sit on it, even tho it didn't have a cushion. Then Mother couldn't use her own bench.

Psyche made herself famous when the morning outside temperature was minus 46 degrees Fahrenheit. That was a cold morning in January. Anyway, while short-haired Dizzy Six was willing to go outside to attend to the call of nature, longhaired fluffy Psyche chose to find a narrow crack between two floor planks, and peed down that. Then returned to her warm cushion. Her hairy paws never had to touch a single flake of snow.

Then Mother got Candy, a Bella Coola mix, a nice little dog with some collie blood but—a good question—what else?

As none of us was up on dog training, Candy spent her entire life on a long chain, part of the time in the house and part tied outside. She was so glad to see someone, anyone, who happened to go outside, she'd race to the end of her chain, be jerked up, lean on her collar, wheezing, leaping, choking, just to get closer to the approaching human sooner. She never learned, or was taught, to sit down and wait for the human to get to her.

Candy also did duty as a strawberry guard a quarter of a mile from the house for a few months during at least one summer. She was tied beside the large strawberry parch to keep strawberry thieves such as robins, crows and squirrels away from the berries. We wanted to sell them to people at Nimpo, Charlotte and Anahim Lakes. Candy was pretty successful, too. When anything came near the patch, she'd dart out of her shelter, barking, leaping, and scare them away.

I remember she was at the strawberry patch during the summer of 1956. Jack, who had walked back into my life in early June, was given the job of going over every day to feed and water the dog and give her a little company and a walk. The rest of the time she was all alone there by the berry patch, night and day. Sometimes one or more of us might go to the garden to get vegetables for lunch and would visit the lonely little dog. As they were everbearing strawberries, she was likely there all summer. I bet she was glad to see fall approaching and she could come home again. Jack didn't mind caring for her. He loved all dogs and liked to visit Candy.

There had not been a dog at The Birches for many years until Candy. Dad had a hunting dog, Whitie, before he went off to join the first war. After his return to Lonesome Lake he had a collie, named Snoops. Snoops got sick, probably with some form of canine flu, and died. Then the family was dogless until they got a little dog called Tupper. He was Johnny's pet. Johnny was a little too young to have to be responsible for an animal and I have to think Tupper sometimes went without his supper.

One night, Tupper, untrained, hungry and not confined in any way to keep him from feeding himself, found some furs and ate them, a crime no dog would be pardoned for. Tupper vanished. Johnny didn't know what had happened to his dog until only a year or two before he passed away. Not knowing my brother never had been told what happened to his pet, I mentioned the little dog's demise one day in relation to something else. He told me he never knew why the dog simply wasn't around any more. Mother had told me sometime in my early life. I am sure the incident had a powerful effect on me. The message was quite clear. If one makes a mistake, they don't get a second chance, and they are no good. This lesson drove me to try to force any animal to be good and useful, and not make too much trouble.

I believe that incident with Tupper may have caused me to try too hard to make the animals that I was training be very good, so I would get worked up too much in my effort to make them shape up and perform well. The more I liked an animal, the harder I'd try to get it to work properly, so it could stay around and be used for work or whatever. I don't think a lesson was intended. I think it could have just happened.

I have always had the feeling that my animals, and by extension, myself, were not as good as someone else's. That caused me to try harder to make them better, and it may have helped me try to face difficulties more stubbornly. I don't know.

When I bought a sturdy black mare in the spring of 1951 and brought her to Lonesome Lake to work with my bay gelding, which I had bought from Dad earlier, he did not think much of her. She was black. Black was not his favorite color. Anyway, to prove to my father that black horses could perform well, I asked her to haul a huge load once. It was a log about 80 feet long and over a foot at the butt, a good load for a team. She hauled it 400 feet to the mill, but he didn't even recognize the fact.

That horse was called Thuja. She was about the best horse I ever had. She was dependable, calm in any emergency, a wonderful puller, packhorse, and saddle horse, and companion.

I am now going to put a bit of fiction in this memoir to illustrate a thought I had one day. Do dogs have a sense of stealing?

Poor Number Five

The sun had just risen and was turning the millions of frost crystals to rubies, sapphires and emeralds that glinted and flashed thru the air as they melted off the birch branches and drifted to the snow lying deep below. The wolves were finishing up a kill they had made in the night. They never saw or paid attention to the frost crystals falling all around and on them as they busied themselves at the carcass.

Number one, the alpha wolf, had pulled off one whole back leg and taken it off a little way from the other four who were still at the kill. His belly full, he sauntered off to a sheltered spot where the sun was shining on the bare ground under a dense tree. He lay down, cleaned his paws, scrubbed his muzzle on the dry needles under the tree, then rose, shook himself, turned around a couple of times, then lay quietly and gazed into a deep ravine just beyond his tree.

Meanwhile Number Five, having gotten very little of the meat, had kept her sight on that juicy leg bone. She crept quietly towards the bone. Once, Number One turned his sleepy gaze on her and then resumed his ravine watching. Number Five, with her instincts yelling, "Grab it, grab it! Quickly!" snatched it up and carried it away to gnaw off what meat was left, all the while hoping the leader would continue his observations of the ravine. As far as he was concerned, the bone was free to anyone who wanted it.

In the Kitchen, Tame Dogs

In the kitchen Number Five lay dreaming on a soft bed near the cook stove. Numbers One, Two, Three and Four and their guests strolled into the living room, drinks in hand, nattering away, leaving a plate of steak thawing on the counter.

Soon Number Five woke up, yawned, sat up, scratched

her right ear, then stood up and shook her coat. A tantalizing aroma caused her to lick her lips and begin sniffing the air.

She was the only one in the room, tho she could hear the rest of the pack carrying on nearby. Her nose told her there was a bonanza of meat just over her head. How could she obtain some of it? She was really hungry, especially now that she had smelled the delicious odor of fresh thawing MEAT!

Hmm, hmm. Her mind worked hard. She knew she wasn't allowed on tables, counters and even chairs. But Numbers One and Two had turned their backs on the meat, so surely it would be all right to take just a little of it, wouldn't it? Instinct yelled, "Yes, yes, take it!" Instinct battled with training. She also knew, from bitter experience, that she was not to get up on tables or counters, at least while Numbers One and Two were present. Numbers Three and Four had allowed her to learn she could do some "bad" things when only they were in the room. Small thefts might not be a really serious crime.

She wandered around the room, thinking. Finally she reared and placed the tip of one paw just on the edge of the counter, near the plate of steaks. She still could not quite reach the meat. With the other paw she reached the far edge of the plate and carefully drew it near enough that she could just raise the edge of one large thick steak with her incisors and get a good grip on it. She pulled it off the stack, dropped to the floor, her instincts yelling at her, "Grab it! Grab it, run and hide, quickly, quietly!"

With the steak dripping meat juice, she fled silently into another room. She lay with her head in a corner so she could eat her trophy in peace.

The eating finished, she cleaned her paws and face, and every drop of meat juice from the floor all the way back to the counter. Then she returned to her bed by the stove and went to sleep again.

Number Five's snooze was shattered by a roar of outrage when Number One prepared to cook the steaks for the guest's dinner. ONE WAS MISSING! He counted again. Yes, there were only three on the plate. He was sure he had taken four out of the freezer. He was certain. He looked at the dog sleeping innocently on the rug, just as she had been when he left the room such a short time ago. Surely she couldn't have snatched a steak. There were no drops of meat juice on the floor that he could see. The plate didn't appear to have been moved, and there were still three steaks on it. SO WHAT HAPPENED TO THAT STEAK?!

Poor Number Five. She rose from her bed and quietly left the room. Soon she returned, just as quietly, a slim piece of steak, now with a few dog hairs clinging to it, clutched in her teeth, and offered it to Number One. He stared in disbelief, not knowing whether to laugh or to cry, as Number Five sat at his feet, offering him the meat she assumed had been left for her. She had not cleaned up the floor to hide her "crime," but to respond to another instinct: "waste not."

The first cat I took to Seven Islands, also known as Fogswamp or Arbordale, came from Bella Coola as a small fluffy yellow kitten. I named her Pacific Queen, for a boat I saw tied up at the docks when I had flown to Bella Coola and tied my plane up there.

At Seven Islands I kept her in my cabin and gave her a dirt box. One day when I went in for lunch there was something on my bed that should have been in the dirt box. I put the kitten outside. She was outraged at being thrown out of "her" house; I was outraged at what she had done on my bed. We really didn't get along too good.

She was going to be an outside cat. Pacific Queen did not want to be an outside cat. I was not going to allow her to be an inside cat. She had to adjust. I was not going to.

The first night of being an outside cat Pacific Queen spent about two hours scrambling all the way around on the top log of each wall, yowling, trying to find a crack she could slip in thru. There wasn't one. And my door remained solidly closed. In the morning she was huddling in a pathetic longhaired heap on the woodpile.

Later we acquired two lady kittens, named Rainbow and Moony. Then later still came Tshombe and Muffet. Tshombe we did not ask for. The people we got the two kittens from just decided to send him along with the female we had asked for. So then we had a tomcat. In time he did what tomcats do. He peed on a riding saddle I had made. He was kept tied up then, at night as well as during the day.

We usually tied our cats during the day in summer to prevent them killing birds, then they were loose at night to catch mice. They didn't mind the tying up, and usually were on hand to be tied and get a dish of warm milk. Each cat had her own nest box to sleep in.

When Susan was around eight or so she tried to make a team out of Tshombe and Muffet to haul a musical toy with a handle she could use like a wagon tongue. She got the two cats harnessed and hitched to the toy. When it came time actually to haul anything both cats lay down and rolled on their backs, one on each side of the "tongue." She couldn't convince them to get up. They just squirmed around good naturedly and purred. She even appealed to her parents to make her team get up and go to work. We tried; the patient cats just weren't into that kind of game.

Once Muffet disgraced herself by sitting over a ceiling crack when we had let the cats upstairs. I happened to be standing under that crack when a stream of smelly liquid splashed down on my head! Outraged, I stamped upstairs, snatched up the innocent looking cat, carried her down the stairs and out to the river. A shallow stream ran right behind the woodshed. Across that channel was an island. Lying from the island to about halfway across the stream was a birch log, mostly out of the water.

I waded across to the log, and deposited the cat on it. She could swim back to the house, or go on the log to the island, then cross back on the pole bridge. It was up to her. She was not going to go upstairs again. Perhaps she was not going to be let upstairs again.

Earlier Muffet was upstairs in the winter and a stream of liquid came down, and when one of us went up to see what was going on, we found her by the stovepipe covered with balls of snow, which were melting. She was a longhair. That was all right and excusable.

The next kittens to come to our place were Dumbo and Cealy, nice cats.

As we had sort of learned—the cats taught us—to keep cats outside, we seldom allowed them in the house. One exception was when Dumbo allowed herself to get trod on by a bull. That must at least have broken some of her small bones in her hindquarters. As she didn't seem to be in severe agony, we gave her a chance to recover, if she could. As she could only drag herself along, we put her in a cage with a litter box and a bed, and set it near the stove to keep her warm. She couldn't have roamed very far, but she could easily get stepped on by one of us, as even the most agile and aware cats seem to believe we have eyes in our feet and that we will avoid them. They don't want to take any responsibility for themselves, unlike dogs, who seem automatically to assume you will want to walk where they are lying if they are, say, in front of a doorway. They get up and move away. This is in my experience. Well, some do.

Anyway, Dummy lived in her cage, ate a bit, drank some milk, and began healing her broken little body. Daily, she improved until she was trying to use her back legs. Not long after trying, she was actually walking again, lucky little cat.

But she still didn't learn to avoid large hoofed animals. Sometimes I would find her sitting, or lying, on the warm bed of a cow who had just risen for her breakfast. She was right under the middle of the cow where a big hoof could easily have been set down on her fragile little body.

Some of the cats seemed to bond with one or two of the horses and would sleep on the horse's hay in the manger. The horse didn't seem to mind the "cat in the manger," and maybe actually enjoyed her companionship. Some horses do seem to like cats, and cats like them. I have a photo of a horse, Spud, wearing a cat hat.

Though we seldom allowed the cats in the house, there was one place where they were allowed to be where they could be close to us and watch what we were doing. They loved to sit on the ledge on top of the window cutout on the front door. We had a window about a foot high by two feet long that we could take out of the door for ventilation. The two cats would jump up onto that ledge from a shelf below and to one side of the door. There was room for both of them to sit there, either facing each other or with both backs turned. They resembled furry, mobile bookends.

Once in a long time one or the other would sneak down the door to the floor and have to be escorted outside again. This didn't happen very often, but the cat who did it was always very proud of herself. Another way a cat could get in the house was to walk along under the dog as she was going out or coming in. We had to watch them carefully, especially if we were going on an overnight or longer trip.

Cats, although solitary hunters, seem to bond to humans. They were always happy to see us when we returned from a two- or three-day trip. When we came across the field to the house at least one of the cats would see or hear us and run, leap, gallop joyously across the grass to meet us, meowing, rubbing around our legs and looking up at us as she kneaded the grass ecstatically.

Then she followed us to the house yard and ran over to her tie-up place, looked in her empty dish and asked for milk and to be tied up.

One time we came home from a five-day mountain trip, which we had cut to a three-day hike. On our arrival we found Dummy badly entangled in a net we had put over the strawberry patch to keep out berry thieves. That was the only time a cat had gotten tangled up in the strawberry net. We had been putting it over the strawberries every summer for years. Just luck, I guess. Dummy was fortunate the weather had not been very hot and that no eaters-of-cats had come along. And also that we had cut our hike short. To rescue the cat was the real reason we returned two days sooner than we had planned. Well, who knows?

One of the last cats to come to Arbordale was a pretty purry creature Susan gave us named Martini, Tinny for short. She was a Siamese shorthair with dark points.

Then there was Melly, a black lady with yellow eyes. She was Jack's special cat and went with us when we moved.

chapter 16

USEFUL PETS

When we sold my place at Lonesome Lake I suddenly had a bit of excess money in my hands, so I kept Bess, mentioned elsewhere, and gave Star and Tempest to Susan. She used them in some of her enterprises and then sold them.

As I did not need a horse, Bess was just a pet. Why do I say, why do people say, "just a pet"? Are pets useless because they cost more to keep than the money they could make? Is a hockey stick useless? Why are pets considered useless? Is a piano or a violin useless? Are skis or skates useless? Is something that improves one's life, but doesn't make a big buck, useless? Anyway I really don't care if it is useless, as long as I can afford it. Why not enjoy something that I get a lot of pleasure out of? And for 10 years I got a heck of a lot of pleasure out of Bess. I won't go into details here as I have done that elsewhere.

I wanted to keep the cows and Bess and live near our daughter and her family. As she had horses also that she needed a farm for, and I needed some farmland, I helped her and Tom buy a 40-acre property in the Bella Coola Valley. We could all live there. I bought three acres of the 40 acres. I built an addition on a small cabin Susan and Tom had sold me along with the three acres. The three acres was for pasture for my two cows and some area for garden.

I also wanted to watch my grandson, Brendan, grow up.

Jack spent the time from mid-September 1989 to mid March 1990 on the south coast. Loneliness drove him to decide he needed his family more than the sea. He asked me to obtain a trailer for him while he was still living on the south coast. In March he moved back with me, and Susan, Tom and Brendan. With his own house to run as he chose, he had no problems and neither did I. With our two residences close to each other we got along fine and could help one another easily.

Brendan got a little brother, Alex, in April 1993. Susan's family was complete, and Jack and I had two grandchildren.

The second autumn after our move down the valley there was a heavy fall of snow in November followed by two or three days of rain. The rain soaked up the foot-thick layer of snow on Susan and Tom's barn roof. I was in my cow barn, milking, when I heard a lot of thumping noise coming from an adjacent building where two of the horses were already stabled for the night. I wondered why Tempest was stamping around so much. Then the noise suddenly increased. I jumped up from my cow and stepped to the door to see what all the uproar was about, and was met by the roof of the adjacent building sliding out right in front of me.

Not knowing how much more of the building complex was going to come down, I yelled to Susan, who was in her house nearby, then checked to try and determine if my cows were safe in their building. I was also concerned about the three horses who might have been under a lean-to roof on the other side of the part that was now spread all over the yard. Thankfully, all the horses were safe. The three outside horses came flying around the corner of the part that had not fallen. The section where Tempest and Star were housed stayed undamaged. Not trusting the rest of the rickety building to stay up, we turned the two stabled horses out and moved my three cattle to a different shelter. It was still raining.

After things settled down a bit I suddenly realized how lucky I was to be still alive. I had been under that fragile roof only a few minutes earlier getting some grain out of a storage container for my cows. Had the roof come down while I was in there, I would not be writing these or any other words now. The roof fell so quickly only a squirrel, a really speedy squirrel, could have escaped.

We had to do a lot of emergency repairs that dark, rainy evening, as the displaced barn roof destroyed the fences and left nails that animals could step on everywhere. We had to protect the horses from all the nails sticking up all over the wreckage.

Much of our hay had no cover then either, except for the snow-covered broken roof parts lying on it. Not very waterproof.

The next day we assessed the damage and put in temporary braces to prop up the part of the building complex that hadn't collapsed. My cows could go back in their barn. I think the horses stayed outside for the winter. We hung up our big freight canvas and plastic sheets to protect the hay as much as possible. All thru the winter, when it wasn't pouring down nasty weather, Jack and I worked at removing roof parts and dragging hay bales out from under what we didn't want to remove then.

I used broken roof parts to build temporary fences to keep my cows in their own pasture and away from the nails. As a further precaution against the possibility of the cows eating some nails, as they would be scattered everywhere, I had a visiting veterinarian put a magnet in the paunch of each. The magnet would collect any iron object she swallowed and keep it from working out of her paunch and ultimately getting to her heart, with fatal results. Years later when we butchered one of those cows I found the magnet, completely surrounded with hay string and some nails, still lying harmless in her paunch, or rumen.

We could simply have demolished the old broken barn and then started again with new materials, but I, being Lonesome Lake economy-minded, suggested that since there was a lot of perfectly sound material in the wreckage strewn all about right there, we could rebuild with that. All thru the winter, with any spare time, I worked at salvaging all the useful parts—and pulling pounds of rusty nails—that could be used again.

At that time I was only salvaging useful materials, but as time went on it became apparent that Susan and I were going to need shelter for our hay, soon. One section of the complex that hadn't come down was a lean-to shed, which would hold my hay. It was open to the weather on one whole side. I suggested we build a new 10- by 20-foot shed against the lean-to part where she could store a lot of hay. So that was done.

Sometime in June there were two or three hot days, then some heavy rain. Soon the Bella Coola River, helped by the Salloompt River, was marching sloppily across the highway, thru the forest, over our driveway and under my house, set about a hundred feet from Tom and Susan's house. The water was all around it, as well as over a lot of the field and a bit of the garden. •

This wet invasion, occurring in the summer, set me to thinking. It was bad enough that the place flooded in the fall when there was a lot of rain, but to have it happen right in the middle of summer was too much. As I continued salvage work, I considered moving to higher ground, later. First, I wanted to build one more barn for Susan.

The old barn had been built in three sections at different times. Some parts were stronger than the sections that failed. Because the parts that fell were so weak, we assumed the rest of the building was weak also. We hired a backhoe to come and knock it down. It wasn't weak at all and bravely resisted the efforts of the backhoe for a long time. By the time it became apparent that that section of the building actually was safe, it had been damaged so much by the machine that we had to go ahead and finish destroying it.

After cleaning up and salvaging more building materials, I built a 20- by 10-foot stable with two box stalls for Susan's horses.

In the fall I looked around a bit and found a four-acre property only half a mile from where I was living, and on higher ground. It even had a small—tiny, actually—lake on it. That would be a bonus. I bought it and began work, getting house logs ready to build a new house. I was over 62 years old then.

Big Lagoon and Head of the Lake area with The Birches in foreground.

Aerial view of The Birches.

Middle of Lonesome Lake.

Ralph Edwards at Stillwater, c. 1940.

Ralph and Ethel Edwards' wedding, 1923.
(L to R) Standing: Aunt Laura, Dad, Aunt Ruth, Grandpa John, Aunt Sarah, the pastor.
Sitting: Mother, Grandma Ida Mae.

West end of the henhouse that the family moved into after the fire in 1929. Wolf pelt hanging up outside.

The rebuilt barn in 1941. Our little house is in the foreground.

The Edwards' family house at The Birches.

The sawmill at The Birches, 1956.   *The barn at The Birches, c. 1980s. Photo by John Edwards.*

Beaver lodge at Lonesome Lake. Photo by John Edwards.

Johnny, age 6, and Trudy, 4, warming up on a sunny rock at Bluff Point on Lonesome Lake, 1933.

Orphaned baby bunnies, their mother killed by a mower. The babies were delivered by caesarian operation and raised by Trudy and her brothers, c. 1936.

L to R: Stanley, age 12; Johnny, 9; Trudy, 6, in front of wolf and cougar pelts trapped by Ralph, c. 1936.

Trudy, about age 10, with her pet rabbit, Peter.

John's first cabin and the skeleton of the new implement shed.

Stanley heading out on his own at 17, c. 1941.

Stanley, about 75 years, near the Stillwater, c. 1999.

*Trudy (left), about 14 years, with her
mother in matching homemade outfits.*

*Ethel with her dog Candy
at The Birches, 1959.*

Ginty and Susan with a load of hay on the raft as Ralph and Stanley take them across the Atnarko River, late 1930s.

Ginty in old age, c. 1942.

Prince and Susan plowing at The Birches, late 1940s.

Rommy learning to work in harness, hauling some windbreak trees for the orchard, c. 1947.

Susan sunning herself in Barn Field, c. 1947.

Susan in the foreground with Ginty behind, then Topsy and Don to the right, winter, c. 1943.

Trudy helps Ralph cut stump roots while Susan and Prince wait with the stump puller, late 1940s.

With the trees all cut down and
the branches burned, we planted
grass between the stumps, often
disking it first.

Grass among the stumps.

Trudy's first cow, Jubilee, c. 1948.

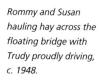

Rommy and Susan
hauling hay across the
floating bridge with
Trudy proudly driving,
c. 1948.

Venturi Bridge that Trudy built over the Atnarko River, 1953.

Trudy with the first outboard motor to come to the Lonesome Lake area, 1948.

Trudy and CF-HEO on the Fraser River, July 1952.

Trudy and HEO at the head of Elbow Lake.

The hangar, still needing its walls, but ready for an airplane.

Ralph Edwards in his glory.

Ethel Edwards and Trudy with Pup, 1954.

The corner of Trudy's first barn, with two 16-inch fir logs she chopped down. "Mac," the McCullough chainsaw Jack brought in, is resting on a log, looking as though "he" wants to take credit for the big stumps, although he did saw the logs up!

Jack with his fishing boat Surfin, c. 1952.

Jack, about 18 years old, near Parksville, BC with his dingy Teal, c. 1948.

Hardworking mare, Thuja, with a giant stump she pulled with the stump-puller, a machine that gives the horse a great mechanical advantage.

Jack at Fogswamp, 1957.

Rommy and Thuja hauling the disk harrow from The Birches to use at Fogswamp, c. 1957.

This picture, looking across the stump-filled field at Fogswamp to Walker's Dome, is a black and white photo that Jack took and his mother colored by hand, c. 1956. Trudy felled all the trees with a double-bitted axe.

The Hibank Bridge, the second bridge over the Atnarko River, built after the Venturi Bridge was torn down, c. 1980s.

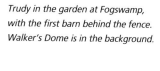

Border collie, Frog, poses on a big double birch stump Trudy chopped down at Fogswamp (Arbordale). This stump, along with all the others, would be pulled out eventually, making room for very productive fields and garden.

Trudy in the garden at Fogswamp, with the first barn behind the fence. Walker's Dome is in the background.

Rommy and Thuja mowing grass at Fogswamp, with Trudy driving.

Frog, looking intelligent.

Barn, henhouse and garden at Arbordale, 1980.

Front yard at Arbordale (Fogswamp).

A winter wonderland at Arbordale.

Fogswamp, c. 1960. The first barn in the foreground, then the root house, chicken house, woodshed and house beyond in a sea of stumps.

*Trudy in the dugout canoe, Amphetrite,
on the big lagoon in 1960.*

*Susan walked at 9 months, and
looks ready to stride off on her
own here. 1960.*

Jack and Susan in Phalarope *on the Big Lagoon,
with Mount Ada in the background.*

Susan at 2½, the youngest farmer, "working the plow" with Rommy and Thuja.

[Inset] Susan at 6, driving the team across the field. This was a big thrill for her.

Another "ticklish" job performed well by Rommy and Thuja, hauling the new plywood boat, Phalarope, *the one and a half miles to Lonesome Lake on the wagon.*

Three-year-old Susan with Jack's parents at Saltspring Island, 1962.

[Inset] Susan, 7, in her new cowgirl outfit, "galloping" off on her wooden horse Trudy carved for her.

Susan and Trudy with Skye, on their first trip up Trumpeter Mountain. The Turner Lake chain and surrounding mountains lay across the valley behind. 1966.

Susan, Jack and Skye on Big Rock, Trumpeter Mountain, 1966.

Susan with Flapdoodle and Trudy with Skye at Junker Lake, 1970.

168

Skye giving Susan a ride, spring 1968.

Susan leading the packtrain on the Hotnarko Grade trail, October 1969.

Beautiful Junker Lake sunrise.

One of the alpine creeks, named Eagle Beak Creek for the beak-shaped peak behind it, which flows into Junker Lake near the outlet.

Susan and Flapdoodle in front of the growing addition on the house at Arbordale, April 1971.

Trudy and Jack. Merry Christmas!

Christmas 1971. Susan and Trudy with Flapdoodle and Skye.

Susan riding a really big bull!

Susan, 12, feeding cygnet, 1971.

Susan, 14, feeding the calf, Valerian,
by the henhouse, 1973.

Susan with her little dog, Kelly,
summer 1986.

Susan, sons Alex and Brendan, and husband Tom at his parents' house, 1998.

Spud with his "cat hat." The cat was put up there on purpose, but looks pleased nonetheless.

*Cealy relaxes atop Guenevere as she takes
a break from plowing, spring 1972.*

*Cealy and Dumbo, bookends
in the window, c. 1970s.*

*Happy Cealy, who thought she could
sleep wherever she wanted, and very
uncomfortable Skye, on the back
porch at Arbordale.*

Open water was laboriously chopped out of the ice for swans to eat, c. 1950.

Swans hurry across the floating bridge to have breakfast.

Feeding a flock of about 40 swans off the floating bridge in 1943.

175

An unforgettable moment; Trudy lets a few extra-brave swans have a big mouthful.

Trudy riding Thuja doing a breakfast delivery for the swans.

One brave swan helps himself.

Towing the grain on the Big Lagoon, with Jack steering the raft. Along with the swan grain is at least one 10-gallon drum of gasoline for winter home use.

Rafting 100-pound sacks of swan grain across Lonesome Lake with the 10 hp Mercury outboard. Trudy steering and Susan as co-pilot, fall 1967 or 68. The boat being towed is full of grain for the swans as well.

Domino. A lot of bull for a 40-pound dog to manage.

Upi, the milk cow, ready to calve, standing beside 8-foot-high deer fence, March 1962.

Upi and a calf stand in a field full of stumps, with the house and woodshed beyond.

Susan with one of the heifers, Vandomar,
and the herd in front of the barn.

Elbow Lake and the meadows
where the cattle ranged.

Thuja with her heavy, awkward
load of stove parts.

Silver Star learning to carry a pack saddle, with Thuja for company.

Lucky Debonair learning to pack, practicing in the backyard at Arbordale, 1965.

[Inset] The packtrain on the Hotnarko Grade, c. 1964. Yes, there really is a trail there!

Rocket and Lucky on the summit of the Hotnarko Grade, October 1969.

An equine water taxi. The packtrain waits for their comfortable ride across the Stillwater. L to R: Thuja, Rocket, Guenevere, Spud and Lucky. October 1969.

Trudy with Lucky and Skye, both packing, at the north end of the Stillwater, 1969.

Susan and packtrain, Guenevere in lead, 1969.

Susan riding Guenevere, leading Rocket, on Trumpeter Mountain. The lovely panorama of Walker's Dome, Mount Ada and the rest of the mountains up the Atnarko Valley is the backdrop. 1972.

Just another day at work for Nugget, packing the frame of the new rubber-tired wagon.

Rocket and Guenevere pause for a drink in the Hotnarko River, fall 1969.

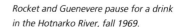

*The horse herd: Star and
Bess on the left, Nugget
and Tempest on the right.*

*Cloud, as a yearling, gets
an early start to her packing
education on the way home.*

Cloud on Trumpeter Mountain, 1977.

*Star with his ladies: Ginger
on the left and Guenevere
and Cloud on the right, 1983.*

*Cariboo Pass in the Rainbow
Mountains, summer 1986.*

Star at 3, 1983.

*Lightning, Guenevere and
hungry Dana, after she lost
her backpack of food, in the
Rainbow Mountains, 1986.*

Trudy's first ride on 2-year-old Bess.

Bess's first harness work, 1986.

Tempest and Bess haying with the rake, 1988.

Bess showing her form over fences with her new partner.

Susan and Lightning, Trudy on Bess,
Fall Fair costumes, 1990.

Sorrow with her new owner giving
Trudy a ride in the Fall Fair parade.

Trudy with her beloved
Breezie Future.

Liesel demonstrates one of the
many tricks Trudy taught her.

Liesel running her
jump course free.

Baby Magi at about 3 months, 2009.

Dove, Magi and Trudy.
Dove, the Aussie
companion for Magi,
came in 2010.

Imagine Lake, *by Trudy.*

Farmhouse with Mount Ada
behind, *by Trudy.*

Rocket on the Hotnarko Grade
on the trail to Stillwater, *by Trudy.*

Pressy Lake, *by Trudy.*

Susan E., *by Trudy.*

Trumpeter swans
in Atnarko River,
by Trudy.

Ant Lake, *by Trudy.*

Ginty and Susan in alpine, *by Trudy.*

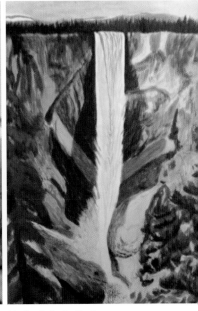

Hunlen Falls, *by Trudy.*

Table, table leg (inset), chair and
animals all carved by Trudy.

The new place was too good to be true. It crowded my neighbor too much, so I sold it to them and selected a more distant property. It had a winter pond on it, and my new neighbors were more tolerant of crowding. In fact we soon were exchanging labor as they were just building their new house also.

I acquired the newest property in January 1992. With some 30 hemlock trees felled to make way for my new house, I began removing the limbs from the fallen trees and burning the branches, snow or rain permitting. All thru the winter, spring, summer and into fall I worked at building my new log house, 24 by 26 feet. A combination stable and hay barn soon followed. Then a woodshed, 16 by 12, was built right against the north end of my house. Thru the summer Jack and Susan hauled about 500 bales of hay and we put it in my new barn. That would feed my two cows, a calf and Bess for the winter.

I moved my cattle to my new place in late October and continued to live on Glengarry, the property owned by Susan, Tom and myself. I walked the one-half mile each day to feed and milk the cow. Then I worked there all day. In the evening, I milked again and fed the cattle, then walked back to Glengarry for supper and to sleep overnight. My new house wasn't finished enough to live in yet. But I got my cows out of their muddy, soggy, wet corral. Bess would come up later.

I moved in on the ninth of November 1992. I had power and heat. That night I slept in my new house.

The ninth of November was a day to remember. As I had help from quite a few kind people in my endeavor, I invited them for a switching-on-of-the-power celebration. We then had cookies and cocoa. Without all their help, kindly given, I would never have made it in so short a time and I am very thankful. And a huge lot of building materials I salvaged from Tom and Susan's broken barn also helped.

My pet, Bess, hauled most of the many logs that went into the house and barn, so even a pet can be useful.

Oh, yes, I almost forgot. Bess was not only useful for hauling my

193

logs, but she and I didn't forget our gymkhanas that summer either. I had to keep my priorities straight and not neglect running in each gymkhana. After all I had to relax once in a while from my frenzied building effort. I even took time to give her practice on my new place where there was room between logs and stumps, using some logs for scurry height jumps.

It paid off, too. She did her best barrel run that summer. And in one gymkhana I won a first place for each of the five events, the only time I did that. I was driven that year, and I think my energy somehow energized my horse also.

Bess still lives, but she is pretty stiff in all four legs now and she is getting thinner as she ages. She is over 25 years old. When she goes all of my animal friends will be gone, and will exist only in a pleasant, tho sad, memory.

chapter 17

PETS & MORE PETS

When I began living in my new house on Dogbane, my new property, in November 1992, all my household items were moved up here, so Jack had to bike up for his milk. He also took the milk for Susan and Tom's family. We got to visit each day. With his daily visits and all my animals here, loneliness was not too big a problem. Then one day I was looking ahead to when winter would melt into spring and suddenly realized when all my cattle and Bess moved back to Glengarry I would be all alone, except for Jack's short visits each day and my short visit to Glengarry to do my chores there. I began thinking about a dog. A puppy. Preferably a border collie.

After a little investigating, I located a litter of Australian shepherds with border collie markings, seven of them. As "Aussies" are sometimes born without tails, there is a requirement that they must all be docked in order to be registered. I didn't want my puppy to have her tail removed and asked my good friend Lori to please leave one pup with a tail. I had no intention of registering her. Lori agreed and kept two with tails. I understood they were all spoken for but there was a slim chance I could have a pup if someone changed their mind.

I can't remember who drove me over to see the puppies, but I clearly remember my first sight of the appealingly heart-stealing little fuzzy babies. They could just sort of tumble around on their unsteady little legs. They were confined in an enclosure with one-foot-high board sides. They could just reach up to the top of it with their snub-nosed heads to greet me and several other people. We were admiring them and making our choices. They could all have been spoken for. I surely hoped not.

I didn't pick a pup, but a pup picked me. She came to me and tried to climb up the board wall to sniff and lick at my hand. I picked her up and made the various tests that are recommended one do on a prospective pup, including cradling her upside down to check for confidence, and she passed them all.

Then I heard something like all the pups definitely had homes. I tried hard to hide my burning disappointment. I turned and walked away from the pups. I wanted to leave, badly. Then someone told me to pick my pup. I couldn't believe my ears. Was it real? But there weren't any pups left, I thought. I was assured it was real. Someone had decided they didn't need a pup right then. I have often wondered if my obvious disappointment was the cause of that person deciding they didn't need a pup. If that was the case, I am forever grateful to them for their kind generosity.

So I went back and selected the little puppy that had picked me. She is Liesel.

Sometime later Susan drove me back to pick up my puppy. There were only two or three pups left by then. I think they were getting a bit apprehensive as one by one they were becoming fewer and fewer. As soon as we were seated in the truck, my little puppy began crawling up my front from my lap. As we drove home she worked herself almost completely inside my shirt. She was frightened, so suddenly away from home and littermates and mum and others she knew.

At home I placed her in a nice bed I had prepared for her, then covered her loosely with something, as she seemed to want to hide. The cover must have kept her in the box, as I don't think I tied her as she would not be safe tied at her age, perhaps five weeks, and left alone. I had to leave her and go and do my barn chores.

When I first had Liesel she didn't need tying, as she could not run away from me with her still unsteady legs. I just picked her up and carried her out to her toilet area and set her down to do her job. When she was finished I could pick her up again—praising her, of course—and return her to her bed. When she had grown enough that she was steadier on her running gear, I introduced her to collar and lead. Then I began training.

When I started the lead teaching, I helped her to learn how to respond to something restraining around her neck, so she didn't have to go thru a terrifying interval of pulling back and choking and gagging. I put a little pressure on the lead as I gently pushed her ahead to relieve the pressure on her neck. She quickly learned to move forward herself to relieve the pressure. Soon she was leading. Then I could tie her up safely and painlessly.

I kept her confined to her bed for several weeks, except when she had to go outside. She soon was telling me when she had to go outside, or I at least kept a close eye on her. If she showed any restlessness I carried her outside. If she did anything, lots of praise and petting was called for, and given, of course. I always took her out if she had just woken up.

The day finally came for me to test her on house training. Confined to one room, she went all over that room, investigating every nook and cranny and everything in between. As she was going about the serious business of learning about her environment, I sort of didn't keep as close a watch on her as I should have and the inevitable happened. She squatted. I noticed and yelled at her and rushed to pick her up and carry her, dripping, outside where she finished the job, and I praised her. I cleaned up the floor, but made no further remarks to her, and kept her confined for a few more weeks. Next time she had the run of that room she never made a mistake again in my house. Not until she was in her old age.

That mistake had to be forgiven, later. There was something going wrong with her warning system that should have told her of an impending evacuation, and something that should have been outside was casually dropped inside. To my shame, I was outraged and threw her out of my house, bitterly disappointed, as she had been so clean for all her life before that. In time I forgave her, but never let her back in the house. I did let her have the run of the barn, which, being part of the whole building, was just on the other side of my back door where my wood is stored. She never made a mistake in the barn. She also had the run of the fenced yard. She even hauled herself out of the barn to do her stuff, when she had difficulty walking and standing up during the last weeks of her life.

Liesel grew rapidly and it was soon time for advanced training, and teaching her to let me have control of her paws and even her tail. I taught her to allow me to lead her backwards by her tail. She also had to learn not to dive into her food dish before I could set it down on the floor. She had to wait until I invited her to eat. She had to learn patience. She learned all her basic obedience stuff quickly.

When she was eight months old I put her in the Bella Coola Fall Fair Dog Show. She lost because I had taught her to "sit" in a down position. She was a sheep-herding dog. Some sheep dogs taught "sit" means for the dog to drop on the ground on her belly, instantly. That is a good position to get into from a fast run, and to surge out of, for a herding dog.

If I had thought faster when the judge asked all the dogs to "sit" I would have asked her to "siddown," which meant to sit on your butt. Then perhaps the judge would have been happy. I knew better than to tell her to "sit" when he asked us to "sit" our dogs. I just automatically used the word he had used. Since she went down as I had asked and remained there until he told us to call our dogs, when she then raced to me, I have always thought he should have accepted her obedience to the command I gave her. She had obeyed me. The judge maybe used the wrong word?

Sometime while Liesel was still quite small I introduced her to the big animals. She was frightened by the huge beasts, especially by the large, scary eyes of the cows and Bess. As I held her in my arms she tried to hide, but she was too large by that age to hide in my arms, and she had to peek out once in a while and take a hasty glance at friendly Bess, who only wanted to sniff at her. The cows wanted to get a good look at her, too. Liesel was a new dog they hadn't seen before. Susan had a dog on her place, so all the horses and cows knew about dogs, just not about this small dog.

Anyway she soon lost her fear of those large animals, except their eyes. She never felt comfortable with their eyes, if they looked at her. Years later while I was riding and lost my quirt, or hat, I would ask her to pick them up and give them to me. If the horse so much as turned his or her head around to look at the little dog, she would back away. Controlling her fear, she still returned and stretched up to give me the item when I asked her the second time.

As she grew, I began taking her with me on a leash as I rode Bess, and she was happy to come along behind.

In time I began training Liesel to find things and to bring me items of clothing, such as sweaters, hats, gloves, shoes and socks, anything she could handle. Even a six-pound sledgehammer she figured out how to bring to me. As she couldn't pick it up in her mouth, she grabbed the end of the handle and backed up to me, dragging the hammer along that way.

She would bring anything I asked for. If she didn't know the object's name, I could just ask for that thing and point to what I wanted, and direct her with hand signals. She never brought me sticks, or any other natural stuff on the ground, unless I asked for a "stick." She would find something that was of interest to me, or anyone else, something that wasn't a part of the forest or whatever, something man-made. She would get other peoples things, too, picking up stuff for my grandson, Alex.

Once, on a Nature Club hike with a group, I asked one of the ladies if I could borrow her glove for a bit so I could show the group the way Liesel could find and retrieve her glove. No, she would not chew it up. I had someone hide the glove behind a tree while I covered her eyes and ears.

I sent her off into the forest in the general direction of the glove, with a request to "find that thing." She started off in the correct direction, looking back to check for more directions. She had no idea what she was looking for. I had to help her some. Using hand signals, I guided her more or less towards the tree, until she was close enough that she picked up an interesting scent, then homed in on it. Picking it up, she hurried back to me, but not to the owner of the glove.

Then I wondered if I could get her to take it to the owner. She could have, with practice, but she clearly didn't understand, so I praised her some more and left it at that. I think finding and selecting someone else's item of clothing was a pretty good job anyway.

When Liesel became full-grown I began her cow herding—or at least bringing—schooling. By then she was no longer afraid of any of the cows or horses, except she still feared those eyes. There was one exception to her fear of cows. That was when the cow had a new calf. When my cow had one of her calves I wanted to get a video of Liesel beside the new calf, but she wouldn't go near the calf. She clearly told me the cow would kill her. I tried to reassure her she would not, as long as she was eating her hay. Liesel hesitated, but reluctantly lay near the new baby and I got a bit of video of the two of them. The cow had told Liesel loud and clear with her eyes that she had better keep away from her new baby.

To train her to move cattle, I kept her on her leash and asked her to move one of the young animals, and at the same time I urged the heifer to move away as we followed. If the cow began to run, Liesel had to "sit." When the heifer stopped running, Liesel could rise and we would follow along. Any time the cow ran she had to "sit" until the beast slowed to a walk. Then I'd tell her to rise, and we continued this way around in my corral. Later I would put the dog on a "sit" in the middle of the corral, then chase the heifer around and correct any attempt on Liesel's part to rise and join in the fun. The only legal reason for her to move was to escape the hooves of the cow. Then she could rise and move, going down again when the danger was past.

Any dog surely has that right. She learned this well. Then I could send her across the pasture to bring the cow to the barn. Off she would dash towards the cow, around behind, and bark an order the cow could not ignore. She headed for the barn, pronto.

Soon the cow learned that if I called her to the barn and she wasn't ready yet to go in and ignored me, I would call Liesel. The cow didn't want to be driven to the barn by Liesel. As soon as I called Liesel, the cow came hustling to the barn. It worked even if Liesel was in the house and couldn't come.

If the cattle went along properly Liesel followed nicely, but if the long-horned old bovine decided she didn't want to be driven anywhere by a little dog, and tried to turn her head to the dog, the dog whipped behind her and used her teeth, gently, and her voice, loudly, to convince old bossy to "Git!"

As commanding as Liesel was with the cattle, she was a model of patience with a couple of goat kids I had here, and a little calf.

Jack and I had driven my truck with a homemade stock pen on it to Williams Lake to get some goats, for milk, as an alternative to cows. We had selected a very pregnant nanny, a young female, and a young billy goat. Loading them on my pickup, we drove home, about a 600-mile round trip. That is, I drove; Jack and Liesel did not have licenses to drive.

The next morning the old goat gave birth to a cute little girl kid, then a cute little boy kid, both the most friendly and entertaining baby animals I had ever seen.

Poor Liesel went into the barn with me and mom goat took exception to a predator in her barn. As the dog was walking by, Old Goat smashed her head into Liesel's unsuspecting side, painfully. Liesel yelped, jumped away, then looked around as if asking, "What was that for?" Old Goat had been quite comfortable with Liesel the day before, so the dog trusted her. However the kids were safe in mom the day before. I told Liesel she had better go outside. She agreed. She held no retaliatory thought.

Liesel could not drive that hornless old battering, um, nanny—we can't call her a battering ram. There was no way the dog could get behind the goat. She could spin just as fast as the dog could, and that was fast. It didn't matter. Lead one and all the others came along, with no straying. They were a lot different than cattle. Go thru a narrow gateway with one and all went there.

I had fenced in a part of my pasture with goat-proof fencing, so they could go loose in that area. It was by the barn, and I wanted to do some work in the barn. To have more light in there, I wanted to keep the door open. The curious old goat wanted to come in, to see what was going on. I didn't want her in with me. Liesel couldn't drive her away, so I told the dog to stay right inside the doorway and not to let the goat in. Liesel put her body in the shelter of the wall on one side of the doorway, with only her teeth sticking out to face the goat. She guarded the entire three-and-a-half-foot-wide doorway. Every time Old Goat tried to enter, Liesel snapped and barked at her, never letting her body leave that wall. Old Goat had to back off, shaking her head in defeat.

As aggressive as Liesel could be to animals that hurt her while she was driving them, she was very tender and caring to young helpless animals, including human young. Newborn calves she would clean as if they were puppies. The kids she treated as if they were precious. One day I had Old Goat on a picket chain. Her kids wandered off a short distance. Liesel herded them back to mom just by moving them with her body, encouraging them with gentle pressure from her side until they were back with mum. Then she left them. She did that all on her own. I only observed. And that persnickety old goat didn't even mind.

Another time Liesel showed her softness was when I had Old Goat and Beauregard, the billy goat, on picket chains, with the kids loose. I was working on the other side of a barbwire fence when both kids, Sandy and Ruby, came under the wire to visit me, leaving mom 80 feet away. I did not want them out there, as there were plants goats were not supposed to eat growing where I was working. I told Liesel to take the kids back to mum. Ruby got under the wire easily enough. Sandy got his collar caught on a barb. Try as he might, he was held fast. Liesel stood patiently behind him, waiting, as he struggled against the collar that was stuck on the barb. Finally he was loose. He raced off to mum, "baaing" as he went. Liesel followed along until he was right back to mum.

I got those goats for milk. My cows were taking a lot of energy to look after, and I thought goats might give me enough milk and would be easier to feed and water. They might have had Old Goat been more cooperative about the milking, and had given more milk. She could only feed her kids; there was none left for me, even if she had been willing to let me have it. For a small animal she had a powerful kick.

And she complained. No matter how much feed she had, she always was complaining. In time I decided to give them away and keep my cows. It was nice knowing them tho. And they were less work to look after once I had my goat fences built. I loved them, but couldn't stand them.

Now I shall mention another of Liesel's achievements. She could jump, and loved it. Now she is coming up to 16 years and cannot do much more than a trot, and she is deaf. In her younger days she was very active. She is gone now, so I must move to past tense.

I made a few jumps for her, most about 20 to 24 inches high. She was only 16 inches high, but she could jump onto a five-foot in diameter log. One of her jumps was a larger folding jump about three feet high with a four-inch-wide level top. Liesel could jump up, stop on top, turn lengthwise, and stand there if I asked her to. We also had a dog-sized hoop for her to jump thru.

Her jump course was set up in such a way that I could stand by the center jump, holding the hoop. I sat her behind one end jump. When I was ready to start her running, I told her to "jump," and she was off over the course as she took two jumps, then thru the hoop, over the A-frame, over two more jumps, then around a pole, then back over the jumps in reverse order to the hoop. As long as I held it for her, she would continue running the course. She would go all the way back to the start jump, turn around and begin the run again. If I lowered the hoop, she just jumped her way back to me. There she stopped and sat down to receive her reward. I never asked her to run the course more than two or three times, as it was hard work and I didn't want to bore her or tire her. I wanted her to enjoy the game as much as I did.

A dog will run this course free because she loves to do it. There is no way one can make a dog do this kind of work if she didn't love it.

Once at the Rodeo Grounds she distinguished herself by running her own jump course and some horse jumps. This was in 1995. Some people were actually into jumping, and they were having a jumping show. As I wanted desperately to jump Bess over their more varied jumps, I invited myself to help them set up the course. They had a big triple bar set up, and as nothing was going on at the moment, I asked Liesel, who was helping, to go over the triple bar. I took her a little way back, pointed her at the jump and said, "Jump." She raced towards the three-foot-high jump, took off, sailed over the big jump and landed about seven or eight feet beyond it, then raced back to me, beaming, tail in a frenzy, to receive her well-deserved praise. The fellow organizing the show was astonished. He invited me to put Liesel in the show the next day when they were going to have the competition. That day had been just for practice.

Since the horse jumps were all decorated with little trees, flowerpots and branches, I decorated Liesel's own jumps, too. She would use one or two of the horse jumps, as well as the triple bar.

She ran her course just before the horses ran, and I was nervous. In spite of that, she did pretty well, especially since she had never gone over the course I set up for her there in the space available. I had to help her by running with her as fast as I could, which compared to her was dead slow. We got thru it and she did the long jump over the triple bar, never touching it, clearing about 15 feet from takeoff to landing. I wish I had a photo of it.

I did get to take Bess over most of their jumps, too, including the triple bar, which I had lowered a little. I didn't want to over face her, as she hadn't jumped that high at that time. And I was not in competition. I just wanted to have fun. Bess eventually took me over a 42-inch jump, cleanly. What glory!

I had worked Bess over a small triple bar at home, to get her used to it before the show. Bess didn't have any trouble with any jumps I pointed her at, including being prepared to jump a chain I had stretched across my driveway to discourage any would-be wood thieves. That was a no, no, no! A chain was not an appropriate thing to use for a jump. I like my jumps to come down easily, or else be solid, such as a big log. Also I want my horse to enjoy the jumping as much as I do.

I had trained Bess over split blocks of firewood, stacked up, about 30 inches high. And crossed poles, hay bales, natural logs in the forest. And a sawhorse with a tarp spread over it. That one she stopped at to examine, then we went over. Anything that appealed to me, I asked her to go over and she did. I even had her going over 45-gallon fuel drums on their sides and the gymkhana barrels. She couldn't compete speed wise going around the barrels, but when I challenged my barrel competition to jump the barrels, there were no takers. Perhaps they didn't have time. They all seemed to be in a sweat to get home. They probably did have stuff to do, what with kids, etc. I had nothing to do but milk my cow when I got home.

Now here Liesel comes back in this story. She not only could jump pretty impressively, but she also was a big help with my work, from building to clearing land.

The way she helped me clear land was to get a good grip on a stump I was digging out with a mattocks and yank, yank, and keep a good pull on it. Every time I hit the ever-loosening stump she'd yank harder, and growl and bark. I think she was pulling down game in her predatory mind as she yanked and lunged backwards.

Once the stump was out she had no more interest in it and came back to attack the next one. We could take out small alder stumps pretty fast that way. When there were no more stumps to help with, she found out how satisfying rocks were as toys, even if hard on teeth. As she assured me she would pay all her dental bills, I let her play with them.

Seriously, I couldn't stop her chewing on the rocks without stopping all the game. If I told her not to bite the rocks she wouldn't play, but just went and lay down as if she was ashamed. I couldn't find any way to tell her it was all right to paw the rock but not to bite it. So I finally let her play with the rocks the way she had to and hoped for the best. She had to have some fun and exercise in her life. Altho badly worn, her teeth did last as long as she needed them.

She used to scent a rock underground and set about digging it out just so she could paw it, growl at it, throw it back between her braced hind legs, then spin and throw it back the other way again. Big rocks she couldn't throw with her paws, she tried to roll by pawing then pushing with her tough nose pad. If that didn't work she would dig a hole under one side, then roll the rock into it, then dig another hole, then roll it again. Some really large rocks she got stuck by digging a hole too deep to roll them out of. Then she left it there after giving it a good growling at. I think she was digging a tunnel, in her mind, and the rock was in her way. That was the way she would cope with any rock she would encounter if she were in fact digging a birthing tunnel. She also snipped off any root or branch that got in her way. As a neuter she could never use a birthing tunnel, but the knowledge of how to dig one would still be in her brain.

Now, a bit on Skye, a border collie I had at Lonesome Lake. I had trained her to carry a small pack. She could take about 10 pounds, or three quarts of chainsaw gas and a quart of chain oil.

When we were building or just clearing trails, Skye's small pack was a big help. Whenever the small chainsaw ran out of gas, Jack only had to call "gas," and here it came running. She lay down beside him. He opened her pack, took out the gas and oil, filled up the saw, and replaced the containers in her pack. She got up and trotted off to a safe place and the trail job went on again.

Here is another dog story I am reminded of and it also goes back to Lonesome Lake and Skye.

Jack had left our house on a trip out for mail in the winter. Some 15 minutes later I stepped out onto the porch for something and saw his hand axe still waiting by the door. He had missed picking it up. He might need it. There was no way I could catch up with him, but Skye could.

I sent her off to "go find Jack." She took off in the right direction down the trail, stopping to glance back a few times to see if I was coming. Satisfied that I was following, she disappeared down the trail. I went as fast as I could, with Jack's axe. When I caught up, about a half a mile from home, they were waiting for me. Skye couldn't tell him what he was missing. He was glad that she came. He did want the axe. That was one more time Skye got huge praise. And when we got home I gave her a whole slice of bread with a slice of roast beef on top. She liked that. Usually her dinner was much less interesting.

Poor old Skye, I never appreciated her enough. I am truly sorry for all the mistakes I made with her throughout her long, loving, loyal life. I am trying to pay for some of my mistakes by being softer and more forgiving with Liesel. Or I did. I cannot help Skye.

For as long as we live it is not too late to learn new things, or correct old habits and mistakes. This was clearly demonstrated to me one day as I watched someone else working with their dog. This person was telling their dog to "heel," then as the dog started off in the correct position the man would say, "now stay heel," whereupon the poor confused dog would stop and lie down, to stay as he had been told. Then the man would get angry with him, for disobeying the "heel" command. The dog, a handsome German shepherd, was getting more and more confused and upset. As I watched this, I suddenly felt like I'd been hit over the head with a club, as I realized that I had been giving the same type of contradictory commands all these years, never thinking of how could the dog possibly obey all of them at the same time? I hadn't understood how tenuous a dog's concept of human words can be. This really opened my eyes to think a lot more carefully about my own dog training.

Liesel asked me to write this bit of "doggerel" as her teeth were too worn from all that rockwork to hold a pen.

Rockwork

I washed my paws this morning, so very clean and white
Then used them both for rockwork, from morning until night.
Now they're cut and bleeding, each toe and claw and pad.
I don't know how it happened,
But they sure are hurting bad.

—by Leisel

chapter 18

SUSAN & GINTY

It is a sad commentary on our interests that the worst natured people and other animals get the most press. Topsy, jealous, stubborn, scheming, mean to cows and any horse she was dominant over, sometimes miserable to work on rake and disc harrow, unwilling to be ridden away from the barn until I showed her she could leave the barn with no harm coming to her, has pages and pages written about her. But gentle, willing, hard-working, sweet, faithful, patient Susan will receive very little, just because she seldom did anything wrong. She quietly went about her life, living in the shadow of her obstreperous teammate. That teammate sometimes ranted and raved and even tried actually to climb over Susan in an effort to make the team turn into the corral when it became apparent Dad was going to drive right on by. She never succeeded.

At four years of age Susan and Topsy had grown into not bad looking young mares. Susan was a bit larger than Topsy, so she was chosen to go in harness with Ginty. The old fellow had done all the farm work alone and he certainly could use some help.

As I seem to recall, he wasn't at all sure about having her hitched beside him to his wagon, sled or whatever. And, of course, before she learned how to pull she probably confused the older horse. He was not used to someone upsetting the order of things he was used to.

It was when Dad started training Susan to harness work that I began seriously helping him. He didn't need anyone to hold Ginty, as he was trained. With an untrained young horse it can be most useful to have someone to stand at their heads while he hitches them up, ties on a load, or whatever and not have to hold on to the lines all the time. Of course I didn't mind. I likely begged for the job. I loved doing anything with horses. Just being near them was pleasure.

Well, except later after Ginty had gone to the "Green Pastures" and Topsy took his place in the team, then there was not quite so much pleasure. Topsy did not want me to hold her bridle. She frequently tried to bite me, and sometimes made it. She much preferred that I just stand there in front of them and keep my miserable, filthy hands a mile from her bridle. I would try that, but then she would reach over and bite Susan on the head or neck, or try to walk away. She really gave me little choice if I was going to do my job.

Sometimes Topsy was more trouble to hold than the stallion, Don, had been. About the worst thing he did while I stood in front of him was to go to sleep while he waited for Dad to fill the wagon with manure. Then he would wake up suddenly and start to walk away, forgetting he was hitched to the wagon.

One day Dad was in deep sh*t, literally, when Don pulled that wake-up-and-walk-off—or in this case, run-off—trick. He had hauled a wagonload of manure out to spread on the field. As it was an unloading job, I was holding Don's lines while standing in the wagon as Dad spread the manure on the grass.

Don went to sleep, as usual, then suddenly was running off with the wagon. He ignored the call to stop. I wasn't getting him stopped, so Dad jumped to the front of the wagon, grabbed the lines ahead of my small hands and began to slow the horse down. As he did, his boots slipped on the dung-covered slippery bed of the wagon and Dad sat, splat, in the squishy sh*t! He did stop the horse, tho. I am sorry, Dad, but it really was funny, some 50 or so years later.

Starting Susan in harness, Dad gave her and Ginty really small loads. Susan quickly learned what was required of her. Soon she was helping to haul larger loads. Finally old Ginty began to appreciate her more and they were developing into a really fine team.

Susan had many sweet little ways about her. One of those was to turn her head when the team was stopped for some reason and she was getting tired. They had had a long day. Looking back to Dad, she'd give a soft little nicker, as if asking to be unhitched and turned loose to graze. She probably was asking for one small favor.

She was quite a talkative little mare and often asked for things, such as oats, hay, carrots and apples. When she had her head deep in her nosebag she kept nickering as she crunched her oats. She would also do this while she was eating her hay. It was if she was saying a horse's version of thank you.

I can't remember Susan ever arguing about anything she was asked to do. She just seemed to want to do whatever one asked of her.

She was lovely to ride, and I don't know why I chose Topsy to be my pet, unless I was smitten by her flamboyant color. She was a bright bay with black mane and tail, and a wide white face mark, and four white feet. She was beautiful. But so was dark bay Susan. She also had a white face mark, only a bit narrower. She had a nicer, more feminine look. Topsy was nice enough to people. And once she learned not to be so darn stubborn, was a better horse than she had been. Topsy really improved much later in life, after she met Thuja in the spring following Susan's demise. I brought the new mare to The Birches and she, with my bay gelding, Rommy, would be my team when I got my own place two years later.

Anyway when Topsy, top horse for too many years, met larger and very confident Thuja, they showed some interesting behavior. Out in the big field, both mares began very industriously pawing the snow off the grass, half facing each other, about 30 feet apart. They were so busy there was no time for any sort of greeting. Well, they were strangers, after all.

As they continued pawing snow and pretending to eat, they gradually moved closer together, but did not actually look at each other, something like dogs do to avoid conflict. Tho I suspect those mares were more sizing each other up for conflict.

When they had grazed close to each other's space they both squared off and began shrieking and kicking—bang, bang—on fat rumps. Then both ran off to begin the mock grazing again, to let their rumps and hind legs cool off, I presume.

Soon they were butt to butt again, shrieking, squealing, and roaring, until they had to rest and cool their guns. They went back to the mock eating. Neither wanted to admit the other was stronger or tougher. Thuja was definitely the stronger mare, as well as taller and heavier, and a lot younger. Eventually Topsy had to admit defeat, but she surely hated to. The first chance she got to get even with Thuja, she took it, but lost again.

One problem those two mares had was that each of them considered The Birches her range. Topsy knew the area was hers as she had lived there since she was two years old. Thuja thought it was hers since there were no horses in residence when she and Rommy arrived. There was bound to be conflict, and Topsy was stubborn. In her mind no black interloper was going to take her property away from her.

When Thuja came to Lonesome Lake, Topsy was 10 miles away at Elbow Lake with Prince, Susan's son. In the fall Rommy joined them, leaving Thuja in sole residence at The Birches. No wonder there was war in the horse herd.

Anyway, later in the winter I rode Thuja the mile or so to the north end of Big Lagoon to feed the swans. Tying her to a tree, I walked the short distance to where I fed the birds, as that section of the trail was not fit to ride over.

The swans fed, counted, and watched for a bit, I returned to my tied-up mare. Something was wrong, however. As I approached along the trail, I thought I could see more than one horse. I had left only one horse tied there, now there were four of them milling around, and one was attacking my mare. And Thuja was quite successfully kicking her off, in spite of being restrained a bit. Topsy was getting angry. Each time she attacked, she was flung off. As I watched I decided not to interfere. I wanted to see if Thuja could, or would, protect herself. Topsy stalked around, trying to think up a way to get in a telling kick without being punished too much herself. Finally she settled on a strategy. She walked up to Thuja, all relaxed, sugar and honey dripping from her lips and ears, really close. Suddenly she shifted and lay herself across Thuja's back legs, hard against them and began biting Thuja's belly with the biting end, while trying hard to kick Thuja's other side with the kicking end. She could not quite bend in a small enough circle to make any real progress in her attack, but she received a real taste of Thuja's power. Thuja coiled, then expanded, lifted Topsy clear of the ground and flung her several feet away. It was an impressive display of power. I was very pleased.

No wonder she could haul a pine log about a foot in diameter and 80 feet long by herself. I didn't know it, but she could have made a great jumper. At that time I didn't know how much fun there could be in jumping over obstacles.

Still, those dominant mares had to find out how much punishment each wanted to absorb. Tied each night in the open shed, with a stout pole between them, they still kicked, throwing the pole askew. So I asked Thuja to haul in a heavy dry log about eight inches in diameter, and 20 feet long. It was resting on the ground on one end. The other end was fastened securely to a pole over the horses' heads. They continued to kick the log, trying to fight each other, but they could do little more than bang deep dents in the hard wood.

Topsy finally accepted defeat and peace more or less returned to the farm.

With Topsy's acceptance of Thuja as the better mare, she began to trust Thuja's judgment in the matter of motor noises. She began leaning on Thuja's calmness, and realized the hum of outboards and airplanes was not a danger that a horse had to hike way up on the side of the mountain and hide under trees to be safe from.

With larger, very stable Thuja by her side, Topsy was much better to work on all the equipment on the farm. It was just too bad that by then she was having a lot of trouble with heaves, a lung condition we thought had been brought on by her hysteria about the first outboard brought to Lonesome Lake in 1947, the first time she had heard one. She ran herself too hard over mountain trails in a vain effort to protect herself from the noise.

She was fine in the summer, on grass, but in the winter when she had to eat hay she'd cough and gag until it sounded as if she would strangle. Dampening her hay was not a very practical solution, as the water would freeze too quickly. She was gently helped to the Green Pastures. With all her faults, she still was a good horse. I had many enjoyable rides on her soft round back, and I did love her, I have to admit now.

Just one more bit about Topsy. When Dad was doing the annual horse packing of their supplies, alone, he let Topsy come behind the other horses, loose. She always followed. One year there were a lot of wasp nests along the trail, difficult to get safely by or to remove. As Topsy was the last horse to pass one such nest, she would get stung more than Dad and the first two horses did. Topsy, being loose, took the opportunity afforded her and tried a novel way to avoid getting stung and still do her job. I think she was more interested in going with the horse herd than in doing her job, but the results were the same.

She simply went down off the trail before she got to the stingers and swam the river, walked up the other bank a ways, then swam back across and rejoined the herd. She gave no thought to what would happen to her load, nor did she care. She didn't get stung. To her that was the important thing. We could cope with the wet flour or whatever she was carrying. Dad didn't put salt or sugar on her.

Flour getting wet was not as serious as it might seem. Being tight in the cloth bag, only a thin layer actually got wet. It was helpful that most groceries were put in cloth or burlap bags rather than useless paper, or non-reusable plastic as they are now.

Are some horses really stubborn and balky, or simply confused? Are they born that way, or accidentally made that way by the trainer?

Animals seem to lean against hard pressure, the harder the pressure, the more strongly they seem to resist. A gentle hint of pressure they will move away from. Especially if your back is cold and you just move up to the side of your horse, barely touching her. Soon she will move away. If you follow, she will move again. She can learn not to move away, but it has to be taught. Horses can learn to move away from pressure, as when you teach your horse to lower her head by application of gentle pressure. Or you can let him learn to push as hard as he can against the collar on a workhorse. Roping horses also learn not to give to the pressure of that big heavy steer on the end of the rope, while still giving to all the signals from the rider.

Perhaps all horses don't resist pressure at the same level. Horses are taught to give to the bit, but not to give to the collar. That must be a bit confusing for them at times.

A horse who appears balky has found out that one cannot stop him from backing up, therefore, since you don't stop him that is what you want him to do. Also, backwards is the only direction left for him to go if he gives to the pressure on his collar. Some horses, having tried moving forward and being stopped too abruptly, won't try forward with any confidence, or will seek back or sideways. If all else fails, they simply stand there and let you do what you want to them, simply because they really don't know what you want them to do. I clearly remember the several confused horses I considered stubborn, and one balky.

I had nothing to do with Topsy's early training, so I don't know how Dad taught her to lead, be shod and to pack. Packing she did fine, couldn't do better, but shoeing or even hoof trimming was always a struggle, often accompanied with broken ropes and frayed nerves and some bad language, Dad's. In those days of the distant past that was how horses were "broken," with brute strength, dust, and terror on the part of the horse. And usually many bent horseshoe nails and more bad language.

The last horse that I trained to have his feet handled, trimmed and shod had those things done while he was standing loose in the corral with his halter rope over his back. There was no dust, no broken ropes and no frayed tempers, tho I did bend a nail or two. That was not the horse's fault, just inaccurate hammering.

I think now that if Topsy hadn't been tied at all, she would not have made the fuss that she did. But how then do you keep her from just walking away? Train her to stand there, the same as one would have to if a pack needed fixing and there were no handy trees nearby. They can do that, so why not for shoeing?

If a horse is comfortable with having her legs and feet handled, it is only a short step to having nails driven into her hooves. One must remember how important legs are to prey animals, as well as to the predators who also must live by speed. The horse needs to learn you are not going to damage his means of escape. If one ties up a horse's legs he instantly is filled with panic, the same as we would be if someone tied our legs and hands together. Your horse must learn to trust you, and that trust shouldn't be betrayed very many times or he will not believe you.

It is difficult for me to absorb just how trusting, sensitive and forgiving horses can be. How much they will do for us, almost all of it of no use whatever to the horse and most of it completely unnatural. About all that we ask a horse to do that is natural is to take a drink after we have led him to the water. Often he will refuse and we can't make him.

I have read some articles about how some horses shy to get their rider off their back. I don't believe it. I have had plenty of shies and I don't think any of them was designed to get me off. After all, all he had to do was just to give a little buck and I would have gone flying, without an airplane. On the contrary, on a couple of occasions he actually picked me up when I was so far off balance there was no way I would have stayed on if he hadn't stepped under me. I was riding bareback.

Shying is an eye-blink response to a sudden threat. It is not a conscious decision to remove a rider. Bucking does that. Shying removes the horse from the danger lying in the shadows along the horse trail.

I have found, mainly by being tested quite often, that if one is totally tuned in to her horse and not daydreaming, is balanced and "with" the horse and relaxed, she will go along when the horse makes that big leap and spin and not be left hanging in the dust in the air which her mount has so recently vacated. My horse taught me that bit of wisdom.

It is true some horses shy faster than others. That just means the quicker horse stands a better chance to reproduce as she would have escaped the cougar, while the cougar would have eaten the slow one.

A horse is a very sensitive creature. Her hairy skin, about 80 square feet of it, can pick up and broadcast many signals to other horses and to predators. Her ears are excellent receivers; her nose is superb. Her eyes, large and expressive, aren't quite as good in SOME WAYS as our own. She can run thru a thick forest at night and not hit anything or damage her eyes. Can a human do that?

Horses seem to be rather poor with imagination. They seem unable to imagine what they can't see. If you change your shape you are no longer you to the horse if he didn't see you make that change, or if he doesn't hear or smell you. If he does, the game is up.

Dogs and cattle can also be fooled if you change your shape, if they don't hear or smell you.

Most non-human animals that I can think of do not live by comparing things reasonably, as, for instance, seeing an animal grazing does not prove it is safe. They can't think, "It is eating grass, therefore it is not a meat eater, but a fellow grazer." If it looks like a bear and smells like a bear, it likely is a bear; better be cautious. However if it doesn't smell like a bear and is eating grass, but still looks like a bear, then it is unknown and very dangerous. Better leave now. The unidentifiable is more dangerous than what they do recognize sometimes.

chapter 19

Floating Bridge

Before I was big enough to be anything but a nuisance in the field at haying time, Mother could do little more than keep an eye on me and make me stay away from wheels and horse feet. She could straighten up the rake-formed bunches of hay as Dad drove the team on the hay rake to gather the sweet smelling dry hay into long windrows. With the rake he would then cut the windrows into ragged bunches along their length.

Mother, Stanley and Johnny could start tidying these bunches up into neater piles of hay, ready to be pitched onto the wagon as soon as Dad had even one windrow bunched, while keeping one eye on me.

Before there was anything to do with the big piles of hay, the boys would haul their little wagon with a hayrack on it out in the field and gather up stray bits of hay left by the horse rake and load it on to their wagon. Of course I continued to be a nuisance. No one ever called me a nuisance, but I surely must have been one.

Finally I grew up big enough to be able to ride on the wagon and walk around on the hay to compact it as Dad and Stanley placed each forkful carefully on the hay load. My job was to try to stay away from the hay coming up, then get my short legs on to it and stomp it down. I don't think I could have done much good to compact the hay at that age, but I at least was out of the way of wheels and hooves. I probably helped some.

Dad always told me when he was ready to drive to the next pile of hay. I'd lie down in the hay in the middle of the load until he stopped there to load it. I seem to remember Dad having both me and Johnny up on the load, but we played so much we threw off more hay than was thrown up, so the idea was abandoned.

I didn't fall off the edge of the wagon very often, but it was a different story when we had to haul hay on a sled with a rack on it.

The reason we had to haul hay on a sled was one of the fields lay across the river and at that time there was no bridge. The river, tho slow, was over 150 feet wide, too wide for Dad to put a conventional bridge over. So he took the haying equipment to the field and stored the hay in sheds on that side.

As both my brothers have passed away and there is no one left for me to ask about these things, I must trust to my rather dim memory. I believe it was in the late thirties when we were storing the hay on the far side of the river in the sheds.

I seem to recall that Dad rode the hay rake across the river. With its large wheels, riding it was no problem. With the mower, I carry a memory of him laying long planks from the shore onto the boat, then pushing the mower out on them and onto planks laid across the gunnels and balancing it there. Then he rowed the somewhat unstable craft to the other shore. Using planks already there, he wheeled the mower off and onto the field.

Thinking back, I believe he tried taking the wagon across with the team and had a hard time getting the wagon out of the mud along the bank and nearly got stuck. He decided to use a sled he had made for hauling heavy things, such as stumps, logs, etc. He could not have ridden the sled, for it would have bucked and thrashed around and probably thrown him off into the water. He must have taken it on the boat.

The sled with a rack on it moved the hay well enough, but was inclined to tip over sometimes, throwing off the hay and me. It would have to be reloaded after the sled had been turned right side up again and I had removed the hay from my ears and down my shirt. I didn't

220

like that sled. It was much rougher than the wagon, on the rougher field. The horses didn't like it either.

Of course, with the hay on the other side of the river from the barn, the cows and horses had to be taken across the frozen-over river to eat it. When the hay was used up those animals would be brought back on the ice or they waded the river.

Two or three people had to go over there every day to feed the stock.

That was another big job. They had to launch the boat down a ramp into freezing water that was flowing just fast enough to keep it from becoming solid. Then row across to the other shore, force the boat up onto a narrow ice shelf, jump out quickly, trying not to slip into that cold, cold water, and tie it up. A short walk took them to the hay sheds where the animals would be waiting. There they'd spread enough hay to last until the next day. There was so much work involved just getting over there, they surely didn't want to do it twice a day.

To get back across the cold, often slush-filled river they had to row somewhat against the current, to land at the ramp, climb out and attach the haul-out rope. Going to a pair of trees where they had a windlass fitted, they could haul the ice-encrusted boat out of the river, high enough that the freezing water would not get to it over-night, where it was then turned over. Then the tired people would trudge back to the house and sit by the warm stove to warm up and drink cups of hot cocoa.

As I was too young to be of much use on that job, Mother left me to do the important task of watching the fire. I was terrified the fire would get going too hot and "roar the house down." I begged her to take me along. She tried to assure me I would be all right, but just do not let the fire get too hot. I think I tried so hard not to let the fire burn too hot, that the house was probably not as warm as it should have been when the cold, tired cow and horse feeders returned.

Some better way definitely had to be thought up. In time it was.

Dad decided to bring up a big cedar freight raft he had somewhere down the lake, up on skids so the logs could dry out. The whole family went down the river in the boat to the lake where the raft was. Working with levers and grunts, we got it off the skids and into the water where it floated high, the logs being dry. I wonder how many grunts I contributed to move the raft.

The raft was 12 feet wide by 36 feet long, built with good-sized logs. With most of us using long, strong poles, the big ungainly craft moved slowly up the river as the polers plied their poles and pushed and grunted and the water gurgled around the square ends of the logs. At last we arrived at the mouth of Homecreek and tied up.

This raft was large enough to carry a team of horses and a wagonload of hay. By the time the grass was ready to cut we were all excited to try out the new labor-saving device.

Dad may have taken the mower and rake across together with the team. The rake could have been wheeled on quite easily by hand. Finally there was a job for the "little nuisance," my words not theirs. I could stand in front of the horses to keep them calm on the raft, while Dad, Stanley and Johnny poled it across the river. I think Mother may have helped me hold the team. I don't believe the horses could have been anything but calm at any time. I really do not remember. What I can clearly recall is that we did use the raft, and I have photos that show the raft with a team and a big wagonload of hay in the middle of it crossing the river, and a person wielding a pole at each end.

With the wagon hauling the hay, there were fewer opportunities for me to fall off. I liked that a lot. And no one had to make that awful cold trip across the river to feed the stock every day. And all the animals could be at the barn and in shelter.

In the early 1940s Dad had an even better idea than the raft. Why not build a floating bridge? Why not, indeed?

He designed a log bridge that was a long, long raft fastened to the riverbank at each end. By using triangulation he found the river to be 150 feet wide where he wanted to put the bridge.

As both Stanley and John were gone from home by then and Mother had a bad back, I was the only help he had. As I had at last grown up, I was able to drive the team, use axes, saws, etc., and be of some use on the farm.

Dad estimated the number of logs it would require to build a raft 12 feet wide and 150 feet long. We set about getting and preparing the logs. They all had to be peeled, sawed to length by crosscut saw. Most were a different length so the joins would not be in line across the raft. No two logs the same length would lie beside each other.

The team hauled the logs a quarter of a mile, more or less, to the river on a sled. When we had all the logs and crosspieces—split in half six-inch cedar poles—at the river, construction began. We used a four-power block and tackle to move the logs from where the team left them to the riverbank. We rolled each one into the water and dogged them and tied them together. They could then be lined up and have the first crosspiece spiked on with eight-inch nails.

As the raft (bridge) grew longer, we moved it up along the river-bank and tied it to sturdy trees. We kept adding on logs at the stern, as it were, moving the whole thing up-stream as it grew longer and longer.

Finally we had a nice cedar raft 150 feet long and 12 feet wide lying along the east bank of the river. Now for the moment of truth. Would it reach the other shore? Excitement, doubt, hope and anxiety churned inside me, and I trembled as we tied a long strong rope to an extra sturdy tree on the east bank and the other end to the bridge. I was on shore, slowly paying out the rope as Dad pushed the "bow" of the bridge away from the shore. Slowly it moved out into the current as I let out tiny bits of my rope. And wonder of wonders, it at last swung into place, exactly the right length. Dad had done a good bit of work with the triangulation.

Now we could get to that big field and not have to use a boat or raft, and the hay could come across the bridge and up to the barn. A big celebration would have been nice, but as I recall we were just too tired to do more than walk back to the house, eat supper, do the chores and go to bed. But we did have a bridge. Possibly the longest usable bridge on the Atnarko River, maybe the only bridge on the Atnarko River at that time.

Sometime around then Dad told me that as I was up on the wagon anyway, I might as well drive. Suddenly I was afraid. I was sure the horses would run away or I'd turn them too tightly and break the wagon. Or I would ask the team to start and they would just ignore me and I'd feel like a fool. Or they would start and I would be unable to stop them. I might even run over the piles of hay, pushing it all down in the muddy ground. Amazingly, none of those things happened. The horses just walked off as if Dad still held the lines and stopped at the next pile of hay.

Dad wanted to drive the wagon across the bridge the first few loads, but as they made no fuss he told me to drive across the bridge, and was I ever proud, tho I tried very hard not to let on.

chapter 20

WHERE TO LIVE

Humans can live in just about any environment on the face of the earth. They build their houses on high, cold, windy, rocky slopes of mountains. They live in hot, steamy, wet jungles, and the sparsely populated burning outback of Australia, and the frozen ice-covered Arctic wastes, as well as the unstable and trembling feet of sleeping volcanoes, and the low-lying flood plains of active rivers. Or they choose to occupy over-populated cities where they are stacked up one on top of another like hens in an egg factory, cells in buildings that can rise a quarter of a mile into the sky; or on small more or less self-sustaining farms miles away from each other, all because they just happen to like something about their chosen space. There is always something to be said for and against living in any environment.

I think it takes a very unusual kind of person to be able to live entirely alone, with no other human within miles for help in case of injury or just companionship.

To live as a family, or even a pair, I believe most of any loneliness would be kept at bay.

Even a group around one does not necessarily relieve loneliness. I was sitting between two ladies whom I knew quite well and we were talking. Then one of them, having asked me a question, which I was partway thru answering, turned to her friend on her right and began visiting her. Then the lady on my other side turned to her friend and started to talk to her. I was there as alone as if there were no others around at all, leaving me profoundly lonely.

Among the advantages of living on your own land and working for yourself is the freedom to do the various tasks that must be done on a small non-commercial farm, as you see fit. There are no nine-to-five deadlines. There are no Monday-to-Friday restrictions on when you can get your hay in, garden weeded, or wood cut. One is ruled by the weather, to a large extent. And if, in your considered opinion, you can afford to make use of the beautiful day to go on a hike to a nice lake with a lovely, long, golden sandy beach, you can do so. There you and your daughter and your dog can race your horses and play on the beach. Oh yes, this would be while your husband rests in the shade, if the dog will let him and doesn't demand he play with her by throwing sticks in the lake for her to swim out and retrieve.

Or if you have been up since daylight mowing a field of grass, and having finished up all the other morning chores, you can read, paint, write, or take a well-deserved sleep. You will be hauling hay until dark and going to bed near midnight by the time you eat and wash the dishes, feed the dog and turn the lady cats, Dumbo and Cealy, loose.

Now on the other side of the coin are some disadvantages to living on your own land, separate from others. The biggest disadvantage I can see in living this way is the lack of transference of knowledge. With no one around us who had knowledge of how to school horses and dogs, I knew of no other way to get these sensitive animals to do what I wanted except with physical punishment. I did not know about soft baby steps and reward, to show them what I wanted, nor did I realize exactly how sensitive horses, dogs, and cows, in fact, are.

I was both deaf and blind to what they were trying to tell me because I didn't know how to read them. Since I couldn't read them, they had great difficulty reading me. I would tell them one thing with my body, as the implement they were hauling told them something else, or nothing. Some of the horses became so frustrated and confused they pranced, sweated, chewed on the neck-yoke, lunged, stopped, reared and backed up, raising heck with the mowing. I had no idea what I was doing wrong and of course blamed the poor horses.

The horses weren't the only ones frustrated, either. I loved those animals and wanted to have them learn what I was trying to teach them. Without exception, those same horses that I couldn't get to haul the hay rake, wagon, mower, or disc properly, would pack, let me ride them at walk, trot or canter with no trouble at all. What in H was I doing wrong?

Finally, after moving to the lower part of the valley and living near where my daughter and her family were, I started to get bits of knowledge about training those forgiving gentle creatures.

Soon after we left Lonesome Lake in 1989 and began living in the lower part of the valley near Susan and her family, she introduced me to her love of the moment, gymkhana and the local riding club, Valley Ridge Riders. We went to several meetings thru the winter and spring and I joined the club. Soon I felt ready to ride in gymkhana. There was only one small problem. I would need a saddle.

Susan acquired a saddle for me and I began schooling Bess in the events so she would not look like the novices we were when we competed. I didn't win many ribbons for a while, but in time we did get quite a few. But Bess and I were not the greatest barrel competition. She was too long and slow. It was hard for her to bend her stout body around short turns and she didn't work off her haunch. She was never made for running barrels. But she loved to jump. She couldn't run quickly around the barrels, but she surely could jump over them. That was delicious fun, especially as the fast barrel racers refused my challenge to them to take their horses over the barrels. In all honesty, they didn't deserve my challenge because I had spent a lot of time teaching Bess to go over short jumps. She had a distinct advantage.

It is now the end of June 2009. Susan, Tom and I were at the Bella Coola Rodeo yesterday, watching the big, burly bulls throw their riders about. We observed a new and novel way to ride a bull.

One big fellow came out of the chute, bucking and spinning with vigor and determination. When his rider was on the ground, the bull came along, scooped his rider up on his horns and head, and trotted off with him up there across his horns. Somehow the lucky man abandoned his high perch and fell to the ground a second time. Then the bull turned and headed for the out gate. That was the grand finale.

chapter 21

ENTERTAINMENT

I have been asked what we did for entertainment way out there in our "dreary" isolation, with no radio, no TV, no newspapers, no movies, no restaurants and no churches. Simple. We made our own. And when you live in God's ultimate church, what more entertainment does one need? We did not need newspapers as we had news magazines for information, and books and other magazines. A good part of Dad's heavy pack from mail trips was reading material.

Some of us could play the violin, some of us could sing, some of us thought we could sing but knew we couldn't really sing well enough to let anyone hear us, so we only sang when we were by our self. But all of us except Mother could whistle, and we did that while working at whatever job we were doing, if we felt like it, or until we hit our thumbnail while nailing on fence rails or whatever; then we sang a different tune for a while. I believe this new tune would have sounded more like complaining. Well, a hammered thumbnail hurts like H*LL!

When I was working alone on my own place I opened up and let all the big and little creature folk in the area hear me, and I really enjoyed the freedom to just let the music fill the outdoor cathedral and banish some of the loneliness, which was usually with me unless I had my horses there helping. I often made up my own songs, and this was my favorite, sung to the tune of *Red River Valley.*

More Water Than She Wants

Oh she built on the edge of the mud pond.
Oh she built by the side of the swamp.
Oh she built on the bank of the river.
Now she's got more water than she wants.

There were times when I was growing up that we had so little money we couldn't afford enough candles or kerosene for the lamp for unlimited light in the evenings. The lights would be blown out by six or seven o'clock, making for a very long night; but we kids were tired enough from working and playing all day that we were ready for sleep anyway. Getting the Pelton wheel changed all this.

Powered by hydropower from our homemade power plant, the small Pelton wheel was constructed from cut-in-half, 28-ounce tomato cans, folded so each half formed two side-by-side cups, and each pair of cups was nailed onto a solid birch core about 16 inches in diameter. This was turned at great speed by three one-inch in diameter pipes implanted in the bottom of the 10-foot-tall penstock, about one foot square, made from lumber from our water-powered sawmill. The top of the penstock stood under a wooden flume, which carried water from Homecreek to the power plant.

We had tried to run electric lights from the big water wheel, which powered the firewood and lumber saws, but the power from the slower waterwheel fluctuated so much the lights flickered wickedly. Although the big seven-foot in diameter waterwheel with four-foot-long buckets to catch the water turned the saws well enough to cut firewood and lumber, it simply wasn't fast enough to generate a steady supply of household electricity. That was when and why Dad built the Pelton wheel. With the higher speed the lights were steady and we could then run a radio without having to pack in very heavy big batteries, which we never did. It simply wasn't worth it.

I can remember staying up until after midnight often to listen to

Seattle radio station KIRO's *Midnight Concert Hour* while I stretched and cleaned squirrel skins. This would have been in the 1940s.

The Pelton wheel was cuddled up in a small, snug split-log cabin built inside a deep pit laboriously dug down about eight feet to the level of the creek bed, to allow the outflow from the penstock to escape down the main creek.

Unfortunately, in the late 1940s high water one summer overflowed the flume and washed out the pit, filling half the powerhouse and burying the Pelton wheel and generator with sand, gravel and rocks. We did not have the energy to clean up the mess and start all over, so we went without electric lights and radio until my future husband, Jack Turner, brought in a Zenith battery-operated radio in 1956. By then radio batteries were much lighter and radios were smaller.

I clearly remember that pit. I dug it. Every cubic foot of it. And my back ached for years, off and on, but only when I got up in the morning. Then, for no good reason that I could see, the backaches ceased, and (knock on wood) haven't returned. Mind you, I'm not complaining.

When I was growing up at The Birches, Christmas was not attended by very many guests, none actually, simply because there weren't any near neighbors to attend. Still I hold memories of how joyful and delicious the food was. Mother made oodles of cookies and boxes of chocolate fudge, boxes of dipped candies and hard candies; also various candied fruits she turned out by the bowlful.

We did not have any kind of roast meat. We could have had roast beef for our Christmas dinner, but Mother never learned the knack of roasting meat without turning it into dense, gray, dry matter. My folks liked their meat well done, or over done. She could fry steak just fine, but roasting seemed to defeat her completely. She could bake delicious cakes, pies, custards and biscuits. Even yeast bread submitted to her kneading fists eventually. And her doughnuts were without peer.

For presents we made things for each other rather than buying and carrying in store-bought gifts. That saved money and a lot of labor, unless they could come in on the horses at fall packing time when the year's supplies came in.

For a number of years we had a tree, and I can remember searching thru the forest for the perfect one. Of course I never found the perfect tree and had to settle for the best I could find without going too far from home.

Our Christmases were not celebrated on Christmas day, but sometime later, in January. It depended on when the ice on Lonesome Lake was safe to travel on. There were no trips out for mail between early November and early January, when the ice was usually safe. We just waited for it to form on the lake.

We did wish each other "Merry Christmas" on the appropriate day, however. The real celebration was held the day after Dad returned from the first mail trip of the New Year. Our relatives and friends always sent something for us, I seem to remember.

Christmas at Arbordale (Fogswamp)

Jack, Susan and I had our Christmas on Christmas Day, and for as long as our airplane was there to bring in mail we received any presents in time for Christmas. After Dad flew away with the plane, to seek some other way of life, I guess, we got our mail the old way, by trail. With Lonesome Lake ice safe to travel on, Jack made the 40-mile hike out to a place farther down the valley than Dad had been going. The mail was not delivered as close to us as it had been in the forties. Often there would be some presents in the mail that Jack carried home on his tired back.

We decorated our tree around the middle of December and left it up until about mid-January and the needles had become quite brittle and were falling off all over the floor. After all the time spent putting the ornaments and icicles on, it seemed a shame to take it down in a few days, and we wanted it there when we celebrated our wedding anniversary, on the ninth.

For Christmas dinner we usually had a nice juicy roast of our own delicious beef, with crisp browned fat on the outside and pink and juicy on the inside, and tender. There were spuds baked and nicely browned in the roast pan. While all of that stuff was cooking, there would usually be a Yorkshire pudding baking to a delicate golden brown. And some kind of salad, and often brussels sprouts, dug out from under the snow where they had kept very well. And over all of that would be spooned a generous layer of delicious brown gravy. Finally, if anyone had any room left, we had fruit cake, either one sent to us by Jack's folks, or one I made out of our own jam. And of course there would be thick cream to pour over it.

Which one of us made Christmas dinner would depend on who fed the swans. Or if we were feeding them that early. Feeding usually started in January.

While I am on the subject of eating "disgusting" meals, I will detail the most awful one of all.

When it was cold enough to have some hope the beef would keep for a decent length of time, we would butcher whatever animal we were going to that winter. With fresh fat beef to cut meat from, we would load up a one-foot-square wire toaster rack with prime steaks and grill these over a heap of glowing birch coals in the cook stove.

A flop-down door-and-draft on the front of the stove gave access to the firebox and took the grill nicely. It was my job to sit on the wood box cover and grill the steaks. Jack's job was to test the meat to see that it was done enough. Susan's job would be to help eat it, a chore I believe she enjoyed very much. The rest of Jack's job was to cut into the steaks a ways, then spread butter all over each steak, where it melted and pooled on the surface. While he attended to the steaks, I browned a grill full of homemade bread, generously sliced. Then the toast was slathered with more butter. Please, gentle reader, don't drool!

A five-mile hike in the cold each day did much to burn off the calories of those exotic meals, and we didn't have them every day, just as often as we liked.

When I growing up at The Birches there were several horses available for me to ride if I so chose, and believe me, I certainly chose, anytime, anyplace, and for any reason, or for no reason. There was the old fellow that Dad started with as a yearling he had got from the Chilcotin country and brought to Lonesome Lake after World War I. By the time I knew him he was called Ginty, though Dad had named him Kid to start with. It was while Dad was working the young gelding, probably as an over four year old, and singing to himself and the horse, a song in which some of the words were, "and down went McGinty to the bottom of the sea," that Dad suddenly decided that Kid was no longer a kid but a grown up and perhaps deserved a more grown up name. So he became "Ginty," a name much more appropriate for the dignified gentleman that he was.

I remember one time when that good old horse didn't act very dignified. It was one fall when his two mares came home from the fall pasture and called from across the river. He was standing asleep in the corral. His head jerked up as he answered, and then he burst into a jumble of bucks, spins, turned handsprings, leapt into the air and dashed about the corral in a paroxysm of pure joy. Ginty had been kept home that fall as he was a bit thin and we didn't want him out in the nasty, wet, cold weather that can, and usually does, happen at that time of year.

Ginty was the first horse that I rode by myself, he was the first horse that I fell off of, and he was the first, but not the last, horse that I fell in love with. He taught me to ride, he taught me to cling to his bony back and narrow withers, even when he shied. I seem to remember this happening more than once, onto hard, stony ground when something caused him to lurch sideways when we were cantering along the old gravel wagon road. He carried on to the barn while I picked myself up, brushed off the dirt and followed on foot.

He didn't intend to dump me. I was not big enough, nor did I have enough balance then, for balance is something one acquires over time. And it certainly helps to have legs long enough to reach down a horse's sides far enough that you can at least use them for some support. I was riding bareback and all I had to hang onto was a bit of wispy mane.

Of course, I continued to ride. A little side-trip to the roadbed was not going to stop anyone as determined as I.

I guess one would have to say my greatest childhood and lifetime love was for horses, except for family. Just going out to the barn to stand beside them and stroke their hair as they munched their hay in the dark was very rewarding.

I remember standing close to Ginty one clear, cold night and stroking my hand down his shoulder. As I stroked his hair my hand left a trail of white light, scaring me. Light, even white light, meant fire, and the light was accompanied by a snapping sound. I did not know about static electricity, but was assured by my parents that there was no danger. I later found out that my own sweater snapped and crackled when I pulled it over my head if the air was really dry.

Sometimes one can't even touch a furry animal without one or the other of you, or even both of you, getting "bitten" when the atmospheric conditions are right, or maybe wrong, depending on how hot the "bites" are.

If I had known in my years at Lonesome Lake what I know now about animals in general, and horses in particular, I would have been able to get a whole lot more pleasure from them than I did, simply because I knew so very little and caused them a lot of frustration. Neither of our parents were raised up with horses, except my Mother's dad had horses for farm work, but I don't think they were ridden very much except just to get from one place to another. In those days horses were expected to learn everything on the job, and no one spent a lot of time teaching them slowly but surely. This is the impression that I carry with me and could be wrong.

As I remember it, only the basics were taught to the rider, that is, pull left to go left, pull it right to go right, pull back to stop, and kick his sides to go forward. And kick your heels on his sides harder to make him go faster or switch him. I never had the concept of learning anything that the horse could teach me, taught to me at Lonesome Lake.

Boy, did my daughter ever open my eyes when we moved down to Hagensborg. When Susan, my daughter, was growing up at Lonesome Lake we subscribed to *Western Horseman* and *Horse of Course,* but with not enough knowledge I could not get much out of the articles, nor could Susan for the same reason. Once she got acquainted with horse people she learned a lot. She and others were able to show me the way and I belatedly found out how much I had missed.

This was one of the downsides of living in such a place as Lonesome Lake. On the upside, I didn't know what I was missing and didn't worry about it. I was happy with getting what I could from the horses.

Some memorable rides I made happened on moonlit evenings. The creek where the horses and cows got their water was about 200 feet from the barn. Sometimes I would go to the barn, open the corral gate, bridle Topsy, halter one of the others, climb onto the manger and jump onto Topsy's back to ride to the creek, leading the haltered horse followed by the others. Done drinking, we all galloped back to the barn in the bright moonlight, flinging snowballs, or perhaps I should say "footballs"—or "hoofballs"?—in every direction. The snow would squeak and the timber would be popping as the cold split the trees from the expansion of frozen sap. Sometimes down on the lake a lonely wolf might begin singing or, more likely, mourning.

On really cold nights, with the river and Lonesome Lake frozen over, the trumpeter swans would have flown 10 miles north to rest on the Stillwater until the sun rose the next day, before returning for their meager feed of grain, some of them still rattling with iceballs they had not been able to wash off their feathers. Swans cannot fly if too much ice adheres to their feathers, and they must clean it off frequently when it is cold so they can fly at any time. To do this they rise up out of the water, then drop down hard enough to sink their body completely under water. As their buoyancy pops them to the surface, a wave of water washes over their back, sluicing off the ice. They do this industriously when planning to make a flight in the immediate future.

I can think of another memorable ride on Topsy. She was nice and round, with very low withers. On some horses the withers can be quite fin-like. Nice to hold a saddle in place but not so good to sit on bareback. But no one would saddle a horse to ride across the field, especially as the horse was on the other side of the field from the barn. Anyway, this particular day some of the field had gone bare, then was snowed on again with soft wet snow. The rest of the field was still covered with hard crystalline old snow. The course across the field ran straight towards the corrals, then just where it reached the new snow was also where the trail made a right angle turn. Topsy and I came flying across the field, started the turn, lost all traction on the slippery wet ground, and she was suddenly planing on her side. I was flung some distance away from her and was myself sliding along on my side, gouging up the hard snow with my face as I rolled desperately to get away from her feet for when she righted herself. We both got up and brushed off the snow, she by a good shake, I very gently. I was not hurt except for a bit of "snow rash" on one cheek. It was a good ride, though, and thank God I wasn't on a saddle!

Writing about that ride reminds me of another mare who went for an unintended journey down an icy slope. This mare was called Thuja, the Latin name for the Western red cedar, a strong and durable tree. She was strong, durable, dependable, patient and lovable as any horse could be. One day when I let her out of her corral the place where she had to go was covered with bare ice, on a slight slope. She walked out of the gate all ready to frisk off to the field, a hundred feet away. Having thrown her usual caution to the four winds, the moment her feet hit the ice she sat on her rump as her back hooves skidded beneath her, leaving her sitting down like a very large black dog. In this posture she swept 18 feet down the slick ice. Reaching the end of the skidway she stopped, stood up, and immediately looked behind herself to me, her whole body language clearly showing acute embarrassment. I tried not to laugh, but had to, I just couldn't help it, though it wasn't fair. She walked away with as much dignity as she could muster.

chapter 22

RUNAWAY

Runaways? Yes, I've had some, several, in fact. I have not had any runaways while mounted that I didn't get stopped at some point, except one. It isn't fair to list it here because the horse I was riding tripped over a pole in a shallow stream and fell, tipping me off in the water. Then he got up and galloped off, taking his teammate with him. I had ridden one horse in the team just to cross the small river channel. As we had planned on doing more work on the other side of the stream we didn't want to separate them and lead the other. I had crossed streams often this way, even hauling logs across water and keeping dry.

My first runaway happened when I was in my teens, not quite adult in age, but as tall as I ever got, five feet three inches, and 130 pounds. This was my first experience driving a half-trained pair of horses, one of them headstrong and the other one "green." The green one was the son of the other.

Dad had plowed a large area of low-producing sandy field, hoping to replant it with better type grass and clover. We had the two mares, Susan and Topsy, and their four-year-old colts, Prince and Rommy. Susan was teamed with her son, Prince, and Topsy was teamed with her son, Rommy. Prince and Susan had plowed the field, taking several days of hard work. To give them a rest, we used Topsy and Rommy to do the disking.

I cannot recall Rommy doing any more work than hauling poles, so he was still pretty green. Dad did not believe in giving horses any basic education, and sort of scoffed at the idea of getting them gradually used to harness and stuff around them and noises behind them. Some horses don't seem to need this slow start, but there are others who do. Tame Rommy was one.

We hitched this pair to the disk. Rommy's head was high, tho Topsy's was low. She was not worried. She was not scared of the disk; she just hated it.

As I had not yet entirely learned what a high head meant, Dad should have known and given me a little instruction on how to prevent a run-away. I was about as green as Rommy in this regard. I had done quite a lot of driving, but the horses I drove were well trained and older. Anyway I drove them off down the field towards a wooden bridge, which we would cross to get to the plowing. Rommy had never hauled an implement with a tongue. Nor had he hauled anything that rumbled like thunder behind him. I did not know what to expect.

As soon as the disk rolled onto the end of the bridge the noise started and Rommy wanted out of there, NOW! I should have stopped them right there until Rommy's head came back down, but I didn't know and I let them proceed. Topsy walked stolidly, Rommy doing a fancy piaffe, a trot in place, almost, as he was going as fast as I was at that time, lifting his legs as in a trot. Nearing the end of the bridge, Topsy caught sight of the plowed field, recognized what it meant, and lit all four "afterburners." Rommy was quite willing to go along.

We were supposed to turn left at the end of the bridge onto the plowing. We didn't do that. Suddenly I was no longer making the decisions. Headstrong old Topsy was. She took control away from me and turned the team right as the pair gathered speed quickly across the field. At one point, before I lost the lines out of my hands, I was on my belly, sliding along on the old grass stubble. The team and disk sped up across Barn Field so fast that the poor old disk was air-born several times as a result of being launched into the air by going over a slight rise, or rock, causing an agonized shriek from wounded high grade steel, adding encouragement to the fleeing horses. They were heading for the barn. Topsy wasn't running away, really. She wasn't even scared. She just didn't want to disk that plowed field. She would have hated just as much to disk an area the size of herself. She hated the disk, not the work. In fact she did better when the disks were advanced and she had actually to work to pull it.

Topsy steered the team into the corral, heading for her end of the barn. She failed to allow for the room Rommy would need to safely pass the corner post of the horse shed. He slammed into the post with enough force to knock it out from under the roof, then before it hit the ground, a projecting piece on the disk gouged a long sloping furrow in the hard fir wood. The horses raced on thru the corral to finally stop at the big gate, with one of Topsy's lines entangled around the projecting end of a fence rail. There they waited for the slow humans to catch up. One horse was just plain scared about the whole thing. The other one thought she might receive some sort of punishment, or at least she acted like it. Mother wanted Dad to unhitch them and not continue with the job. Dad thought we should go on as planned, but at a much slower pace.

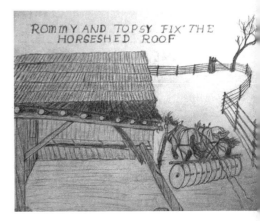

Rommy and topsy 'fix'
the horseshed roof.

After getting them disentangled from the gate, Dad drove them back to the field, advanced the slightly dulled disks, mounted the machine and did a couple of rounds. By then they had slowed down considerably. He turned them over to me again. To have done otherwise could have stopped me, possibly forever, driving horses again.

Dad was right. I had to get back on and finish the job. The only advice he gave me was to keep them from going too fast. Believe me, I didn't let them go too fast.

Dad still didn't seem to know that any time horses get upset, worried, even uncomfortable, stopping them seems to help them get their brains working again, then they will work better. If you keep on when they are acting silly, they only get worse, not better.

A short time later I was taking the disk somewhere and had to cross a bridge. I had the same team, but a different bridge. When we neared the bridge, apprehension cropped out all over Rommy's body. He remembered what had happened at the last bridge he had crossed with the disk. He had had to run like crazy and got hit on the shoulder, hard, then had to do a lot of hard work for hours on end without much rest. He really didn't want this to happen again, but he didn't know how to avoid it. So I had to show him.

The fidgety colt walks across the bridge.

Starting them onto the bridge, I thought to myself, "This time you bloody well aren't going to get away from me! You will WALK across if it takes the whole darn day." And it nearly did. With the team on the bridge, I stopped them. Rommy piaffed. Topsy stood. I stood. Topsy usually liked to stop, unless she saw a good reason not to. A good reason, to her, that is. In fact one of her nicknames was Stopsy.

When Rommy stopped piaffing and stood quietly, I asked them to walk. Rommy managed to do that until the disk started onto the bridge. As Rommy's head went up I stopped them. Rommy piaffed. It was a really neat piaffe, too, much like a Lipizzaner doing Airs Above the Ground.

Finally Rommy stood still. I asked for a few more steps, Rommy gave one or two, then started to piaffe. I stopped them. Even that few steps caused the disk to thunder on the wooden bridge. We waited until Rommy stopped trotting in place and stood. That was how we crossed that bridge. Each time I started them, Rommy took a few more steps before his fear took over his normally stable nature and made him do what he could to satisfy the natural instinct to run. His legs were moving, therefore, he must be escaping the perceived danger.

I used this strategy on every bridge we came to. In time Rommy walked across any old bridge, including the 150-foot-long floating bridge spanning the whole Atnarko River, hauling mower, hay, whatever.

It was when I was driving a big wagonload of hay across the floating bridge with Susan and Rommy that one of the logs disengaged from its nails and dropped Susan thru the bridge, up to her belly. I was up on the load of hay; Dad was following behind. Obviously the team came to a stop. I hollered to Dad what had happened. He squeezed past the load of hay as I climbed down. Susan was calmly resting on the bridge deck, with her weight pulling down on the neck yoke, and Rommy. I went to Rommy's head, as we certainly didn't need him trying to go anywhere. With a few moments' study of the situation, Dad got out his sharp pocketknife and began cutting every strap that fastened Susan to the wagon. She was putting so much weight on those pieces of harness there was simply was no way to unhitch anything except her lines, reins to a riding horse. Rommy just looked over to Susan, more curious than frightened. In fact I don't seem to recall that he indicated in any way that the position Susan was in was anything but normal.

With Susan disconnected from the wagon she made a prodigious effort, exploded out of the hole, wavered on the edge of the bridge, side-passed into the river, then swam 15 feet to shore. There she made another prodigious effort to leap out of the water onto the top of a vertical bank, dripping and trembling. But she got out safely.

Then we unhitched Rommy, led him off the bridge, and took the two horses to the barn. Unharnessed, the horses were let into the pasture for the night. The hay would have to sit there until we could repair things. That would happen next day. We were tired, but so thankful neither horse had been hurt.

With the bridge back in shape, we led each horse out on it to the wagon, wondering how they would feel about going on a bridge that had let at least one of them down. They both showed complete trust and faith in our judgment and acted no differently than they would have had the accident never happened. We hitched up; I climbed back up on the load and drove to the barn. Rommy had indeed learned how to cope with bridges.

Another horse who had to use a rather unusual method of learning bridges generally were safe, if we said they were, was Lucky Debonair, a coming three-year-old brown gelding. We had bought him out of the bucking horses at the Anahim Lake Stampede in July 1965.

I had halter trained this young, partly tame horse in a small round corral the stampede people had loaned us. We got more attention from the fence sitters, who should have been watching the stampede, than the stampede did. Jack helped, while Susan, our daughter, kept out of the way outside the corral. With very little gentle urging, Lucky D was soon following me around with the halter and stopping when I asked him to.

We thought it was time to head for home. As it was near dark when we started out we didn't go very far, only as far as the first wooden truck bridge. There we stopped. LD didn't like the bridge. To us it looked safe enough, and solid. LD had not learned to trust people yet. He simply had not had the experience, as he was range raised. He seemed quite a compliant colt.

After trying unsuccessfully to convince LD to walk onto the bridge, including using the time honored method of the old whip, which only caused some jumping around and a bit of rearing, we had to think of a better way. LD was not going to set foot on that dangerous bridge. Period. Then one of us suggested a blindfold.

Neither of us had tried that before, so it was worth a try. Nothing else was working. Dumping our bedrolls out of a gunnysack we placed it over his eyes, fastening it securely to his halter.

There was quite a large clear area in front of the bridge. I led LD, now sightless, around and about until he was following nicely. Then I headed directly for the center of the bridge. I didn't want him to get too near either edge. With him unable to see, I was totally responsible for him.

When one of his hooves came down on the bridge he stopped, blindfolded head high, and pulled his foot back off the bridge. I pulled very gently on his rope. Soon he lowered his head and clomped across the bridge. On the other side I removed the blindfold and turned him around to show him what he had done. He stared with astonishment, shook his mane, then wanted to continue wherever it was we were going. His trust was complete.

In the following years, I seem to remember a few times when he questioned our judgment, but I don't remember him actually refusing again.

Lucky Debonair was a rather lackadaisical workhorse, but a good pack horse, saddle horse, and could always be caught. He was friendly, very friendly. And he had disgustingly fragile hooves, but with iron shoes on he did his packing well.

I will relate one more runaway where the horses were not panicked; just one of them had heard an airplane, distant and high.

I had taken the team, Topsy and Thuja, over to the Pen field to rake and bunch the dry hay. The rake work finished, I tied them to a willow bush near the end of the floating bridge, so I could spend a bit of time tidying up the bunches. That field is about a third of a mile long, but as I had raked only the south half of it, I was quite a way up the field when an airplane flew over.

I wondered what would happen. I didn't have to wait very long to find out. As I had tied only Thuja, the boss mare, to one of the trees in the willow bush, I looped Topsy's crosscheck line around Thuja's hame, hopefully securing both of them. Topsy, in her frenzy, shoved herself between Thuja and the tree she was tied to, breaking Thuja's line and turning the team loose with the rake still attached. From where I was I could not see what was going on until they appeared out in the field, turning towards the bridge. More by luck than design, I believe, they made the correct turn to approach the bridge. They were out of my sight and out of my control. There was nothing I could do but hope like heck they didn't get hurt.

I ran down the field and got to the bridge in time to see them haul the rake off the other end, and start up the field, first at a fast walk, then at a trot and finally at a canter. They were getting frightened by then. There was no one to give them instructions, but they didn't panic and stopped at the corral gate. Once again Mother came out and caught them and soothed them.

The only damage to the rake was one slightly bent axel caused by one wheel slipping thru a crack between two of the outer logs, which we hadn't filled, as ordinarily the rake wouldn't be that close to the edge of the bridge. The bent axel was not serious. Dad just turned it over and it was fine.

My runaway with Rommy and Topsy on the disk was not the only one that spring. It was only a few days later that Dad had his own. He had built a horse-drawn brush to cover sowed grass seed. It consisted of a frame to hold the branchy tops of birch trees. A cross piece with holes drilled thru about a foot apart was attached to a piece of wire going from one end of the cross piece to the other with enough slack to form a loop, which was shackled to the double trees, and which the team pulled the brush with. The branches were inserted thru the holes in the cross piece and nailed.

Dad had hitched his plow team, Prince and Susan, to the brush, then started for the field, about 400 feet away. He had to drive thru a wide gateway. While passing thru the gateway, the brush started brushing one side of the gateway, making a frothy sound. That new and unusual noise was all Prince needed to energize him considerably. He burst into a run, taking his mother along. She didn't have much choice. Dad was in a bad place to set his feet and try to stop them. He was caught between the brush and the open gate. He had to let them go. As the young horse had been working so quietly up till then, Dad allowed himself to get in a bad position. Mother and I were right there, but there was nothing we could do either, as the team and brush disappeared out the other side of the corral, heading for the plowed and seeded area.

Passing the seeded area, the team made a gentle sweeping turn around the edge of the large field and returned to the barn, where they were caught. Then they had to go do the brushing and rolling.

Now I am reminded of the runaway in the orchard. It was at the start of haying. Dad had brought the mower out of the part of the 40-foot-square mill building where he housed the haying equipment until he built the Imp Shed a short time later. Out in the yard he inspected and oiled up the machine, ready to hitch up. I was there to hold the horses while he hitched them up. All was ready; the cutter bar was folded and secured, as he was going to drive over to another field. I believe the orchard had already been cut by hand scythe.

With Prince and Susan hitched on and Dad on the mower seat, he asked me to let them go. I did and stepped back, on the safe side. Dad had taught me very early in life to never leave the heads of the horses on the cutter bar side, something I never forgot. After I stepped back he started the team. For maybe one second after they began walking nothing unusual happened, then as a harsh clattering blasted out of the belly of the mower, the two horses were in full flight, Dad was yanking grimly on the lines and yelling, "Whoa!" It seemed nothing was going to stop those panicked horses. On the way thru the orchard, suddenly, right in front of the frenzied horses, stood a good-sized apple tree. Dad steered them into it. When they hit that tree with their lines tight, the impact made their high heads slam together with a loud thud. They stopped, shifting and snorting and shaking. They were scared! So was I. Dad wasn't, tho. He hadn't time to be scared. He quickly put the mower out of gear. Mowing machines were not intended to be run in gear with the cutter bar folded!

There was a bit of damage, quite a bit actually. Two or three young apple trees had been cut off. At least two of the dogs in the right wheel were smashed, and part of the inner shoe hinge was broken. Quite a bit of damage, but, hey, they didn't get away or injured. Dad had to do a lot of metal work to repair the damage.

Quite a few years later Dad had his second mowing machine runaway. This one happened after I was married and Jack and I were living on my place, and we were loaning our team to Dad when he needed them.

It was Dad's last runaway and was a rather mild one. It started when he drove the mower over a log left lying in the field. The sudden lurch as one wheel went over the log threw him right off the seat. He lost the lines, and the mares were loose in the hay field with the mower still in gear. Dad got hurt some, I never heard how much, but he got up and followed after the horses. All they did was to run to the end of the field where there was a closed gate. There they stopped and waited for him to take control again. Those mares were Thuja and Rocket.

A little later he got a tractor. I don't know if that runaway was a factor or not, but it was better for each farm to have its own power, especially during haying.

The last runaway on my place happened the summer before we left Lonesome Lake. We were hauling hay with Tempest and a new mare Susan had found and brought in, in the hope she would work better than Guenevere did. Well, she did for several years. So I gave Susan Guenevere and her filly, Lightning, whom she very much wanted. Then the new mare began acting up almost as badly as Guenevere did.

Anyway the new mare, Nugget, and Tempest were hauling hay. We had the wagon over one-half loaded when the two of them decided to head for the barn without asking for my permission. I had their lines wrapped somewhat snugly around the top of the ladder at the front of the hay rack to kind of suggest to the horses they were not free to go yet. For no apparent reason, they started down the lumpy field, gathering speed as they went, pulling the nice rubber-tired wagon as much by their lines as by their traces. I was near the back end of the load when they started. I ordered them to stop and was ignored completely. I tried desperately to get to the front end of the wagon and grab those lines. The bouncing hay slowed me down too much. Then I was flung off the load along with my pitchfork and a bunch of hay into a rusty, muddy creek, face down, when the wagon ran into the same creek. The rack capsized, unloaded a good portion of the dry hay into the creek, then was hauled out again, now with the rack resting heavily on the top of the nice rubber-tired right wheel, adding a really good brake to those two idiots. At last they had to stop, tho they had hauled the wagon all that way with their mouths, mostly.

I hauled myself out of that muddy, sandy creek, scraped the mud and sand out of my eyes and off my face, so at last I could see again. Jack was at their heads, the hay rack was on its side, and much of the hay was in the creek.

As we had 30-foot-long half-inch ropes to bundle the hay with still on the wagon, I took them around and tied each horse to a stout fence post of her own. Then we began unloading the wagon so we could put the hayrack back in place, then reload all the hay. We were a bit late getting to the barn that evening, and tired. And I probably still had to milk the cow.

I had two more runaways after we moved to the Salloompt area, one as violent and scary as the other was quiet.

The first one happened when I took Bess out to the river to give her a drink while I was waiting for things to get started for our gymkhana at the Rodeo Grounds. I had my little Aussie puppy, Liesel, with me, on a leash.

Where we watered our horses there is a narrow, shallow river channel one can ride across to a small sand bar. At the top of the sand bar the water is deep enough for a horse to wade into and get a good drink.

Downstream is a much longer sand bar, partly clear of logs, but some of it has several water-worn logs lying about. Beyond the sand bar hurries the main channel of the Bella Coola River, muddy-white in summer. The shoreline across the river is a vertical rock bluff, which the river smashes into as it swirls past.

I rode Bess into the white water; she lowered her head all ready to drink when a dreaded sea-monster flicked its tail in her face. She did a 180-degree turn on her haunch and exploded out of there at 40 miles an hour. That was the start and speed that I needed for gymkhana, which she never gave me, fortunately, for she was out of my control and her own. She raced away down the sand bar leaving her brain in the grass with my puppy. I could not stop her. She tore out onto the big bar heading for the main channel of the Bella Coola River, across which perhaps 200 or 300 feet away stood that vertical bluff. I did not want to go there. I couldn't stop her, but I could, and did, bend her in a U-turn. We then raced back up the bar where she jumped up onto a three-foot-high bank, only to leap back into a deep pool, then out of that to go crashing into a dense alder thicket, causing a few gouges and scratches to appear on my face. Finally she stopped, trembling, tossing her head and fidgeting. She could go no farther into the thicket without doing some serious land clearing. She allowed me to hold her there for several minutes until her head came down a bit. Then I cautiously backed her out, rode across the small channel to where the whole exercise had started and, hopefully, my pup still waited.

When we were near the grassy patch I asked Bess to stop. She did, as if nothing had ever happened. On the ground I led her as I looked for my little Liesel, and called. Soon she crawled out of the tall grass, looking scared and abandoned but uninjured, thank God. I had visions of her being smashed and broken from Bess's violent departure.

Untangling Liesel's leash from the tall grass, I remounted Bess and we three returned to the rodeo grounds. That was the only time I have ever been really scared while riding a horse. She was out of her own control and never heard me.

Now for the quiet runaway, in complete contrast to the one we just witnessed.

I had started riding my new horse, Breezie Future, when he was a bit past two. By the time he was three we were making long rides up a logging road way up where logging had taken place the year before. Lots of rich grass was growing all over the logged area in the Salloompt valley. On the way to this area we had to go up quite a long hill called Woodlot Hill, as people went up to cut firewood out of leftover stuff the logging company didn't want. Many times we made that pleasant ride up there. It was so quiet and Breezie really seemed to like to go off with just Liesel and me. By then she was a grown dog, who always came behind us and never ran off anywhere.

While Breezie grazed on the sweet, tall grass, Liesel usually busied herself poking into any small creek she could find. There were many creeks there. She didn't go very far from us. I either remained mounted while Breezie grazed, or sometimes I got off and held his rein while I sat on a handy stump.

On the return from one trip up in the Woodlot Hill area we were walking calmly down the relatively steep grade (not too steep for an ordinary pickup) with Liesel trotting along behind. Suddenly she dashed past Breezie as he burst into a downhill canter. I ordered him to stop, once. He didn't. I tried to bend him in a circle, but the road was too narrow; I would put both of us in a deep, muddy ditch. I decided to let him continue to the bottom of the hill where there was room to bend him into a circle. At about that time I thought maybe I didn't want to stop him anyway, as I didn't know what had set the dog off to begin with. Liesel maintained her position, about 20 feet in front of the horse. He was not running at anything like his top speed. Liesel could not keep up if Breezie just cantered fast, never mind galloped.

As we cantered on down the road I began really to enjoy the ride Breezie was giving me. He felt so completely in control of his body, even if he was not in my control. I had never cantered a horse down any very long descents or any very steep downgrades. I always thought there would be a large potential for a horse tripping over something and falling heavily on his front end.

That ride made me fully aware of how well he was carrying practically all his weight on his back legs. When he felt he was far enough away from whatever had scared Liesel, he simply stopped, as I, sensing he was going to stop, told him to, so he had to obey me, finally. I think he could not have run more than 400 or 500 feet. I don't like to tell a horse, or dog, too many times to do something that there is a good chance I can't enforce, and show him that I really am a paper tiger after all and lose a lot of respect.

As he was stopping he stared back, trying to see what had scared the dog. Seeing nothing, we walked on down the hill. Liesel returned to her place behind. She could have caught a glimpse of an owl or it could have been a cougar.

Another situation that I found myself in one day happened near the bottom of the Woodlot Hill where the logging road forks.

I had ridden Breezie up to there and then turned off to the left to go a short distance from the road to where I could get right to the bank of the Salloompt River. I liked just to sit there on my horse and watch the sparkling clear water as it tumbled and frothed over the rocks that lay scattered all over its bed. This time, however, I didn't go right to the bank.

About 15 feet short of the river something alerted Breezie. He wanted out of there, quickly. I couldn't see anything to worry about.

Liesel wasn't concerned, but she was behind him and on the ground. He, being much higher, might smell something the dog couldn't. He was full of adrenalin. His heart was pounding; I could feel it as I sat on his back. He was as taut as a properly tuned violin string, the "E" string. To me he felt as tho a leaf falling would cause him to blow sky high. He was one tense horse, yet he stayed there. All I did to keep him in that place was not to let him depart. He trusted me enough by then to believe me against all his instincts to flee. I did not want to ask him to leave until he relaxed and his heart had slowed down to a normal rate.

To help him see that a cedar block lying under a dense cedar tree, some 15 feet away, was really not a cougar, I asked Liesel to walk over to it and get up on top of it. As soon as the dog lay on the block, quite comfortably, I could feel his heart rate begin to drop. I think that with Liesel on the block and not being eaten, and me sitting on his back, relaxed but very tuned in to him, made him feel that maybe there really wasn't anything dangerous there, after all. Finally he relaxed, gave a huge sigh, then I walked him slowly away and on home.

All the tense time I was sitting on him, I was not scared. Unsure, maybe, as I really did not know how much he would trust me. Obviously he trusted me a lot, and I trusted him similarly.

chapter 23

MINK, BEES & BEAVERS

In the early days at Lonesome Lake Dad was trapping for the money the family needed to survive there. With no other source of income, Dad bought the south end of the Ratcliff trap line. That gave him access to the furs from the middle of Lonesome Lake south to the north end of Knot Lake, which is about 15 to 20 miles of valley. He also trapped part of the Turner Lake string and a mile or two up the east fork of the Atnarko River, which drains Charlotte Lake. As that required a lot of time for him to be away from home, and a lot of work for Mother, they decided to try farming mink and some other furbearers. Having obtained permits and information to do with farming mink, martens and beavers, Dad also had to buy, and horse-pack in, woven wire for the pens to hold his breeding stock.

The wire came in rolls, some weighing 140 pounds and some were just 100 pounds. As he did not have an even number of each, some packs had to be loaded on the horse with the 100-pound roll of wire lashed to the packsaddle horizontally. The 140-pound one had to be put on vertically, with enough of the weight over the center of the horse to balance the pack. It is essential that horse packs be balanced; if not, your horse will get a sore back. And the pack stands a good chance of turning, with the whole 240 pounds plus the saddle winding up under the horse hanging only by the cinch, now over his back.

Also if a pack is going to turn, the chosen spot for this to happen will be on the steepest, roughest down grade, the reason being that on a down grade a pack rocks the most as the horse eases carefully down over the rough trail.

The pack trail along one of the many grades on the way to Stillwater carries along on the hillside about a hundred feet above the rock-strewn valley floor. At one point the trail angles into a rather sharp turn where there is a more or less permanent landslide path, which always leaves a heap of sand, rocks and broken tree parts in the trail.

In attempting to negotiate this uneven trail bed, an elderly horse, Dick, either stumbled, or bumped his pack on the hillside on his left, and with his 240 pounds knocked off balance, he went off the trail and down the slide path to land, cushioned somewhat by his pack, on the rocky river bed. Dad watched in distress, thinking of at least a broken leg. The old horse untangled himself from his pack, stood up and whinnied, asking where everyone was.

My memory is not clear on how Dad got Dick's pack back up to the trail, or Dick himself. He could have left Dick and his pack where they were while he took the other horses the one-half mile to the Stillwater and unpacked there. Then by following a piece of trail, which descended to the riverbed farther upstream, with one of the other horses he could have taken Dick and his pack back up to the regular trail and on to Stillwater.

I say Dad could have done what I have outlined here, but I simply can't remember.

Dick wasn't seriously injured, but he was pretty stiff for a while. I believe he continued to take a pack each day, maybe a lighter one. Dad really could not afford to let him off entirely. Lonesome Lake would not hold off freezing over just because someone might want to use it to haul freight on.

Without any more serious interruptions Dad got all his fur farming materials home. He could then begin assembling pens for the wild mink and beavers he hoped to catch in live traps.

The live traps for the mink were wire cages about two feet long and some eight inches square. A sturdy door was hinged to the top of one end of the cage in such a way that it could be opened up against the top of the cage. To set the trap, the door could be balanced lightly on a bent piece of wire that was attached to a triangular piece of heavy wire fastened to the top of the cage at the back end. The triangular piece was then attached by another wire to the end of a piece of board lying on the bottom of the cage. The animal had to walk on the board to take the bait that was hung from the wire at the back end of the cage. Depressing the board would pull the wire bit off the edge of the door, allowing it to close behind the animal. A spring on each side of the cage would engage behind the closed door in such a way that any animal inside the cage could not pull the door open and escape.

Pens for the mink to live in were made with the same kind of wire as the traps were. The pens were 10 feet long, four feet wide and four feet high. A two-foot-square door set in the corner of the front end of the pen allowed access by mink or humans, for cleaning or any other reason.

At the back end of the pen there would be a single mink bed box for non-breeders or out-of-season breeders. The single bed boxes were built out of two-inch-thick cedar planks, hand split and planed. There was a four-inch in diameter entry hole near the top of the box, and a roof of another two-inch-thick plank lay over the top of the box to keep out snow and rain. On top of the pen over the bed box was a shake roof covering one half of the pen, giving the mink extra shelter and security.

The bed boxes were half filled with fresh, dust-free meadow hay. The mink quickly made his or her bed in the hay. Only one mink could live in each pen, except at breeding time, and then for only a brief, very brief, time. If she weren't quite ready for him, she'd chew his head off, or at least sound like she would. Their problem, of course, was the pens. Fences make a lot of trouble for animals that can't go away when told to by a dominant one, so mink ranching can get rather frantic at times. And the mink do often hurt each other because of the fences.

The whelping boxes were much larger than the single bedrooms and had at least two rooms, sometimes three. These boxes were also built out of two-inch-thick, hand-split and planned cedar planks. These birthing dens were three feet long, 14 inches deep and 18 inches wide. I am guessing now, as I have not seen one for over 50 years and the 2004 fire took them all. The entry hole for the mother mink was near the bottom of the box, so the little kits could get in and out easily once they got old enough to toddle outside and see their world. As mink babies are born hairless and with their eyes closed, it is a while before they can make their way outside.

We laid slabs of cedar bark under the wire on the bottom of the pen, for about half the length of it, to prevent baby kits falling thru the one-inch mesh of the woven wire bottom of the pen.

Mother mink are very protective of their babies and will attack a great horned owl if it lands on top of the mink's pen. Owls just love minced mink. Mamma runs along upside down under the top of the pen, trying to scare the owl away. The owl doesn't scare, but reaches his talons thru the wire and rips the belly out of the poor mink. After one horrifying tragedy of this kind, we put a roof over the entire pen rather than just over the bed box.

The wild-caught mink took quite a while to learn to trust people, but the ones we raised there were quite tame, tho they never became really tame. Some of the ones born in the pens I believe were tame enough to begin eating their food as soon as it was set down for them.

They sometimes tried to escape. I clearly remember one attempt. Mother had just opened the door to set the mink's dish down when she came flying in about two leaps the length of the pen to go out the door, diving under Mother's right arm. In an eye-blink reaction Mother clamped her arm down on the escaping black streak. She held it there as each end wiggled franticly releasing a pungent aroma from one end and, I believe, trying to gain a red-hot tooth hold with the other. Mother flung the struggling creature back into her pen and slammed the door. The air reeked!

Food for the mink was prepared daily, so it would be fresh and appetizing. When I was too young to help much with the preparing, I seem to remember one or both of my brothers grinding the meat and carrots thru the meat-grinding mill, hand powered, of course. If we didn't have beef, squawfish or fresh squirrels, we opened up a jar of canned horsemeat to grind up with the carrots. To this Mother added some sort of cereal to make a balanced and attractive dish. That was when I learned just how delicious horsemeat really was, just as good as beef, better than some. Each mink had a one pint enamel dish to eat out of, and half of a 28-ounce tomato can hung on the side of her or his pen to drink out of.

Mother always fed the mink. Non-breeders were fed once a day. Mother mink ate two times daily, and more in each feed if they were nursing. I believe they received a richer ration also.

When the mothers were getting ready to whelp, they were moved from the area near the house where the non-breeders lived to a special maternity ward way back in a dark cedar forest along the upper reaches of Homecreek, where there would be a lot less disturbance to worry the mothers with their babies. Mink like their environment to be quiet and calm, especially when they have their kits.

When the young ones were weaned and on their own, mum no longer felt responsible for them. Then they were all moved back closer to the house, making the feeding job much easier.

While the mink feeding was not a hard job, it often was a very cold one in winter. With frost on our house windows, the snow squeaking with every step and the trees popping all thru the forest, Mother and I went out to feed the mink. She carried a bowl of prepared warm mink food in one hand and a big teakettle of very hot water in the other. I lugged a container of cooler water.

Each mink's water can would be frozen solid and needed taking out of the pen to have hot water poured over its bottom to thaw the ice enough that it would fall out of the can. New warm water was poured in and given back to the mink. This was done while the mink was eating. That mink fed and watered, we could move on to the next pen to repeat the process until all the mink were taken care of. Then we could return to the house and warm up. At least we didn't have to cross any icy foot-logs or wear snowshoes as trappers often had to do.

To catch squawfish for the mink, often the whole family would cross the river in the boat, hike up the pen, then continue around the shallow south end of the Big Lagoon, and along the shore to where the water was deeper and the fat squawfish would come to our hooks, often baited with bits of mice caught the night before. We fished with long, slender pine poles with a length of fish line attached to the tip. When a fish grabbed the hook, the lucky person jerked the pole and flung the fish out of the water and far up on the bank, sometimes catching his or her fish line in an overhanging treetop. Then the line got broken, the fish fell to earth, and another hook had to be tied on so the fishing could continue.

We fished until we had as much as would keep without refrigeration, then took our load of food home. There were many squawfish in that lagoon. One could see them swimming slowly along near the boat if you just let it drift.

Dad had quite a few mink, all penned up and producing kits every year. He could have made a lot of money, but with the capricious fur market and the fact that the customers of furs—fine, rich ladies who desired wild mink coats—our ranch mink couldn't compete. There isn't a lot of difference between farm-raised mink pelts and wild-caught ones, but there is some. The pelts of wild mink are usually longer furred, due to the fact that they spend a lot of time in the water and rubbing themselves in the snow. Also they have a bit more shine to the fur than the confined ones do.

Then the Great Depression finished us. For all the work raising the animals, in the early thirties mink prices crashed along with everything else. A mink pelt that should have brought 20 dollars would sell for a disappointing three dollars. It was time to pack up the mink venture. The martens and beavers had already been put to bed.

The beavers escaped too many times. They simply were not content to stay in captivity in a small 100-foot-square fenced-in pond on a creek. They wanted to build their own dams where they chose, on their own. Determined to get out of their nice big pen, a beaver would select a section of the fence and begin working on a single strand of wire, using his very effective orange chisels single-mindedly until he simply wore it out and he had a small hole in the fence. Encouraged, he continued chewing, strand after strand, until there was a beaver-sized hole. Then out he slipped to waddle off down the creek to freedom and the river.

Dad tried several times to improve the fence, but with those ceaseless endeavors of the beavers, it always failed.

In spite of the escapes, they did manage to raise one kit. I don't remember what happened to it, but I do remember feeding the youngster carrots thru the wire fence. I'd push it thru the fence to the kit, who took it, sat up on his haunches and nibbled away at the carrot as he held it in those manipulative hands.

The martens were even more unsuccessful than the beavers. They didn't escape, but it took too much fooling around trying to get the girls bred. Martens don't mate in the winter, then whelp a couple of months later as mink do, Dad found out. They mate in the middle of the summer, then give birth about eight months later. This is called delayed implantation of the embryo, something martens, fishers and other members of the weasel family do. The martens were just too much trouble and he quit trying to raise them, tho there was one kit born in the pen.

For the martens Dad used one pen the same size as the mink pens, but, in addition, he stood another similar sized pen on end with a doorway between them. In the vertical pen he put a branchy tree for the martens to play in. Martens love trees and are as handy as squirrels.

The one kit they did raise became a tame pet and ran around the house free. She liked jam or any fruit. She loved to curl up in a round-bottomed bowl, after rocking herself in the bowl for a while. The fruit sauce she liked we called marten sauce, but we ate it too.

Martens are quite social and in the wild often come together to play and talk to each other. And they sometimes sleep cuddled together and wrapped in each other's arms. As they hunt singly, they constantly travel and cover a vast area, running over the snow on a circuit that brings them back to where they have a short visit. Then they are off again, separately, thru the woods. I have never seen more than the tracks of a single marten at a time on the many miles I have traveled in the winter just hiking to Lonesome Lake to feed the trumpeter swans each day.

Martens are very gentle and tame up easily. They will accept an offering of meat from one's hand on very short acquaintance with a human who sits quietly—and gentle. They will take a piece of meat from a person's fingers without touching those fingers with their own sharp teeth.

Altho in the mid-summer breeding season the males give off a rather strong odor, the rest of the time they are very odorless except for a very mild scent of tree bark and woods. Well, they live in trees, dash thru the branches, up and down tree trunks as they chase after equally adroit and speedy squirrels.

My brother John gave me much of the information I have written here. He had martens coming to his house, sleeping in his cupboards, and taking meat out of his hands, sometimes a marten at each hand. He kept a record of each one that came to him. They can be identified easily by the orange markings on their throat and on down between their front legs. They are all different, he found. He made accurate sketches of each one. So when a new marten came he could check to see if it was an old one he had a record of, or a brand new one. They came to take meat from him so soon after arriving, sometimes he would not have known if it was one he had fed before or not if he hadn't had the sketch. They are very interesting little creatures.

One other venture Dad tried at The Birches was bees, thousands of them. And honey by the quart, no, by the pounds. We had 180 pounds of honey one year. We could cook with it. We could spread it on our bread. Mother made honey drop cookies by the dozen. They were good! We had lots of honey.

As the fields were producing clover, and there were many other nectar producing plants around, such as the hated and persecuted dandelion, fireweed and some other wild plants the bees could find, why not try them?

Again, Dad sent away for materials and instructions for building beehives, and frames for the bees to use for egg laying and storing honey. He built two hives with hand-split and planed lumber, and then ordered a couple of packages of bees, about 60,000 of them, to come to Atnarko by mail.

The packages were wooden boxes about a foot long, six or eight inches high and four or five inches wide. I believe both sides were of fine screen so the bees could get adequate ventilation. They needed cooling as much as they needed to be warm. The queen was in a small cage with several attendants. I seem to remember the mail carrier was quite concerned about the bees getting loose and attacking en masse, but that didn't happen.

Dad packed the bees home and soon had them in their new hives. It was up to the bees to release the queen by eating away a plug of honey, allowing her to get out and begin her job of laying millions of eggs.

We had a honey extractor and with it we harvested the honey from the filled and capped combs. With this hand-operated machine we could extract the honey easily. We collected the liquid honey in large containers.

We had bees for quite a few years, but in time the honey producing plants seemed to become fewer and fewer. Then the bees couldn't find enough nectar to feed on over the winter and give us any, so we ended up stealing all the honey and giving the bees sugar candy. That was not a very good exchange. The sugar had to be bought and horse-packed in. In time the bee venture ceased also.

Over winter the bees' activity does slow down, but they don't hibernate. They form a ball of bees that can move in or out, as some get too warm and others get too cool. On warm days in late winter, when it is over 50 degrees Fahrenheit they come out of the hive, have a drink and fly around in the sunshine. Then they return to the hive and wait for spring.

chapter 24

DON & TOPSY

When my father started at Lonesome Lake he didn't have any horses there, but he soon corrected that lack. He did have two horses, but they were at the Stillwater, 10 miles away. At that time there was no trail around Lonesome Lake. Later Dad would correct that little matter, too.

To get a horse to Lonesome Lake Dad hiked over the mountain that lies east of Lonesome Lake to the Chilcotin Plateau, where many horses could be had if they could be found in the meadow-dotted pine clothed vastness of the area.

At one rancher's place there were several young horses in a corral, seemingly just waiting to go to Lonesome Lake. Dad was very interested in those young horses and with the rancher, looked them over. The colt my father settled on buying was a yearling that seemed like he would grow up to be a large enough horse to do the work Dad would have for him. After some time spent halter training this youngster, Dad headed for home with the light brown yearling, later called Kid.

Of course Kid had to grow up before he could do any farm work, so in the meantime Dad acquired some other horses. One was elderly, another one was too small to do much in harness, tho she was a good packhorse and she was nice to ride. She was called Queenie. The other one was Old Blue, an ornery plug from the Cariboo Road where he worked in a stagecoach team. He could carry a pack well enough, unless it rattled. If it did, then he would unload it and scatter it about along the trail. He especially liked to do this if he was on a rocky piece of trail and his pack was jars. More than once he did that.

Sometime after Dad settled at Lonesome Lake he improved the game trail along the west side of it so he could get horses to the north end of the lake. I do not know when this happened. It was not a pack trail, but it was easy to move horse gear and supplies across the lake by boat.

When Dad and Mother decided to try raising mink, martens and beavers, one of the things they had to learn was what diets these fur bearers needed. Feed for the beavers could easily be obtained on the farm, but the mink and martens required protein. The cheapest source of this was horsemeat whenever they could buy an old horse cheaply.

On one meat-horse buying trip to the Anahim Lake area, Dad bought a mean adult bay mare with rickets. She could hardly walk, tho she seems to have been quite capable of kicking cows and horses. In addition to "Wobblelegs," he bought two yearling fillies for five dollars each. Wobblelegs cost 10 bucks. In those days it wasn't uncommon to buy a 40-dollar saddle for a 10-dollar "hoss." Wobblelegs became mink feed right away. The two little fillies would have to grow up some before they could fulfill their supposed destiny.

Needless to say the family fell in love with those pretty, sweet little girls, and their new destiny was assured. One, a dark bay with a narrow white strip down her face and one white hind foot was Susan Ann, called Susan. The other, something of a tomboy, was Topsy. She was a bright bay with four white feet and a broad white face mark.

I can still see them as skinny little hungry things pulling dry and brittle moon-vines off the poles on the sides of the porch the vines had climbed up the summer before. There was snow on the ground and all their ribs showed thru their winter coats. My people were short of hay and were trying to winter too many animals over too long a winter. They tried to balance the feed and stock better after that winter.

Susan and Topsy grew up to quite good-sized mares. Susan became the teammate for Kid—Ginty by then. Until that time he had been doing the horse work alone.

Topsy was used for packing, along with Susan and Ginty, when the year's supplies were brought in. While Topsy waited to do her packing job each fall she spent her summers at the Stillwater, alone, but with lots of good grass. The area where she lived had been mostly cleared and seeded with good grass and clover by one of the half brothers to Uncle Frank. On that good feed she grew fat, round and sassy.

When Dad was bringing in the year's supplies each fall he would have the truck bring them as far up the road as possible. He met it there with the horses. He then began moving the stuff to Atnarko, a very small settlement of just two or three inhabitants. At Atnarko Dad could put the freight in an out-building owned by my Uncle Earle, his brother, and my Aunt Isabel (writer of *Ruffles on My Longjohns*). The horses were turned out in the fields to graze.

From Atnarko, Dad could begin packing it to Stillwater. There the slow job of taking it up that weed-filled river, in a rowboat, began with about 800 pounds to a boatload. How Dad would have enjoyed an outboard motor.

With all the freight at the south end of Stillwater, the horses would also be moved to that end. The last stretch of trail would be covered faster than the others had been, as Dad could make two trips to Lonesome Lake each day and he would leave some of the swan feed at Stillwater.

Finally, with the supplies all at the north end of Lonesome Lake, the horses could go home and the boating would soon see the freight home.

After any fall work that required horses was finished they would go to the fall pasture at Elbow Lake. When the snow became too deep, they would be brought in to the farm for the winter.

On one of Dad's mail trips out to Atnarko there was a black, ungainly, skittish colt grazing in the yard where he stayed overnight answering mail. After learning this colt was for sale, he began thinking about the fact that old Ginty wasn't young any more and maybe he should buy the colt and try raising a replacement for the old fellow.

That fall when Dad came home at the finish of the packing job he had the young stud colt with him. At 18 months, he seemed to be gangling and all legs and head. Topsy hated the youngster, even tho he was very polite and did his best to keep out of her precious way. Topsy was nice to people, but seldom passed up an opportunity to bite or kick any horse or cow if she thought she could get away with it. Except Ginty. Ginty ruled, and would punish Topsy if she kicked other animals. Or him.

One evening the four horses were lined up along the manger, eating their supper. The young stallion, Don, was at one end of the manger, as far from Topsy as he could get, quietly eating. Topsy left her food at the other end of the manger, walked past Ginty and Susan to where Don was, then stopped and sized up the situation. Seeing Don was trapped in a corner at the end of the manger, she turned deliberately around and began disciplining the helpless young horse. There was no place Don could go and she was kicking him with machine gun rapidity. We all were in the house at the time, about a hundred feet away. Racing outdoors, we yelled at her.

She shot out of there as if we had touched her with a high powered stock prod (an electrified implement commonly used to move cattle at rodeos). After that all the horses were tied up while they were eating.

Don matured a lot thru the winter. By spring he was starting to arch his neck and fuss the mares. Topsy remained bossy and mean, sometimes kicking Susan if Don wasn't close enough.

I seem to recall Dad worked Don and Ginty together on some of the spring work. Finally Susan was bred, so we took Don and Topsy to the Stillwater. As soon as they were across the river, Topsy had her brief moment of sex.

Ginty and Susan did the rest of the spring work and the haying. Then it was time to do the fall horse packing. Ginty was failing and tired, but Dad thought he at least could manage a light pack. He might have, too, if we had just kept him away from Don. But Dad sent both Ginty and Susan across the river to where Don and Topsy were, then all hell broke loose.

Don was now a stallion with a band of mares. He wanted that sub-standard horse as far from his mares as he could send him. It probably would have been all right if the mares had just allowed Ginty to escape, as he wanted to do. However, Susan considered Ginty hers. She had lived and worked with him for years. She insisted on following the old fellow away from Don. All of Don's instincts drove him to punish the gelding. Finally Ginty escaped back across the river, and Don and the mares let him go.

Poor old beaten-up Ginty tried to go home. He made it to about halfway between Stillwater and Lonesome Lake. There he staggered off the trail and died beside a shallow creek. Of course we blamed Don, but it was really human error, due to a tragic lack of knowledge about how horse families worked. Ginty should never have been taken down to the Stillwater.

That was the first year that I helped Dad on the packing. He certainly needed help with two mares and an un-mannered, lively stallion. He couldn't lead them together on the pack trail without the risk—almost certainty—of at least one of them being pushed off a grade and killed or injured. There was no way Dad knew about to keep the stallion from playing with the mares without separating them with two people leading them all.

With the three horses we began the work of moving the freight to Atnarko from wherever the truck delivered it. There was an old log cabin there where we could store the freight and live in ourselves. There was a stove to cook on and two beds in the cabin. We stabled the horses in the barn and fed them hay. Don lived in a box stall with a strong door.

It was at that cabin that Dad learned another thing about horses. Don was tied to one corner of the building. Dad was ready to finish packing up, doing Don last because he, being new at the job, tended to fidget if he was packed and then left while the others were getting their loads on. And Don sometimes ate some of his pack.

Dad stepped quietly to Don's side and began doing something to the saddle when WHAM!

Dad backed, or was flung, away and he rolled on the ground, uttering some expression of surprise and pain. Don, badly startled, backed away from the building. I was in the cabin, and hearing the commotion, rushed to the door. Dad was still on the ground, I think. Don had wandered off a bit. I caught him, then helped Dad into the cabin to his bed. He had received a pretty good blow to his right leg just above the knee. I am a bit hazy here, but I think we did not make a trip to Stillwater that day.

I believe there was some talk to the effect that Don should have been gelded five or six months earlier, but the cause of the accident had nothing to do with him being a stallion. The gentlest mare might very well have done the same thing under the same circumstance. Dad had received what is known as a cow kick, a forward kick employed to protect the animal's tender belly. Don was asleep, with his head past the corner of the building. He could not see Dad and not know he was there. He just felt something touching his side and gave an eye-blink reaction.

The forgoing reminds me of a similar response, many years later, from one of my own horses. This horse, Breezie Future, was eating hay with his head in his manger and couldn't see me clearly unless he turned his head towards me. There was a pole along his side to keep him straight in his standing stall.

To put sawdust on his floor for the night, I just put the bucket over the pole and kind of under his belly. Well, you should have seen the fast footwork that little palomino gelding exhibited! He kept that old pail airborne for several seconds. His leg moved so fast it was a blur.

I moved close to his head, speaking to him. Then he seemed to wake up and let the bucket fall to the floor, tho he still kept one eye on it for a bit longer. The sawdust should have been put on the floor when the barn was cleaned.

I retrieved the pail with a long pole. I could have reached my arm under him once he knew it was just me, but I felt better using a pole. He had been frightened.

I think Dad had recently put nice new shoes on Don, making the kick worse than a bare hoof would have, tho not much. A horse can kick with so much power.

After taking a day off for Dad's badly injured leg, we went back to packing the next day. It would be weeks before his leg would be healed.

When we got a raft load to the north end of Lonesome Lake, Mother, John and Stanley brought a raft and the boat down the lake and took home a good lot of the freight. Then it turned cold. Before we could get all the stuff off the lake Mother and her crew managed to get a second raft load to within two miles of home, then ran into ice. The lake was frozen over from the Narrows right to the head. They arrived at the Narrows after dark, cold and dog-tired. They tied up on a sandy beach.

As there were no outboards on the lake at that time, they had moved the big freight raft—12 feet by 36 feet—by towing it from the boat, a slow and extremely exhausting job. Fortunately Dad had left some of the swan feed at Stillwater. They went ashore to camp.

It was so dark the only way they could find firewood was to search thru the forest until they found a birch tree, by feel. They stripped off some loose bark and got a little fire going. With an anemic little fire to give them light they could find some wood lying on the ground. Also, they broke dry branches off of several fir trees to make a better fire.

With the packing finished, and Dad still pretty sore, he and I started around the lake on the improved game trail, rough but usable. I took the two mares ahead, the same as we did when packing, and Dad came behind with Don in front of him. Don needed holding back so he could not push the mares off the narrow trail. Dad had tried taking Don ahead of the mares, but he wouldn't go at all then, he just wanted to keep turning around to watch them.

Poor Dad, the agony he suffered as he was pulled willy-nilly down steep grades and had to keep up. He just couldn't let the horse go loose. He was screaming as all the injured tendons and muscles were stretched at every step down the slopes.

It turned out later that as painful as it was, it was the best thing that could have happened to him. The leg had healed with those tendons and muscles shortened and grown onto the bone. After that rather severe treatment, the leg finally healed properly and he could walk without pain, as far as I know. But it took a while—a painful while.

Finally, we all arrived at the Narrows, where we would normally swim the horses to the east side of the lake. There was no horse trail over a series of talus and bluffs south of the Narrows to the head of the lake except about a quarter of a mile to a sharp spit, called Sandspit, jutting into the lake. We had to tie the horses there and leave them for the night. We could continue on around the lake on the rough going, where it was not possible, or safe, for horses.

As the boat was locked north of the ice, we had only the old Indian dugout to use for transportation. We used it to transport sacks of hay to the hungry horses, for three or four days, until we could build a trail for perhaps a mile along the rocky shore to where the horses could wade across to the willow and sedge meadows at the head of the lake.

We still couldn't get the last of the freight, boat and raft home. We began horse packing on the east side with Susan and Topsy. As soon as we did that, a warm south wind howled thru the valley and melted all the ice. We got the rest of the stuff, raft and boat home at last.

The next job, after putting windbreaks behind the apple trees, would be to take the horses to the fall pasture for a short time until the snow got too deep. Then they and the cattle would be brought in for the rest of the winter, where they would be fed hay from the barn.

Before spring it became obvious that both mares were expecting. Sometime in the early spring they were taken to the summer range to have their foals. Don stayed home to do the spring work by himself.

In due time, in May, Topsy gave birth to a bay colt; then Susan birthed a huge bay colt, also in May. Both were healthy and strong.

While Susan and Topsy were on pasture having their babies, Don finished up the spring work. Then he decided that as there was no more work at The Birches for him to do, he might just as well hike off down to the Stillwater. Perhaps there would be a mare or two just waiting for him to show his handsome black face. Don, despite his unpromising appearance as a gangling yearling, as a three year old he had grown into one beautiful creature, with shining eyes, arched neck, and powerful carriage, and still gentle.

Alas, there were no mares there. So he had a long, rough hike, including swimming the Narrows by himself, for nothing.

With two healthy colts on the ground and doing well it was finally time to turn him into a gelding. Dad would have preferred to have him at home in case he got infected from the operation, but as he already had gotten himself to the Stillwater, Dad decided to leave him there and geld him where he was.

We all went down with lots of ropes, as that was one job where you can hardly have too much help. It is very difficult to convince a large, strong animal to lie down quietly. We got the job done, then came home, hoping for the best. Our hopes were in vain.

A week or so later Dad went to Atnarko for mail, checking Don on the way. He seemed healthy enough, but the next day when Dad returned Don was dead. Just like that and no obvious cause. It was a heart-breaking loss. He was a good and handsome horse.

chapter 25

Susan E.

As I write this in the winter of 2008 it is almost 58 years ago Susan E. lost her life in the icy water of the north end of the Big Lagoon, just five feet from dry land. For all of those nearly 58 years I have carried a burden of guilt for forgetting to take an axe with us when Mother and I rowed the boat down the river to look for a missing horse.

I had been in the process of putting the cattle in the barn for the night when I heard a horse whinny on the field across the river. As horses usually don't whinny unless they get separated for some reason, I hurried down to the river, about 300 yards from the barn, and crossed the bridge to see what they wanted.

They seemed to be telling me that Susan was in trouble somewhere. I rushed off down the long strip of land that lies between the river and the Big Lagoon, checking for the little mare anywhere she could be tangled up, or whatever. Following the fresh tracks of the three horses who had run up from the lower end of the meadow land and islands that they lived on, I came to an open channel separating the land I was on from an island. I assumed the missing horse was on that island or on some other island beyond. The grass on both sides of the channel was well eaten down, and the muddy ground was tracked up as if the horses had spent a lot of time there.

Not wanting to wade across the icy channel, and also not knowing but what she could have been on any of several islands, which I couldn't wade to, I rushed back to the house to get mother and some rescue equipment. She could have been stuck in a ditch or braver hole, of which there are many there. Thinking only to look on the land, I didn't even glance across the ice on the lagoon. Our rescue stuff did not include an axe, either.

Away we went to the river, launched the boat and headed downstream. With the boat we could at least roughly search the islands on the other side of the river. Then just as we were passing the channel that I didn't want to cross, Mother spotted a dark horse head sticking out of the ice several hundred feet away near the west shore of Big Lagoon. It was Susan.

Even rowing as hard as I could, we required too much time getting to where she was. We had to go too many hundreds of yards to the closest place we could land the boat. Then we had to go another several hundred feet along the shore until we were opposite the cold, exhausted, shivering mare, swimming endlessly in a pond about 15 feet in diameter and 140 feet from shore. A desperate whinny welcomed us there.

Since we had no axe to chop out a channel for Susan to get to shore, Mother hurried home to get one, a trip of about three miles by the time she returned, very tired. In the meantime I got a pole to lay on the ice to try to keep me from joining Susan. I used another shorter pole to break the thin ice near the open water. Then I spent the next span of time trying to get a loop of rope over Susan's head. As I wasn't a roper, it took a long time. I wanted a rope on her so I could keep her on the shore side of the pool. Then, with a pole, I broke what ice was weak enough, to start a channel to shore. I hadn't achieved much until Mother returned with the axe, but then we made better progress.

Susan had stopped swimming and shivering. She was just too cold. She lay in the water and let Mother keep her head out of it as we moved along as I chopped the channel out. I don't remember any concept of the passage of time as I chopped the three-inch-thick ice into blocks and shoved each one away under the ice.

When we were near the shore Mother went to the boat for the

rescue stuff. It didn't look like Susan would be able to walk out of the water herself as she was so cold. So much time in that ice water must have weakened her greatly. She had been in there for about two hours by then, I think.

Before Mother returned with the ropes Susan's feet hit bottom and she stood up, only to collapse onto the water again, sticking her nose into it briefly. I pulled her nose out, then dropped to my knees there on the edge of the ice and pulled her head onto my lap and cuddled her as the life went out of that courageous little mare that we couldn't save.

At the moment she died it seemed the surrounding forest stood still, and in silence, to honor a brave mare. Then across the frozen lake a small group of trumpeter swans trumpeted a muted requiem for her.

All the time hunting for her and trying to make a rescue, I felt energized and tireless. Then suddenly, with nothing more to do in a hurry, I felt utterly drained, completely flat and profoundly sad. I imagine Mother must have felt much the same. Of course we didn't talk about it. We had to be strong.

We still had to row back up the river for a mile, against the slight current. Walk up to the barn, finish the chores, have supper…I can't remember…then fall into bed and try to sleep. For myself, I did not do much sleeping for seeking an answer to the question: Why? There is no answer.

Dad came home from the trap-line a few days later, tired and wet with sweat, as usual. Mother and I waited until he at least had a night to rest up before he had to hear about the death of his favorite horse.

Having heard our account of the demise of Susan, Dad just remarked that her time had come, he guessed. This was not what I needed to hear. We all three remained sitting on our respective stools, as alone as if we had been 10 miles apart. I believe what I needed, what we all needed, at that moment of shared loss was a three-way hug and a good old family cry.

We couldn't, because one had to be strong. Even a loss as upsetting as this one was, it was still nothing to cry about. Dad's apparent calm acceptance of his favorite mare's death made it appear like he didn't care. But he did care. He didn't seem to know how to express it.

After running this tragedy thru my mind for nearly 58 years, trying to figure out why she went across the ice in a direction away from the other horses and why she didn't cross the channel with the others, I am no closer to an acceptable answer than I was when it happened.

Now as I scour my memory to set down this story about the sad end of a well-loved friend, I have to admit that even if we had taken the axe it would have made very little difference to the outcome. There was just too much time required to get to her. The distances we had to travel were just too great. Mother and I were both exhausted, partly from stress, but mostly from physical labor.

I will lay that guilt burden down and acknowledge we did the best we could with the knowledge we had. If I had seen her when I first went looking for her, it still would have taken too long to get her out of the water and home. That water was cold.

Susan was about the same age as I was and we had known each other for nearly all our lives. With no other companions besides family, the horses and cows were also family and friends.

One can become as attached to some of our non-human animals as one can to human friends, and closer in some cases. A loss, totally unexpected, can be as devastating as if the friend had been a human. Tho the pain of loss does diminish over the years, it never goes away entirely and is very easy to bring back in all its original aching sorrow, even after over 50 years.

chapter 26

TAME MEAT

On a small farm one can have only a few animals. A team of horses is essential for doing all the work these animals perform. To have milk, butter and cream, and meat, a few head of cattle is nice. At Lonesome Lake my parents kept many cattle and had several calves each year, but on my place Jack and I just kept a couple of cows. We did not have as extensive fields as Dad did, nor the ambition to make a lot more hay than we needed for the rather few stock we did have. Anyway we usually had enough cattle that we could have beef each winter for canning and fresh meat for as long as it would keep in winter. We had no refrigeration except for what the weather provided.

With all the cattle my parents raised, sometimes around a dozen head, I don't see now why Dad ever had to hunt deer, except to get fresh meat before it was cold enough to kill a large beef later in the winter. Both Jack and I and my family wanted to have fresh meat as long as possible. We weren't short of food; we would be short of fresh meat. We had canned meat, but it can get a bit boring after eating it for several months.

My people had tried burying hard-frozen beef quarters in snow, on frozen ground, and covered with three or four feet of snow. Expecting something good, they dug the snow off in a month or so and there was only a slimy, stinking mess, completely thawed!

Many years later Jack and I tried building an insulated cupboard on the back wall of the house. With six inches of sawdust for insulation, that small cupboard kept frozen beef frozen for three or more weeks, if it didn't get too warm. Any time it got cold, we opened the door and allowed the meat to cool down again, and that helped.

In the early years when we children were young, and a beef animal was being readied for eating, Mother would play a gramophone record very loud in the vain hope we would not hear the shot, but even in the house we heard it. Then we knew there would be an empty stall, and one fewer animal to feed that night. A sad glance into the empty stall confirmed this.

However, we also knew no animals would have to be rationed and be hungry for the rest of the winter. And we knew there would be fresh beef for dinner. The first meat we would use was the thin diaphragm, sliced thinly. We would look forward to the fresh steak with drooling anticipation as it sizzled and spit in the frying pan and the delicious aroma filled the house. Just thinking about those far off days makes me drool.

Also, when I was young Mother didn't want me to help with the slaughtering of the animals selected for that fate. She told me that I would become hardened to suffering and death and would be unable to feel sympathy for anything. There were many times in my life that I wished to God she had been right. I can't even stand the suffering and sorrow involved in our wonderful wars and other forms of violence.

I think that of all the jobs on a farm, the taking of the life of an animal that you had known from the moment of birth, or one that had become a real pet, such as a grand old milk cow, or was a sweet young heifer that you had trained to lead and was friendly, was the hardest. I feel that the pain and sorrow we feel on the loss of something we love is in direct proportion to all the good stuff we get from that animal while it was alive. Nothing is free.

Even when you know the heifer is destined for the table and you try not to get too emotionally involved with her, it doesn't help much. A lot of the misery we suffer is caused by the sense of betrayal. You have spent the animal's life since birth showing him or her that you can be trusted. Then one day you turn on her and take her life, hopefully painlessly.

I used to think the victims were quite unaware that we had predatory designs on them. Now many years later, and after a lot of thinking about how non-human animals communicate non-verbally, I have to wonder how much of our thoughts and intentions and feelings we can really hide from the sensitivities of our fellow creatures.

When trying to get close to a horse who doesn't want to be caught because she isn't trusting, you approach very off-hand, glancing all around and only very casually looking at her body, never her eyes. She still seems to know you are hunting. You are telling her by your body. It is saying "hunting made," and she reads you loud and clear.

How the horse responds to your instinctive messages is usually a matter of her making a conscious decision. You can see her choosing to run or not. If she doesn't run, she has decided to take a chance on you. She will allow you walk right up and put her halter on, then receive a carrot, apple or some oats. A horse like this one should never disappoint.

We had one at Lonesome Lake for quite a few years. She would let us catch her more easily for work than to put her in the barn for her supper. Once caught, she was a good worker and packhorse. In fact she was our safest jar-packing horse. After she learned to avoid hitting her pack on trees she never hit anything. It took just hitting a schooling pack of blocks of firewood to teach her to watch and take her pack well around any obstruction along the trail. She also was a very excellent and intelligent puller, who did her utmost to help her teammate move the load. This was Rocket.

When Rocket was in her early twenties she began having trouble lifting her back legs when backing. Her forward gear worked perfectly. The main work finished for the year, we put Rocket, Cloud and Guenevere out on fall pasture where they would be able to find food for a month or so.

Around Christmas time we went out to bring them in for the winter. Rocket was having a lot of trouble walking, as her back end was not working properly and it would drift off to one side or the other, and it was with great difficulty that she could get herself straightened up again. She had to put her head low and use her shoulders to force the rest of herself straight. As the trail along the lakeshore was quite narrow and had several short steep pitches, tragedy was almost inevitable. Going down one particularly steep part, her back end lopped sideways and carried her off the trail and down the slope to the lake, where she landed on her feet in two feet of water along a narrow beach, about 20 feet below the trail. There she struggled along close to the shore, finally coming to rest draped over a large boulder, with her right hind leg crossways over the rock and under her belly. Her front legs supported the front end of her.

The other two horses stayed up on the trail. Jack came down to the lakeshore to see if there was any way we could get her back up to the trail. I had already gone down with Rocket, as I was leading her. We discussed the matter of rescue, and as it didn't look at all promising, given her failing rear end, we decided the kindest thing was to put her out of her misery. And one look at her totally defeated, exhausted expression convinced me that she was almost, if not expressly, begging for a quick end to her suffering. At that moment she might even have welcomed a wolf. She knew there was no hope for her. I never had seen such a look of lost hope. For once, giving her the only relief, or release, possible under the circumstances was almost painless to us.

On the way home with Cloud and Guenevere, and seeing many worse places where Rocket could have fallen down the hillside into the boulder-filled river, we were very thankful she fell where she did.

On the way up to get the horses a strange thing had happened to me. It lasted only a few seconds. At the outlet of the lake, not Lonesome Lake, but Rainbow Lake on the Atnarko River, about five miles south of Lonesome Lake, the trail comes out on top of a small bluff where one can look up the lake about three miles. Going along this trail, and pausing just to gaze up the lake, suddenly everything around me went almost dark, and a clear picture of two dark horses struggling in the lake formed in my mind. Rocket was black, Guenevere was bay, both dark.

A few hours later one of them was in the lake. What did it mean? Did it mean anything?

While on the subject of meat, I am going to mention a funny thing that happened at my folks' house when the young man who became my husband was at their place the first time he came to Lonesome Lake, in April 1955. As Dad was trapping beavers for furs, we were using the meat for our dinner. Beaver meat is not too bad if one soaks it in salt water for a while before cooking it. We had done that and Mother cooked up a pan full for our dinner.

I guess that was the first time Jack had tasted beaver meat. Sometime later he told me how much he enjoyed the meat. It seems like he really didn't enjoy it very much—he had carefully slipped the fat, greasy lumps of strong meat into his shirt pocket. Later he fed it to Mother's dog, Candy, and no one knew the difference.

chapter 27

Start Seven Islands

I seem to remember that I was about 19 when I was bitten with the "get-out-and-find-a-job" bug, and wanted desperately to leave home. I even had an idea that I could make enough money to hire someone to come and help my parents in my stead, but Mother wanted me to stay just a little longer. She really did need some help and I thought I could wait a year or so, then go when Mother's health might be better. I was young yet. I had lots of time, I thought. But it was not to be. Any longing to leave the nest and fly on my own untried wings evaporated like a puddle on hot pavement.

An alternate to leaving was to get my own preemption and remain in the area. I would be available, then, to render any help that was needed. I really did want to stay by then. As I was well aware of the old surveyed lots in the valley, I obtained blueprints of the ones that interested me the most. Choosing the one that looked to have the best possibilities for a farm, I applied for it. I would call my new place Seven Islands (and also eventually known as Fogswamp). I think this move suited my parents very well, for a while anyway.

With an OK on the preemption, I began work on materials for a bridge across the Atnarko River. As the good land on my preemption was on the west side of the Atnarko and my parents' place was on the east side of the river, I had to have a bridge to get from one place to the other. On February 23, 1952, I began preparing logs for a 65-foot long bridge, 10 feet wide, and high above the water. I would build the bridge about half way between my place and my parents' place across a narrow spot, called a Venturi.

Preparing the materials for my bridge meant chopping down 8-to-10-inch-in-diameter fir trees, removing the branches, sawing them to the required length, and stripping all the bark off. Off the logs, and too often off my knuckles. No chainsaw then.

When I had the required logs ready to go to the bridge sight, I took my two harnessed horses across the river at a shallow place, with Rommy carrying the double trees and chain on his hames while I rode Thuja and led him.

The bridge logs lay all about the mixed cedar and fir forest, just where I had felled them. There was not much trouble for the team to pull them out to a more-or-less cleared roadway to the river. The forest was open, with little stuff on the ground except the branches from the trees I had cut down.

Dad helped me build the bridge. We put in the piers, resting against large rocks on the river bottom to support each end of the bridge. There was an approach section from the shore to the top of the piers. Then a central section, 33 feet long, connected the two piers. The 18-foot approach part on the south side of the river was quite steep, but possible for the team to haul a wagon or sled up.

The materials for the main stringers, approach stringers, decking and braces for the south end of the bridge I cut on that side of the river. That material I hauled with my team. On the east side of the river the materials were farther away and had to be hauled over a narrow trail. I separated the two horses and used them singly. I hitched Rommy to his load, then Thuja to hers, and sent them off down the trail to the bridge, while I came along with my peavey in case a load got hung up on a rock or stump. Those two horses were very calm and probably as trustworthy as horses ever can be.

A short way downstream of the Venturi bridge site, the river suddenly is very wide, rock-strewn but shallow, with small rapids. During cold spells this piece of river slushes up and rises several feet, building fancy ice formations here and there on branches that hang down over the water and catch drops that are flung into the air as the river hustles past. In time it might freeze right over with a foot or more of ice, if it stays cold long enough.

With the thaw that always follows a cold spell, the ice jam melts, the water level falls and the ice drops into the river, leaving a foot-thick shelf along the bank two feet above the river bottom. This had happened in February 1952.

To make it possible for my horses to get into the river from the ice shelf I had chopped steps in the ice so they could step down to the rocky river bottom and not have to jump down on the rocks. Also, as I had tools and harness to get across the river, all on the horses, I surely didn't want them to jump.

One day, going across riding Rommy and leading Thuja, she stopped out in the river just when Rommy climbed up the ice steps. Rommy didn't "whoa," Thuja didn't come. I was being stretched between them as Rommy continued to walk. Thuja's rope wouldn't stretch at all and she had her head up, so she could not see where to put her feet. I was damned if I would let her rope go. I didn't want to have to wade into that icy cold river to retrieve her rope and her. Only one thing could happen. As Rommy wouldn't stop, I was being slowly pulled off his back. I fell onto the ice on one shoulder, cracking a small bone on top of the shoulder joint. Rommy stopped then and looked around, as if he asking what the heck was I doing down there.

I still had Thuja's rope, tho. With her head released she could put it down to see where to step in the water and agreed to come up the steps. Going over in the morning she didn't have a problem and stepped down very nicely.

I finally got the bridge finished on November 5, 1953. Then horses could go across the river and not have to wade. I named it for the narrow place in the river—the Venturi Bridge. It stood there for

20 years; then we removed it, piece by piece, as it was getting old and could be unsafe.

With the removal of my bridge I felt a sense of loss. It had served us well. Even with all the braces pulled off and both approaches removed, it refused to fall, with a team giving their all to try to pull it over so we could haul off the central stringers. We didn't want the parts to go down the river and hang up on my parents' floating bridge. We did get it removed, but it sturdily resisted destruction.

Before the Venturi Bridge could be used to cross with horses, I began work on a small 8- by 14-foot cabin in the spring of 1952. Abandoning the bridge for the time being, I made my cabin usable for cooking my lunch each day that I worked on my place. The first time I did that was on April 23, 1952. I do not remember what I cooked, but I am sure it was a real meal not just a little feed of quick-to-prepare food, as lunch usually is. It was the mid-day meal. As I was working hard I needed food to sustain me in my labors.

About a month later I started on a small shed in which I could store hay. There was an acre of natural meadow, already cleared, from which I could harvest meadow forage for hay. It would be by hand, of course.

With my small shed filled with my small amount of hay, I moved my two cows to my place in the winter of 1953, to feed them the hay. Soon after moving them to my place, they became three cattle. The first calf to be born on my new home I named Naseka. I do not know why, now. While I had those cattle there, I lived on my place, but I had only a small amount of hay and it was soon gone. I took the cattle back to The Birches then.

I began riding to Seven Islands each day it wasn't pouring snow or rain. I worked there clearing land, falling trees and cutting the branches off the logs. They would be used for wood, buildings or fence rails. As evening came on, I'd get aboard my horse to ride back to The Birches to milk the cow, then have supper.

I did the feeding and milking in the morning. While my horse ate her breakfast, I had mine. After turning the stock out for the day, I fed the swans, then raced off to Seven Islands. I had my lunch there.

Looking at this account of my days, I seem to have been too busy. Too right. I was working too hard, but I didn't know it then. I felt young and strong, chopping down trees, sawing up logs with a crosscut saw, sometimes called a "misery whip" appropriately enough. But I was getting my farm going. When I quit work for the day, my back would be really tired and sore, but after a one-and-a-half-mile canter on Thuja I felt fine.

In March 1953, with Venturi Bridge still unfinished, I hauled some birch logs to The Birches to be milled into lumber by Dad's sawmill. I hauled them on a sled I had built. It had a tongue hinged to the front end of the runners so the horses could keep the sled from ramming into their legs on a down-slope. It also stayed on the road better than a sled pulled by a chain fastened to the front crosspiece did. Without the use of the bridge, I crossed the river with the sled load of logs, the same place where I crossed when riding, where it is wide and shallow.

Even tho I seemed to be working long hours, progress was slow. One reason for this was because a lot of the time I was helping Dad with getting and preparing materials for a 40- by 40-foot hangar for the airplane we hoped to get.

With six mudsills in place on the ice, we could begin the real construction. The sills, posts and braces for the floor of the hangar could all be hauled out on the ice, ready to be put in place.

Just getting the materials required a nearly one-half-mile drive up on the lower slopes of the east mountain, to where there was a good stand of long, straight young firs, the result of a forest fire about a hundred years earlier. There were many such stands of young trees throughout the valley. We needed many timbers 42 feet long for sills and plates, as straight as possible.

The floor was 40 by 40 feet, but the hangar itself was 30 by 40 feet, leaving a 10- by 40-foot porch on the lagoon side, so the big double doors would have some place to stand when open.

With the timbers cut, trimmed of branches, peeled and sawed to length (no chainsaw then) we could begin hauling them to the building site. A round trip required a mile of traveling. Fortunately they didn't all come from so far away, but a lot did. As most of the way was downhill, it was fairly easy for the horses coming down loaded. I remember kind of panting, as I had to keep up with the team going up to get the logs. It wasn't that they were going fast; I was going slowly. I have never been able to race up any kind of a slope, and horses seem to want to speed up a bit on hills; and the steeper the hill, the more they feel the need to keep moving right along.

For the six big, strong roof trusses we needed the best timbers we could find. We also needed smaller long, straight pine poles to lay from one end of the roof trusses to the other, parallel to the plates, to be nailed to the sloping members of the trusses. These would have the shakes nailed to them. We found them up on the mountain also.

With the main structure in place, all but the shakes being put on, it was time for me to head for Vancouver and my pilot's license. Dad had to get the shakes on by himself.

On April 25, 1953, I left Lonesome Lake to find my way to the Union Steamship's *Catala*. It would take me to Vancouver. There I would have to find the Vancouver Airport so I could attend flying school. A big job for someone who had never been anywhere farther away from home than Ocean Falls, where it would be pretty difficult to get lost. But as word spread I was met at every corner by concerned and helpful people who guided me in my quest. I am forever thankful for their help.

When I landed in Vancouver, I was met at the docks by my Aunt Isabel's friend, who took me to her home for the night. I cannot remember who it was, but the next day someone took me to the airport on Sea Island where the flying school was. I think the first thing on the agenda was to have a medical check, which I passed easily enough. I was only 24.

Vancouver's U-Fly was the flight school of my choice. The instructors soon had me up in an airplane. I believe there was a small matter of a student's license required before I could take the controls. So, with license in hand, I was up in the air again.

In addition to trying to learn how to fly an airplane, I sort of paid some attention to the males who were present in the school with me. To say I was never interested in any young, handsome or otherwise, men would be a complete lie. The instructors that I had were all quite friendly in a very polite way. They were professionals, after all, doing an important and responsible job. I respected them and trusted them. And I didn't think a single one of them would have wanted to live on a farm at Lonesome Lake; and I believe most of them were already married. But even if I have no intention whatsoever of buying a horse, I still might be interested in looking at one.

After about 40 hours of flying a Cessna 140 around, taking off, landing, practicing, practicing, practicing, the instructor simply got out of the airplane and told me to take it around and land again. I was suddenly afraid. I hadn't had enough practice, I just knew I wasn't ready; I really needed that security blanket. My heart hammered. My mouth went dry, but I did as he asked and somehow took off, circled the airport and landed, still in one piece. It was wonderful. I made more solo flights. Then they gave me a written test. I passed that. Then we went out for the flight test. Passing that, I received my pilot's license.

Weeks later everybody thought I had gotten stuck up there over the airport. I had been flying around the circuit, coming down on an approach to land, only to put on power and go around again. After I had done this three or four times a plane came up and joined me. Those planes did not have radios, so they could not contact me to tell me what to do when I got stuck up in the air. And I couldn't tell them what I was trying to do. As the traffic did not seem very dense, I thought that might be a good time to see if I could just pick a spot on the runway and set my plane down there, instead of just landing any old place the plane wanted to make its way onto the runway.

After an embarrassing discussion in the school about wrong turns, etc., I continued to fly and tried not to break any more rules, and still tried to get my landings more precise.

It was time to find an airplane to buy.

All the time I had been practicing flying I had been staying with either Johnny and Midge Hatch, or Roy and Nancy Moulton. Both Johnny and Roy were pilots who had been to Lonesome Lake several times and were good friends of ours. They were instrumental in locating a light aircraft in Mount Vernon, Washington. I was flown down to look at the plane. As my pilot recommended against it, we flew back to Vancouver and waited some more.

Not too long after that a Taylorcraft was located and flown to Vancouver. I was very interested, but knowing so very little about quality, or safety of used airplanes, I pretty well had to take the advice of those with more knowledge that it would be a good buy at 2575 dollars. I bought it, on floats.

At the time I bought the plane I received word that Mother had gotten her arm either broken or dislocated, doing something with the bull. She needed a trip to Bella Coola, the sooner the better for her. Roy and I took off for Lonesome Lake the next day. Roy flew the plane, as I had no float training.

Landing at Lonesome Lake was wonderful. Dad rushed down to the Big Lagoon and we met there by the new hangar. It was good to see Dad again. Then we all trooped across the field to meet Mother; it was very good to see her, too. I had been away from my parents for about three months, the longest I had been completely away from them, and we had many things to talk about, especially about how she had been hurt by the bull.

It seems it was just an accident. Mother was in the process of tying the bull, named Spicy, from outside his high sturdy fence of large rails when he just moved his head a bit and her arm was in the wrong position for a second. The slight movement of his large and heavy head, with her arm thru the fence to do something with the rope, damaged her wrist.

Mother had just wanted to tie Spicy up to get a cow bred. To tie him one would put some food down for him to eat and catch him while he was engaged in that job. With Spicy secured, the cow would then be let into his corral. He was not a lot of trouble to tie, but turning him loose was the worst job. With the cow in the corral with him, he would be in a "swivet" to get loose and just didn't seem able to learn that standing still would get him loose sooner than yanking on his rope would.

Now to get back to Mother. The next day Roy took the Taylor-craft CF-HEO off the lake with himself, about 210 pounds; Mother, about 140 pounds; and me at 130 pounds and sitting on her knees. He did take a long run to get the plane on the step, but it finally staggered into the air with the 65 small horses giving their all. We landed at Bella Coola and sent Mother off to the hospital to get her arm attended to, and Roy and I headed for Vancouver.

Back at the Vancouver Airport, my float flying could begin. Roy kindly offered to teach me. I guess I was not a very good student; more than once he became rather irritated with my stupid mistakes. One day he actually kicked the rudder, then swore an awful word. It seems he had already bumped his toe on one of his daughter's toys left lying on the floor and his toe was a bit tender. Kicking the rudder pedal didn't help it.

Roy was kind, generous and very helpful to we Edwards, but I don't think he was designed to be a flying instructor. I appreciate all the help and hospitality he gave me.

Anyway, when he kicked that poor rudder and sort of yanked the wheel around, I simply sat quite still, took both feet off my controls and folded both hands in my lap, clearly stating he could fly the airplane for a while until his tantrum was over. Then we went on with the schooling. We didn't have any more disruptions and in a few days Roy considered I could keep the airplane in the air, then land it more or less safely on the Fraser River and dock it there. Soon I had my seaplane endorsement. I was ready to go home.

On my first flight to Lonesome Lake, I felt I made enough mistakes that if Roy had been with me he not only would have kicked the rudder, but my backside as well. Somehow I survived them and didn't even dent the airplane much less bend it.

Arriving at Lonesome Lake, I elected to land on the main lake rather than on the Big Lagoon, as it looked so tiny. That gave me a long taxi to get to the hangar, which was at the south end of the lagoon. I parked the plane as close to dry land as possible, leaving me only a short distance to plow thru the sticky mud to reach that dry land.

After a few landings on the main lake I got a good hold on my courage and set HEO down on the lagoon. By then it had grown a lot and didn't seem so tiny any more.

Soon after returning to Lonesome Lake I flew to Bella Coola to see how Mother was. Her arm had not been broken; her wrist had been dislocated, which was worse. Four days later Mother and I returned home with HEO. Mother's wrist was still pretty sore, but was improving.

With me home there was less work she would have to do and I could write the daily record. Mother had been keeping the record written up, using her left hand. The writing she did with that untrained left hand is surprisingly good and I treasure it.

I had been keeping a daily record of what we did each day, as well as the morning temperature and other weather conditions, and the amount of milk each cow gave each day, since 1947. I still do this, except for the milk; I have no cow now, but I had stopped recording milk amounts before we left Lonesome Lake anyway.

Shortly after I arrived back at Lonesome Lake I flew Dad to Nimpo Lake and Charlotte Lake to visit people there and ask if they'd be interested in having me fly fresh farm produce up to them. We could offer carrots, peas, greens, broccoli, cauliflower, green beans, cabbage, milk, butter, and cream. Would they ever! One day I asked Pat, the lady on Smith's Inlet if she would like some lambsquarters. She said she sure would. Her enthusiasm tipped me off. She was thinking of meat; I was talking about greens. We didn't have the lamb; she didn't want the greens.

I made a lot of trips to those Chilcotin lakes, taking our fresh vegetables and apples to those people who, even living beside a road, could not get anything as fresh as our produce was, and they gobbled it up. It was all quite illegal, of course, because as private pilots we weren't supposed to fly for money, but no one complained, and who were we hurting?

On one of those trips to Nimpo Lake a fellow who had helped me gas the plane a few times and swung my prop to start the engine, as it didn't have a starter, asked if I would fly him to Lonesome Lake. I guessed I couldn't refuse; he had helped me. He was at The Birches two or three days, but on one of those days he got a bit too familiar and chucked me under the chin, right in front of my parents. In my best cow-scolding voice I told him to behave or he could WALK back to Nimpo. I guess he didn't want to walk those 30 miles. He behaved. I did return him to Nimpo.

I also made frequent trips to Bella Coola for mail and supplies, including gas for HEO and outboards. Dad had a five-horsepower outboard by then.

In March 1954 I flew Dad to Ocean Falls so he could take a boat to Vancouver to get his own pilot's license. I headed for home.

Taking off at Ocean Falls, 60 miles from Bella Coola, I set an almost straight course to Lonesome Lake. Climbing all the way to Mt. Stupendous, about 25 miles up the valley from Bella Coola, I was at 10,000 feet and just above the mountain, which is a bit less than 10,000 feet. I swept over the snow-covered summit with barely a hundred feet clear. In a few seconds I was out over the valley, nearly 10,000 feet straight down. What a long way to fall! I reduced power and went the rest of the way to Lonesome Lake on glide. I landed straight in on the Big Lagoon ice. It was warm there in the sun on the ice. Over that high mountain it was cold, even with gloves and warm clothes on.

When Dad returned with his pilot's license, which he had no trouble earning despite being over 60 years old, I checked him out on HEO for a few flights. He was eager to go on his own. I guess he was happy when I let him go. I just hoped he was really ready.

As Dad was in his sixties and I was still young, I let him do most of the flying, thinking I might have a chance to do more flying later in life. It was not to be. I still love to be up in any aircraft, fixed-wing, as well as helicopter. I have never flown in anything larger than 21-passenger DC3s, thru circumstances rather than choice.

chapter 28

PUP, BORDER COLLIE

For years I had wanted a dog. Except for Candy, a young dog Mother had, there hadn't been a dog at my parents' home for many years. Candy was my mother's dog. I wanted my own dog that I would be free to become attached to. It is a very risky business to get too fond of some other person's pet. I was allowed to have a cat or two, but I wanted a dog, a collie dog if you please. That was probably because collies were about all that I had had much acquaintance with, and I had liked just about all of them. I yearned for a dog. I needed a dog.

With my own property, perhaps I could at last have a dog. I wasn't thinking about the fact that as long as I was feeding my cows and horses at my people's place, I was not quite as independent as I would have liked. As I had very little hay on my place, Seven Islands, I pretty well had to help putting up the hay at least, and with lots of other work, too, which involved horses anyway. By then I had the only team in the area. I had stock, but not much hay then.

Anyway, as my parents did not seem too averse to me getting a dog when I did have my own place, I wrote to my Aunt Laura asking her if she could locate a collie puppy for me. She could be brought to Lonesome Lake on our Taylorcraft on one of our trips to Bella Coola. She wrote back that she had found just the puppy for me, and she was free. Aunty Laura told me who had her. All excited and itching to go get my very first dog, I could hardly wait until Dad wanted to make a trip to Bella Coola. At last we went.

Arriving at the home of the people who owned the puppy, I had a great surprise. The puppy was a full-grown dog and was black and white! I had wanted a white and sable collie. I had never heard of black and white collies. It turned out this little dog was what was known as a border collie. And they wanted someone to take her off their hands. I didn't know why then. Anyway, I thought beggars can't be choosers, so I accepted her and hoped for the best.

No one asked the dog how she felt about being taken by complete strangers to a strange place in a strange conveyance. We treated her as one would a vegetable instead of the sensitive being that she was. It never entered my head how she would miss her people. She was three years old, not a good age to change people and homes I wouldn't imagine now.

Concerned that a dog might get scared enough in the plane to bite one of us, I decided to muzzle her with a rope-halter style of restraint. We certainly didn't want a 40-pound scared dog bouncing around in the cockpit at 5000 feet in the air and no place to land short of Lonesome Lake.

She got into the vehicle that had brought Dad and me to the farm, without any problem, and we had no trouble stuffing her into the tiny airplane. She did not seem to worry too much about the flight. She just kept quiet and looked worried, or perhaps betrayed by some of her family.

Arriving at Lonesome Lake, I removed her muzzle. A mistake as it turned out when we met the first cat, tho I didn't turn her loose. Even so, she didn't know that a well-trained dog never pulls on the leash; when she saw the cat, she almost pulled the leash out of my hand in her mad dash for that cat. There was an outraged hiss from the cat, yells from me, Dad and Mother, and a futile yanking on her leash, and more verbal abuse on the confused dog. Some welcome to her new home; but she had acted like an extremely unmannerly guest, what could she expect? You don't chase your host and hostess's cat! No one had taught her that. So that was why they wanted to get rid of her. Actually it wasn't; she had puppies sometimes, and I guess they were tired of that.

The cat having fled from all the noise and fuss, my parents told me to bring the dog in the house and shut the door. That would at least make the cats stay outdoors.

I tied the dog to a table leg and we gave her a blanket for a bed. The table leg would make a good hitching post, as the table was very heavy and the floor was rough. The sorrowful dog sank down on the blanket, laid her muzzle on her paws and silently cried her distress, refusing to look at me or to come out when I called her. She was not only missing her people and her home, I believe she was also upset by having been yelled at, yanked around and sworn at. She was actually a sweet little dog and very sensitive. She just hadn't been given an education on manners, or my conception of them.

I did not know much about how to handle dogs then, and when I told her to come out from under the table, she just lay there and growled at me. And I did not learn much about the art of teaching a dog until about four decades later. But I did have enough sense just to leave her be, there under the table, until she felt like coming out, after she had had time to sort out her feelings. I put a dish of water and some food by her bed, then ignored her. And she ignored the offerings. I know now that she was sad, lonely and felt betrayed. And I felt very sorry for her, as I was the one who had hauled her away from her home and family, making her sad.

Then a couple of days later I was sitting in my chair at the end of the table, right next to where she lay on her blanket, reading out a cake recipe to Mother. One item called for "one cup" of something. Out from under the table that poor little dog came, having heard for the first time since leaving her home a word she knew. Her name was Duchess, but her people must have called her Pup. She hadn't responded to Duchess at all. Anyway, her tail was wagging and she looked up at me, and her eyes lit up with joy. Then she accepted food and started playing and acting generally happy at last.

The next thing Pup had to cope with was the cattle. Outraged, longhorned and banded into a hard-eyed defensive group, they stood shoulder-to-shoulder, cheek skin wrinkled into high ridges, and snorting. They tossed their heads and made distinct hooking motions and lashed their tails. They were dumbfounded to see the humans they trusted standing, seemingly unperturbed, RIGHT NEXT TO A WOLF! The only dogs the cows knew about were wolves, and they certainly should not be allowed to get that close. Wolves were danger.

The cattle learned this little dog was no danger at all, but it took a while.

Pup got even a short time later.

Dad had made a set of steps to make it easier for short people to get stuff in or out of the airplane when it was resting on its floats on the ice or hangar floor. He and Mother and Pup and I were carrying the steps across Barn Field, where there were four or five curious cows. On our way to the hangar we had to cross that field. The curious cattle came galloping over to meet us and see what we had. We set it down. Pup cringed against my legs as the cows investigated the steps. Soon we picked it up and headed once again for the river on our way to the hangar. The cows ran around, bucking and tossing their heads and generally getting in the way. We put it down again and they crowded around once more, had a good sniff, then stood there. When we started once more, the cows bucked and got in the way some more. Not thinking she would do anything, I told Pup to take the cows out of there. Like a shot, she raced around them as they were milling about. She tried to get behind the longhorned defenders, but every time she tried that they all spun around to face her with their horns. Since she couldn't get behind the cows that way, she raced out in front of them, inviting them to chase her. Which they did, happily.

297

When they were all going nicely across the field, running at a furious clip, Pup whipped behind them, barking commandingly, and drove them to where there was a right angle corner in the fence. There the frisky cattle halted, blowing, wild-eyed, heads high, tails lashing. They swung around to glare at her as she dashed back and forth in front of them, holding the critters there until we got to the floating bridge. I called Pup just once and she left the cows and streaked back to me, panting and proud.

I was proud, too. She had courage to face those cows with their wicked-looking horns. And she had done that bit of herding while wearing her muzzle. How can a little 40-pound dog tell five long-horned cows what to do? Speed, intelligence and agility. There was absolutely no way one small dog could bring down even one cow, never mind five. Her strategy was to get them running, but that would be a wolf's strategy also. I have to wonder how we were able to run our cattle out in wolf country for so many years and have so few losses. Wolves would be working in a group, and being so much larger and stronger than the little border collie, it is hard to see why they didn't bother our cattle very much.

Perhaps the fact that we had horns on our cattle helped, and we let them wear bells. After a bit of leg-hold trap education, wolves became very wary of anything that smelled of iron. Dad set traps in his trails and the wolves learned not to travel on any trail that Dad had walked over. If they had to get from one side of the valley to the other, they made a flying leap over the trail, then went on their way, safe.

We also tried to have the calves born at home, and that helped. We did have a few injuries, but no deaths, due to wolves. One cow had several holes punched in one ear and another one lost a rump roast, but survived. Several lost part of their tails.

Pup was too quick to drive the cows without specific directions to do so, and I hadn't yet learned to be more careful of what I said in her presence for the first few weeks that I had her. She and I had gone to the huge raspberry patch and picked a gallon or so into a can of some sort. This patch of thornless raspberries was about a hundred feet long and 15 feet wide. They produced generously and were very delicious to eat. Their berries being large, it did not require much time to fill a pail, unlike those confounded currants of my childhood.

The pail of berries and Pup's leash in one hand, I opened the garden gate where two or three cows stood just outside, glaring at the very polite little dog inside the fence. As soon as I stepped thru the gateway the cows converged on us. Not wanting to be caught between a fence and a set of long horns, I thoughtlessly said to the cows, "Get out of here." The cows knew I wanted them to go away, as they knew I was the dominant animal there. However they had forgotten that fact for a brief moment, but quickly remembered who was boss when that little black and white snip of a dog once again put the run on them, jerking my hand that held her leash and my pail of berries. A good lot of them spilled on the ground. But the cows moved. I think I made some uncomplimentary remarks to Pup as I went back to pick more fruit. She should have picked them. Oh, but then they would have been covered with dog drool. Yuk.

The way Pup had responded to my people's cats reminds me of another cat-and-dog encounter in my parents' house.

Harry Grainger was on the annual sockeye salmon spawning inspection trip to Lonesome Lake–Atnarko River area and had brought his black spaniel with him. Dad had gone to Atnarko to guide the Fisheries Officer to our home where Harry would overnight. After greetings and introductions were attended to in the yard, Harry was invited into the house, with his dog. Offered a chair, he sat down, tucking his dog close.

Soon a cat wandered into the house. Instantly an aggressive dog and a very scared cat were flying around the room, bouncing over and around obstacles, knocking some wildly about, as the barking dog sought the cat and the hissing cat sought refuge. The cat made a couple of circuits of the house, going higher as she leaped from shelves to shelves, even the hot stove felt a brief contact of the cat's furry paws as she streaked away to a higher perch. The barking dog kept up bravely as he followed, sometimes on the floor, sometimes in the air. Finally the cat was "treed" on a cupboard high above the table, up next to the ceiling.

Harry eventually got control of his dog and tied him up, apologizing profusely for the manners, or lack of, of his dog. It was a long time before the cat descended from her refuge, where she had done a lot of growling while she sat up there and glared at the chastised and apologetic dog.

I don't seem to remember arguing with my parents very often after I had grown up, but one day we had a lively one. I stomped off angrily in a huff, leaving Pup, who was in the house, behind. Upset, I had just wanted to get to my own place and relax. I assumed my dog would be all right until I returned in the evening. I did not think they would mind.

Soon after I got to my place, she arrived, panting hard and still wearing her muzzle. I was glad to see my little dog, but not so pleased that they had left her muzzle on when they sent her off to me. She could have gotten tangled up with it and perhaps been eaten. No one would have known, as I wouldn't know they had sent her to me until I returned in the evening. To protect the cats, Pup's muzzle had to be quite snug, and it must have interfered with her panting, to cool herself, on that mile-and-a-half fast run. Still, when she flopped down at my feet I had to forgive them. They had sent a message on her collar.

Some dogs keep one awake all night barking incessantly, but Pup was keeping me awake by licking herself incessantly. Finally I asked her to "Shut up, Pup." Surprising me again, she stopped licking and didn't make another sound all night as she lay on her bed beside mine. I never thought she would consider the sound of licking to be barking. In some things they had trained her well.

If I had known then what I found out later, I just would have gone to sleep and ignored the licking. Pup was not neutered, so she had to clean herself frequently during a certain stage of her reproductive cycle. The poor dog could not use a washcloth for the job. Her tongue was all she had. She and my later dogs, all entire females, showed me this. Sympathy was what was required, not censure.

chapter 29

PUP & SILVER STAR

Part of the time I was in Vancouver learning to fly and waiting to buy an airplane, I was staying with Johnny and Midge Hatch in the Fraser Valley farming country. They had a short-legged paint horse called Shorty. His story is told elsewhere in these memoirs. As the Hatches wanted two horses, Midge wanted me to find a colt that I could train to be a nice saddle horse and then ship it down to them. Then Johnny and Midge could go riding together.

On one of my flights to Nimpo Lake in the Chilcotin country, when arriving at Stewart's dock I was met by a man and a brown, nice-looking mare and her two- or three-month-old filly, also good-looking. As I was prepared to look at any young foal that I came across, I asked the mare's owner a few questions about the filly. His answers made me think perhaps she was just what I was looking for. If she grew up to look anything like her mother she should make an excellent saddle horse. I asked him if she was for sale. Yes, she might be, but the man would have to go to Anahim Lake and ask his wife. So I waited until he returned with the answer.

In a while he was back, and yes, she was for sale. So I bought her. As she was quite small and probably did not weigh much over 150 pounds, I thought I could tie her legs together and put her in the airplane and fly her to Lonesome Lake.

Trussed up like a turkey ready to roast, and with Bob Stewart helping me, we got the filly in the plane. There was one problem. I did not have anything to put on the floor of the plane to support her back quarters. She put too much weight forward and I could not get the plane up on the step. Also it was a calm, hot day, and at 3600-feet elevation there was no way I could take off. It was probably just as well. She could have gotten loose and caused a bad accident.

I returned to the dock, unloaded the little filly and sold her back to the owner, who returned my money. I hated to let her go. She was really very pretty, but at least her mother was happy to have her baby back by her side and nursing. The mare's joy took away some of my disappointment.

Since I could not fly a filly to Lonesome lake, the only alternative was to get Dad to fly me to Nimpo Lake, and from there try to find a filly I could walk in over the mountain to the east of Lonesome Lake, Trumpeter Mountain. It would be possibly a three-day hike. I believe I had some knowledge that there was a six-month-old filly for sale at Towdystan, 15 miles from Nimpo Lake. I seem to recall that a good friend of mine from Nimpo Lake, Ginny Stewart, drove me and Pup and my camping gear to Towdystan.

Arriving there, Mrs. Engebretson took me out to the barn where the filly was in a small corral. She was not halter trained and was a bit timid. We got her in the barn, where I could put a small halter on her dark gray-black head, then begin to teach her to lead. Pup stayed somewhere out of the way while I slowly got the filly to move around the corral. I did not confront her with a direct head-on pull, but by gently asking her to take a step to one side and releasing the pull when she did. Soon she got the idea and was turning nicely. By encouraging her to move forward as well as in a circle she gradually learned to follow my rope. In time she was walking with me outside the corral. I thought we were ready to head for Lonesome Lake.

I stayed at Engebretson's that night. The filly was easy enough to catch in the corral the next morning. I soon was on my way to Charlotte Lake with filly and dog.

The filly went well enough for a mile or two, then began stalling. To start her moving again, I'd pull her sideways and head off along the road. Pretty soon she stopped. Again I started her by the side-pull and we would progress for a distance. However, the distances were becoming shorter and she was taking longer to get started, until she finally fell flat on her side when I tried to get her to step sideways. And there she lay, as flat as a rolled-out piece of piecrust, all four legs stuck out straight and her head back as far as possible. Trying to roll her up on her brisket was like trying to stand up a big, heavy six-foot-long log. I tried hitting her. No response. I swore at her. No response. I wondered if she was having some kind of seizure. I didn't know what was wrong with her. I even told Pup to "get her," but she just looked at me and shrugged. She was not going to jump on poor, tired little filly. The filly could not have been tired. We hadn't gone that far. (I learned many years later that Pup had been trained not to bother horses.)

After I had heaved her up on her legs, which I had folded for her several times, she would get up and walk along the road for a ways, then repeat the whole game all over again. Then Pup started fooling around and running off in front of me. Finally, tired, frustrated, alone with a problem I didn't know how to solve, I roared at Pup, "Get be-bloody-hind!" She did and not once did she leave that position for the rest of that long, tiring day, as I struggled with that recalcitrant immobile piece of "piecrust." After a hard 14 miles we arrived at Smith's Inlet on the north side of Charlotte Lake, where I planned to spend the night.

The Smiths had kindly taken my pack in their truck to their home on Smith's Inlet. At least I didn't have it to carry while I was arguing with the horse. She spent the night, the rainy night, tied to a pine tree. Pup spent her night in a hollow she dug at the base of the filly's tree, I presume to be with the only thing of mine she had access to. Or maybe that was the only place she was safe from the Smiths' boxer dog, who didn't like her.

I had spent the night in Smiths' beautiful log home, with a huge fireplace at one end. They fed me, too. I had become acquainted with those friendly, helpful people when flying vegetables, milk and butter to them.

In the morning the filly was hungry and followed me eagerly to where there was some fine grass growing along the lakeshore.

When we left Smiths' place there was a well-marked trail to follow along the north shore of Charlotte Lake for several miles until we came to a fair-sized creek. The creek was where I turned away from the lake and headed for the alpine country of the east end of Trumpeter Mountain. There was still a trail, well marked, by a group of horses having recently made a trip to the area where I was heading.

We had hiked up close to a sub-alpine area of small pines scattered loosely over gently sloping soft land, with here and there the odd small, grassy meadow where the filly could eat. I let her have some time to feed, as there wasn't a lot to eat for most of the way where we had traveled. I had my lunch also.

This day had been as easy as the day before had been difficult. Silver Star, as I named her for her improved performance, came along as if she had thought about our struggle of the day before and finally figured out what I wanted her to do. She likely had. Soon after I continued our slowly ascending way thru the pines I suddenly became aware that there was no horse in my halter, which was dragging on the ground. I stopped, glancing back to see my little horse wandering off thru the pines. How could I ever catch her with not a fence or even a natural obstacle in sight? Only empty forest in every direction. I began to follow, but she started to trot. I slowed, she slowed. That was how we wandered among the trees, going in no particular direction. The terrain and the trees all looked the same. Slowly she let me get closer to her as we wandered until she finally stopped. I very carefully came up to her shoulder, slipped the rope over her neck and quickly tied it there.

I rebuilt her halter, which had become loose enough that she just shook it off her small head. This time I put an additional rope around her neck, so if the halter came off her head I would still have a rope on her. Then I tied an additional knot on her neck as well. I didn't want a repeat. I was totally responsible for her and I surely didn't want her to get loose again. She would starve up there. I didn't think she could ever find her way home over all the miles we had traveled. She was only six months old.

I knew where I was heading from having flown over the area and observed a pretty little lake just at timberline. That was where I had to go to get up on Trumpeter Mountain. The creek I had been following had vanished shortly before my horse got loose. Fortunately I could see my destination briefly thru the trees from time to time as we went towards a sort of funnel to where the lake lay. I had a compass and a map also. With horse in hand and my direction relocated, we hiked off thru the anonymous forest, every tree looking like all the others and all of the same species, pine.

It wasn't long before the forest began to change. A few balsams appeared among the endless pines, telling me we were getting close to the lake. And night was suggesting I make camp soon. Moments later the trail that I had lost way back where Star got loose suddenly lay under my feet. At that instant a white rabbit dashed past me. I told Pup to get it. She streaked by me in hot pursuit, a few feet behind the fleeing hare. They disappeared in the forest. Soon Pup was back, rabbit-less, and my vision of having roast bunny for supper shriveled. I would have to eat whatever junk I had in my pack. It really wasn't junk; it just wasn't grilled fresh meat.

Now in balsam forest, we continued along a good trail that followed close beside a creek channel, some 15 feet below us. It should lead us to the lake. And it was time to camp. I tied Star to a tree, then selected as sheltered a spot as was available to build my fire and bed down beside. At 5000 feet, nights can get cold in October.

After cutting a supply of dry wood and balsam branches for my bed, I started my fire and laid the balsam tips. My supper finished and Pup fed, I lay down on the aromatic evergreen mattress. The fire was warm. I was tired, so I soon was asleep. Some time later I was awakened by some strange noise. As I had made my camp a short way from where I tied Star, I decided to move her closer to the fire. I didn't know what made the noise.

Returning to my bed I found a black and white dog lying on it. As there were lots of balsam branches readily available, I simply built myself a new bed on the other side of the fire and went back to sleep. As my fire needed frequent fueling during the long night, Pup had several chances to steal my bed. Every time I got up she would steal it, so I just took hers, which was mine to start with anyway. And so we got thru the night.

Leaving camp shortly after daylight, we were soon at the lake, lying calm and reflecting the clear blue sky. A poor trail wound around clumps of short balsams, over large rocks and several steep little pitches along the south side of the half-mile-long lake. At the head of the lake was a rough mass of ice-shifted loose rocks, leading up to the more gentle area where alpine plants grew. Grass grew over much of the land. Flowers, now frozen and dry stuck out of the thin layer of snow, which lay on the higher levels.

From where I was then I would travel west perhaps six miles to where Trumpeter Mountain overlooks Lonesome lake, crossing over gently rolling country, open, and on this trip, windswept. As we hiked along the spine of Trumpeter Mountain, at times the wind almost blew Star and me off our feet and did shift Pup sideways more than once. It must have been blowing at close to 80 miles an hour.

The farther west we traveled the snow was deeper, until it was almost a foot deep and drifting. Some places were drifted bare; there the snow would be deep in any hollow that held it. I was mighty glad to get down in the timber and out of that cold, ceaseless wind. Down in among the trees we were also below the snow line.

On the headwaters of Homecreek we followed along where it wandered across grassy meadows for miles, to near the top of the slope into the valley. There we entered pine forest and found a trail. As most of the trail was blocked by windfall we could not use much of it.

Shortly before we were to head down the steep mountain slope to the valley bottom, we hiked along the top of a chasm into which Homecreek Falls roars in times of snow melting on its head, but in low water times barely murmurs. Homecreek never goes dry any time of year. In winter, the falls that barely murmur can build up a huge pile of green ice from the top of the falls and down for perhaps 500 feet, to where it is hidden in its well-timbered creek bed—or it was well timbered before the terrible wildfire that destroyed our beautiful valley, in the dry, hot summer of 2004.

As the old trap trail which followed a ridge running down close to the creek's valley was so filled with down trees, it was not possible for me to get Star down it. So I simply picked a route among the small trees where we could safely make our way until we were down. It was only a short, easy hike to my people's place once we were on the valley bottom. We made it just before dark.

I left Star in one of their corrals for the night. She was tired and so was I. Pup wasn't, tho.

Star spent the winter at The Birches, along with my other horses, Rommy and Thuja, and my cow, as I did not have much hay yet on my own place. I did not do much training on her except to introduce her to a packsaddle. She had to grow up before she could carry very much. She was quite tame by the time she arrived at Lonesome Lake and was no trouble to catch.

To save pasture, Dad wanted me to put her up on the summer pasture at Elbow Lake in the fall when she was 18 months old. When he brought his cattle home, Star could not be found. Dad made a flight to the area to look for her when there was snow on the ground and saw nothing. I made a flight over the whole area, looking for any tracks that would be visible in the deep snow, but I saw no sign of her and I was flying as low as I dared.

So that was that. I had lost her. Poor little Silver Star, gentle, well-built, calm. She would have made an excellent riding horse for anyone. She should never have been put out there by herself.

308

I believe now, after thinking about Star's refusal to go too far from her home the day I took her from Towdystan to Charlotte Lake, she was waiting for her mother to come and take her home. The farther we traveled away from home, the harder it would be for her mum to find her, so the best thing to do from her instincts was to stay in one place and wait for mum.

The next day mum had not come to find her. She was alone, except for me. All she had to cling to was me and Pup, to make any sort of herd. She needed a herd of some kind, even if it is only a dog and a human as well as herself. Horses do not like to be alone. They are in danger alone. This thought never crossed my mind back when I was struggling with her. Pup was right. She was a poor baby. I failed to think about how she might be feeling or thinking. I had to wait about 55 years to see this.

chapter 30

PUP & THUJA

I got my first dog, Pup, in the summer of 1954, then lost her in 1955, about seven months later. In that brief interval of time I became very attached to the little border collie. She always went to my place when I went there to clear land or whatever. In the summer she swam the river behind Thuja, if I chose to cross it. If I crossed the river in the winter when the water was very cold, I let her ride in front of me across Thuja's withers. To get her up there, I just called her after I was aboard and she stood up, resting her paws against Thuja's side. I could reach down, gather up a good handful of neck skin and lift her 40 pounds onto the mare's back. Pup thought that was a great way to cross the cold river.

Thuja came to Lonesome Lake in the spring of 1951. She was my second horse, giving me a team to help me on my place, Seven Islands. Thuja seemed to love all the dogs I had during her lifetime with me. After losing Pup I adopted another young dog, Kilo. Thuja went so far in her friendship with that little dog that once when there was a strange dog trying to fight with Kilo, Thuja allowed her to hide under her big sheltering body. Every time the stranger tried to make Kilo go out where he could get at her, Thuja put her ears back and thrust out her head towards the stranger, making him back off. She was protecting the little dog as if she were a foal.

Thuja was a big strong mare with a lot of grit. She packed some mean and cumbersome loads. One of the meanest was the oven part of a cast-iron cooking range. It was placed over the top of her saddle and resting on a 60-pound box of nails on each side of her, then roped on with a special hitch. On one section of the trail she was going along very carefully, so Jack and I stopped the other horse and investigated.

The stove had shifted and was banging down on her back with every step she took and had worn a bloody hole in her skin over her spine. She had not complained or tried to remove the pack. She just walked more carefully. We repacked, trying to see to it the stove didn't repeat the shifting. It didn't.

Thuja's saddest burden was Pup's body. Four days after I accidentally dropped a tree on her, killing her, I carried her home on Thuja as I rode. Arriving at her corral, I lowered Pup's stiff body to the ground and then dismounted. I moved Pup a few steps away so Thuja would not step on her friend. Thuja stepped around, lowered her head and began nosing all over Pup's body and ruffling her fur, sniffing, acting as horses often do to each other. She did this for several minutes, then just stood, her head hanging over Pup. She must have known her friend was dead. She and I shared a poignant moment as I stood beside her, resting one hand on her withers. Then, with a deep sigh, Thuja turned around and wandered into her corral and began to eat her supper. She must have been hungry, as I had no hay at my place and it was a long time since breakfast.

Leaving Thuja to eat her meal, I walked shakily to the house and told Mother and Dad I had brought Pup home and would like to lay her to rest in main field, if they didn't mind. The ground on my place was frozen, as it did not have a pelt of grass to keep it thawed thru the winter. They said it would be all right.

The next day I carried her across the field, found a spot that was not frozen and buried her below plow line and left her there in an unmarked grave. Yet, I believe I could still find the spot today where she sleeps.

Four days earlier I had had the painful task of telling my parents why Pup did not come home with me. I had to run outside for a while to gather myself enough to tell them while I was out in the yard. Then I returned to the house and I am afraid I did make a bit of an emotional display. I had been taught to face these things alone and preferably in silence. I have to admit a parental hug would have been very comforting. Things have changed a lot since those days, thank God.

Life would not be worth living if every loss was not followed by quite a few joyful incidents or situations, and it can take many joys to balance just one loss. Tho most of my losses have been painful indeed, I also have had many joys. Some of those high points were flying an airplane; nursing and just sitting quietly with a sweet little baby sleeping in my arms while my loving husband cooked lunch; listening to good music, and trumpeter swans; the first glimpse of my mate returning from a few day's trip. And riding a gentle jumping horse, Bess, over a complicated course and feeling a part of her as she canters, changes leads for almost every jump and doesn't knock anything down. There are many things that have given me joy in my life. Even the running of my life all over again in memory is pleasure in spite of the pain. So, tho most of my losses have been painful indeed, I am still on the joy side of the creek.

chapter 31

WEDDING TRIP

I imagine most young ladies meet their future husbands at a movie or in the course of daily work, or some such situation. My future husband hiked into my life, quite a few miles into the Lonesome Lake outback.

The first time Jack Turner and I met was on April 7, 1955. Mother and I were in the kitchen when she looked out the window on the west end of the house and saw a tall young man walking towards the house from the direction of the barn. Very interested in who would be visiting us that early in the spring, we went to the door to see who it was and what he wanted. We met in the yard.

This young man said he was just looking around BC, sizing up localities he might want to preempt. Someone he had met told him about the Lonesome Lake area. He thought he'd take a look at it as he had a few days to put in between jobs.

Mother invited him into the house and offered lunch, as it was close to that time of day. Jack seemed quite shy, but admitted lunch would be quite welcome, after saying she didn't need to bother and that he had food with him. Of course, she insisted. We both wanted to visit with this new person. Not too many people hiked in there in any time of year, and never in spring break-up. I wanted to see more of the handsome, soft-spoken young fellow, anyway.

After lunch, Jack wanted to know if there was any work he could do. I think Mother told him he didn't need to work. Jack asked about wood and Mother reluctantly admitted he could split some wood if he really wanted to. So, he spent the afternoon splitting up a big pile of firewood. I was impressed, but didn't say much. He obviously was an outdoor person who knew how to use an axe.

For the next three days he helped me clear land on my place. Then he had to leave to go on another job. I wondered if he would ever return. I was interested.

During the few days he was with us Jack told us a bit about his life. He was born in Vancouver, but he only lived in the city for a few years until his dad went off to the Second World War. In the 1940s Jack and his mother moved to several rental places, seeking as economical housing as they could get. Money was short due to the Depression. Leaving home at age fourteen, Jack moved about the province, taking any job he felt he could work at. He was definitely an outdoor person.

On June 9, 1956, Jack hiked into my life again. He spent the summer helping me on Fogswamp and on my parent's place, The Birches, with whatever needed to be done. He became the official breakfast cook. A good one, too. Jack had to leave in early September to get more money over some of the winter. We were engaged by then and I never questioned if he would return. I knew he would.

Over the long months we kept in contact by mail, so I was expecting him before he actually arrived. I had marked some weak places in the Big Lagoon ice, so he would avoid them and hopefully not fall thru. Then, on January 4 he once more hiked into my life.

Dad had slaughtered a couple of cattle the day before and I was helping cut and wrap the quarters when I became aware that someone was walking towards the building where the beef was. I had bloody, greasy hands and I still had my butcher knife in my hand when I rushed off to meet my intended.

We were both a bit shy after being apart for four months, but soon settled down. We were very glad to see each other again. A few days after Jack's return the weather looked nice, so we warmed up the airplane, then took off for Bella Coola to get married.

314

About 16 miles from salt water, near where Salloompt and Nusatsum Rivers meet, there is an intersection of valleys, which often seems to encourage snowstorms to develop. A healthy one was there that day, blocking the valley firmly. We returned to Lonesome Lake, hangared CF-HEO, shouldered our packs and set off down the lake on the ice.

That night we camped at the north end of Lonesome Lake in an old cabin. With a fire to warm the place up, we rested for a while, then went to bed. The fire had just about burned itself out and we were getting cold.

Warm in bed, and not too tired, we talked for a bit about several things. One of the items of mutual interest was Jack's fishing life with his troller, *Surfin.*

As he had grown up on the coast, fishing sort of came natural as a way to make a living. He acquired a troller and set off to catch a fish or two. I do not remember how many years he pursued this watery enterprise, nor do I know how financially lucrative it was, but he did enjoy sea life, except once, when he had to cope with a wild storm, a dead engine, and no place to escape the agitated sea. He put out a sea anchor and tried to get the motor going again, to no avail. He continued to drift before the wind until a big freighter interrupted its voyage to help him. With the wild sea all the big ship could do was to provide a windbreak so Jack could get *Surfin* into a small bay behind an equally small island. A small refuge, but enough shelter that he could anchor safely for the night. The wind howled all night, then fell in the morning. Then Jack could contact a tug to tow him home to his float. I may not have all the details of this account correct, as it was a long time ago when he told me about it. This is the best my memory can do. Remembering his story inspired me to write this poem.

Surfin

He loved the smell and the sounds of the sea
It was the only place that he longed to be
The howl of the wind and the crash of the waves
Gladdened my heart and made me feel brave

But alas, with no power and the shoreline all steep-to
His bravery sought refuge in the toe of my left shoe
Up the wave tops, then down in the troughs
His good ship Surfin *was spun and was tossed*

With a sea-anchor made fast his ship rode more mild
He went down to the motor tho the waves were sure wild
Unable to fix it, he came up from below
There lay a big freighter offering him a tow

Safe in shelter he could at last take his ease
Tho over the small island the wind punished the trees
Out in the open the waves galloped along
With the wind snatchin' the tops off as it shrieked its wild song

The wind howled all night; in the morning it slept
So out of his shelter he thankfully crept
By rowing his dinghy he moved his ship
So a tug could tow him back to his slip.

Some time in the night we smelled smoke. Investigating, we found our blankets on fire at the foot of the beds near the fireplace. We found some old cans and packed in snow and dumped it on the smoldering blankets and rotten punk of the cabin logs. As it seemed to be out after we had dumped a lot of snow on it, we went to bed again.

In not very long we were alerted again by the smell of smoke. Out of bed we got and packed in more snow. This time we tore out all the old dry humus, fir bark, cones and anything burnable we could find, and threw it all out in the snow. Then dumped more snow on the frozen ground where we had raked all the dry stuff off. We stayed up then and watched it for a while before we tried to trust it again.

Nights are long in January. We did get back to sleep, but were glad to see daylight creep back into the valley. As it was too cold to eat without a fire, we simply packed up and started down the trail. Sometime after we had hiked long enough to get warmed up, we had our breakfast.

We had to cross the Atnarko River between Lonesome Lake and Stillwater as the river was frozen over farther downstream, so we couldn't use the boat. After searching around in the snow for a while we found a nice long log covered with about a foot of crusted snow. It would take us to the other side of the river. To be able to cross safely we had to kick all the snow off as we went. It had been on the log so long that it had bulged out on each side until it was twice as wide as the log, under it. We couldn't even see the log until we had kicked the snow off, in large chunks.

We were able to use the ice on the lower end of the Stillwater, as it was frozen thick enough.

I think we stopped at Atnarko and visited Bert Robson a short time. When we were talking to Bert, he phoned Peggy Matthews and she invited us to stay in her house, about a mile farther down the trail. We thankfully did that.

In the morning we left the Matthews house and hiked on down the trail. We had a cold breakfast near the bottom of the hill, after a hands-and-face wash in a cold, cold, rocky little creek. Having eaten a cold breakfast of sweet Christmas cake, and something else, we continued on down the road.

Sometime later in the day Uncle Earle drove up to meet us and took us to his and Aunt Isabel's home. Someone kind must have phoned them that we were coming. That was January 9, 1957. They gave us a warm lunch, and then Uncle Earle drove us to Bella Coola.

We were married in the minister's house, in a very simple ceremony. Outdoors, an evil east wind howled. It was colder than anything I had experienced except when the morning temperature was minus 46 Fahrenheit in late January in the 1940s. Oh God, it was cold!

I seem to recall we had a reception at Aunt Laura and Uncle Frank's home. They had lamb stew. There was quite a gathering of cousins and other relatives and friends. I think there was singing and Uncle Frank played his violin. They gave us a very nice time. I still can taste that lamb stew. Then Uncle Earle drove us back to his home, long after dark.

To further pamper us, Uncle Earle and Aunt Isabel went over to the neighbors for the night and let us newlyweds have their snug house. Very kind of them.

The next day Uncle Earl drove us to the bottom of the hill. As they had only a jeep, there was not room for my aunt to go along. From there we hiked to the Stillwater, carrying a nice piece of mutton they gave us. That night we camped in the Ratcliff cabin at the north end of Stillwater. For supper we had delicious mutton steak and bread and butter.

We stayed there for three days doing nothing, at least nothing that is anybody's business. One thing we did do was burn up some of their wood, so we replaced it before leaving. One never leaves someone's borrowed house without replacing any wood they use.

To replace the wood we had burned Jack felled a tree, which went wrong and got hung up in another tree. I thought I might become a widow before I had a decent honeymoon, but he got the tree down safely. Hung-up trees always worry me, whether they are someone else's or mine.

Having eaten all the sheep meat, we decided we might as well come on home. Tho at the Stillwater there was no nasty east wind.

Between Stillwater and Lonesome Lake we were well protected from any wind, as the three miles of trail runs thru heavy sheltering forest for most of the way. Only when getting near the outlet of the lake does the forest thin out, over the boulder bed of Hunlen Creek.

It was a different story soon after we were out on the frozen lake. Only a quarter of a mile from the forested north end of the lake, we were in a nasty cold north wind with only our relatively light packs for shelter. As it was quite warm when we left home to fly to Bella Coola, I hadn't taken my really cold weather protection, such as a warm wool hat. Out on the open ice, my ears were soon feeling the cold. There was nothing to do but keep plodding across the lake. Jack had better equipment, but I was not going to borrow his, as I should have brought my own even if the trip was supposed to be for only a few hours. That would teach me, maybe.

Back at my people's place, I believe we were invited to spend the night instead of going to our own place. We accepted gladly.

The next day saw us home in my little cabin on Fogswamp, now a unit rather than two individuals.

Soon we began preparing materials for building a house.

chapter 32

HOUSE LOGS & GARDEN

Home at Fogswamp, we began the task of preparing logs, etc. for the house we would build. Thankfully, Jack had the chainsaw to fall all the trees we needed. We still had to use axes to take the bark off. The saw wouldn't do that, but it could remove the branches. We had to pile them; the saw would not do that either. By late winter we had a good lot of the materials required for a 24- by 26-foot three-room house, all cut quite close to the house site.

As our cows and horses were feeding at The Birches that winter, I just went down and fed the swans around noon. After lunch we both worked at the log job, day after day, when it wasn't raining or snowing too much. Some days we went together to feed the swans. On those days lunch would be a bit late. I think we did this only on warm days or the cabin would get too cold during our absence. We didn't like to leave a fire burning in the stove.

One night Jack asked me why I called my place Fogswamp. I explained that I wanted to change the rather cheery name, Seven Islands, to something more somber because of dropping a tree on my very first dog and I thought Fogswamp suggested that. The name would remind me of the reason for the change and keep her memory fresher for me. I didn't mention that I felt it would be a memorial to Pup. I also named the island where she died "Pup Island," and so it remained for as long as we were living there.

Some of my relatives in Bella Coola were shocked by me changing the name of my place and were quite determined that I change it back. I refused. It was my loss and my place. Years later I changed the name again, after my book *Fogswamp* came out. I was disappointed and unhappy at that time, as the publisher, or editor, had edited out too much of my own life. I really don't know how changing the name helped, except I didn't have to say "Fogswamp" anymore when referring to that scrap of land I called home. I chose a nice name that time—Arbordale, "Tree Valley"—and so it was until the summer of 2004 when fire destroyed the entire area.

With my father and myself both holding pilot's licenses, Jack thought he ought to join the club and become a pilot too. On the first of March we flew in CF-HEO to Pat Bay on Vancouver Island, then took another plane to Vancouver Airport, leaving HEO hangared at Pat Bay.

The first order of business was to find a place to rent for several weeks while Jack was learning to fly an airplane. I seem to remember the first place was on Clarke Drive and I shopped for groceries on Commercial Street, which ran at right angles to Clark Drive.

As Jack was spending most days at the airport, or waiting for decent weather, I had nothing much to do all day. So, to use up some time I got a city map and went for a hike. Part of that hike was along East Hastings. Other streets I do not remember. Most of what I can recall from that voyage of discovery, taken on my own two feet, is all the nasty-natured little "ankle-biters" that came roaring across the street from their yard to try to drive me from their property. I felt I had as much right on the streets as they did. It wasn't that I was trying to invade their yard.

That was the first and only time I attempted solo navigation of the city, even a small part, except to go shopping on Commercial, and I was confident going there because I could see the store from the house anyway. When I was in Vancouver area earning to fly I never had to do my own navigating around the city, as there always seemed to be someone kind and generous to drive me to wherever I wanted to go, and I am forever grateful to them.

For Jack to get his license required nearly six weeks as he could not fly every day due to rotten weather. Some days he would be there from morning to evening, waiting for an hour of decent weather, then come home disgusted and a bit crabby because of the delays.

When I was learning to fly it was later in the spring and the weather was generally better. Most of the two months I was in the Vancouver area was spent waiting for the right plane to show up or be found. Some of that time was spent learning to fly.

The longest sojourn in Vancouver was when we were waiting for our child to be born. That took about two and a half months. We left home shortly after the first of January, and didn't get home until mid-March with baby Susan. That winter, 1959, Dad had to feed the swans. It was the only time he had to do the swan feeding after he gave me the job when I was about 12.

All the time we were in Vancouver I had made Jack do all the navigating, as he had grown up in the city and knew where everything was, what bus to take to get there. So why should I have to learn what he already knew?

We spent some time at Jack's folks' home on Saltspring Island before flying home. I got to know my father-in-law and mother-in law a bit. Jack encouraged me to follow him across a narrow channel to a small island where I believe there were some oysters he wanted. The only trouble was the water was deeper than he claimed it to be. To me it was darn near chin deep and COLD. We did get the oysters, but from my taste they weren't worth walking on dry land to get, never mind practically swimming for.

My folks had asked us to bring 25 day-old leghorn pullets when we came home. I remember landing at one place on our way up the coast. Tied up at the dock, we spread newspapers over the airplane's bench seat and let the little yellow chicks out in the plane to eat, drink and flutter around, and of course crap a whole lot. That was what the newspaper was for. While the chicks were having fun in the airplane, we went for a hike along the beach. Then we gassed the plane and it was off for Lonesome Lake.

That same spring we borrowed my folks' plow and disk to prepare our first garden. We hauled those implements to Fogswamp on a sled, with the team hitched to the disk, which was chained to a short sled. Behind the disk we had a longer sled chained to the disk harrow. On that we tied the plow.

With the garden area plowed and disked, we were ready to plant some seeds. I have no memory of what we raised that first year, except some spuds, but we must have had at least peas, beans, radish, lettuce, greens, onions and transplants from my people's greenhouse. Those we transplanted in our garden.

Thru the summer we worked at the house, when we weren't helping my people. By the third of December we were able to move into the building, with only half the roof on.

We had bought a McClary range while we were in Vancouver in the spring of 1957, when Jack was getting his flying license. With the stove set up in the kitchen, under the roofed-over part, we could cook. An airtight heater would be set up later. Getting the roof on was more important.

We had already secured many sacks of moss out of a swampy pond to stuff in the spaces between the logs as soon as it was dry. That happened sometime during the summer. Jack chain-sawed long, straight poles into quarters to nail over the moss, making the house quite snug. The window holes were filled with sacks of hay until we could build more window sashes. We had three windows my dad had made for me to put in my cabin. One was in my cabin door. We put it in our house front door. The other two went in the south wall, near where our bed would be when the last of the roof was put on.

The window holes filled with sacks of hay were not the best kind of window if one wanted light, so we started on them, making the sashes by hand, carving the groove for the glass with a chisel. Shortly after moving to Bella Coola I acquired a small chainsaw and used it to cut out the groove for the glass. Much easier and faster.

With the house more or less finished, we could start tomatoes and pumpkins under the stove. Soon after they were up they could be set on the windowsills of our front window and the big window over the sink on the east end of the house. It received early sun. Later, when it got warmer, we carried the flats outside and put them in a small frame with plastic-covered windows over them. Even on cloudy days it became quite warm inside the green house. We had to bring all the flats into the house at night. Starting the plants in late March helped to lengthen the growing season. As the growing season is short at Lonesome Lake, every advantage is worth working for. By covering the plants any night that frost threatened, we were able to raise all the tender things that can be raised at Bella Coola without covering, most years.

The next big project was the barn. We had been keeping our two or three cattle in the shed I had built in 1955 after a run-away clearing fire destroyed the smaller shed I had made in 1953. The 1955 shed was 30 by 20 feet, and had room for a lot more hay and stanchion room for the cows. My horses were still wintering at The Birches, as we hadn't enough hay for them and the cows. However, it was a few years before we got going on the barn.

In the meantime we acquired a wagon in the spring of 1958. Then we made a dugout canoe to use on Lonesome Lake. It was quite large and would take a 10-horsepower motor mounted on the stern. It was not the most stable of crafts, so we didn't go out on the lake any more often than we had to. In a few years Jack packed in plywood on his back and we built a real boat.

In 1958 we put a phone line between our place and The Birches. We bought the wire and my people bought the phones and installed them, one in our house and the other one in their house. We strung the wire—one and a half miles of it—and maintained the line. That phone was a great help and was of entertainment value also, especially when Susan got big enough to talk to her grandparents.

In 1961 or 1962 we finally got going on the barn. It was 30 feet by 48 feet on the ground. One half was for hay, a 24- by 30-foot shed. The other half was a stable, also 24 by 30 feet.

The stable part had room for four stanchions, two large ones for grown cows and two smaller ones for younger cattle. On the same side we had two straight stalls for horses. Then a four-foot-wide hallway with room for two more horses, also in straight stalls. Coming off the side of the hall opposite the cow stanchions was a 10-foot-square stall for a bull, then a similar sized maternity stall. There was a four-foot-wide door at each end of the stable to let animals in or out. Access to the hay was up a ladder against the seven-foot-high wall under the seven- by eight-foot doorway where the hay was slung in, using the same system Dad used in his barn. Sometime we built a lean-to porte-cochere in front of the hay door to park wagonloads of hay under.

Land clearing, fences and bridges, one place or another, were always clamoring to be built. It seemed like we would no sooner get one project finished than something else had to be done, or re-done. Posts would rot, fences would get broken by trees falling on them or by fat bears squeezing themselves thru, or even being blown down by violent, wild south wind. And one time by a helicopter landing too near our garden fence. It flattened about six panels. All had to be repaired.

And if repairs didn't keep us busy enough, often we would decide to re-route a fence.

Then there were many bridges. Not all for horses and cows, but for us to cross to get to islands in the river where we had pasture, and had to get to twice daily to milk the cow. These bridges just consisted of two or three long logs put up on high enough piers to raise them well above high water.

Our enterprising stock made us build drawbridges over the various river channels to keep them from wading a long way down the river from a beach or other handy place to get into the water. Climbing out of the river, they would be in the cow pasture, where we did not want them. The drawbridges were built with three logs so we could hang sections of fence under the bridge to stop river wanderers. The fence sections could be raised for high water, or lowered for critters, from the top of the bridge.

In the fall we took them up as high as possible for winter. The highest water could, and did, occur in that season.

Then suddenly it seemed like there was no more land to clear, there was no more moving of fences, no more place to move one to. The older fences were beginning to need replacing. That was just drudgery, replacing what we had already built years earlier.

Now I believe that was one thing that helped make me want to move from my home and seek some new adventure. Jack never was really satisfied there and always missed the sea. With me kind of uprooted I guess it truly was time to go and find a new challenge.

I have to believe now that a lack of any new challenges is what made Dad leave his beloved Birches. He also had nothing new to do on his place, which would be an exciting challenge. He had done it all before.

chapter 33

DAILY SCHEDULE

I have read some stories about our daily activities in which it was claimed, somewhat derogatorily I thought, that we had no regular schedules in our lives and did things any old time, whenever we pleased. Actually it was much different.

Our daily tasks were done on a pretty even schedule, allowing for the ever shortening and lengthening of the days. Our activities were hinged on the milking time—cows do much better if they are milked at the same time each day—and on news times on the radio. In winter, the swan-feeding time and stock turn-out time were very constant, close to noon. Meal times were slotted in to round out the day, with bedtime right after the evening news. School time came between breakfast and lunch, and between lunch and supper.

Of course there were times when we had to rearrange things, such as when we wanted to mow the grass to make hay, and we wanted to do that as early as possible to get finished before it became too hot and the noisome little biting bugs began to annoy both the horses and the driver. On those days, milking was usually a little late, as was breakfast. When we started really early we could sleep in the afternoon.

As there is a three-hour cool period in the morning, and a similar length of less hot period in the evening, we could haul the hay in then and not have to work in so much heat, unless there was threat of a thunderstorm. In that case, we worked right thru the heat. Summer temperatures can reach over 90 degrees Fahrenheit in the shade, and that is really too hot for me. Too hot for anybody, really. The sweat pours off you, and hay chaff sticks to sweaty skin while pitching big forkfuls of hay up on to the wagonload of hay. Of course I had it much better, as I was up on the load and got only a small part of the dust and chaff on myself.

Another time when we would have to rearrange our schedule was if we were going on a trip, maybe to the area where the stock were ranged, to salt them and possibly bring one home to calve, or perhaps we would be getting the work team in to do the haying.

There could be many reasons for us to get an early start, aside from haying. Any time we wanted to make a trip away from home, we tried to get an early start. In the summer we liked to make hikes to the alpine country if the weather looked like it would be nice for a few days. Lonesome Lake is surrounded by much alpine area and nice lakes, on a higher level, where we liked to go.

When we made hikes to the alpine, milking would be done earlier in the morning when we left home, and later in the evening when we returned. While I did the milking, Susan and Jack would get supper, unless Susan chose to help me milk.

Jack also cooked breakfast every day, whether or not I was mowing. If the horse-work required only one person, I, having grown up with horses, did it. It would have been rather stupid to do it the other way around. Jack's background was of boats and the sea, and he was a good cook. I remember the summer of 1956 when I was mowing a large field on my parent's place. It was about a four-hour job. Sometime during those four hours, Jack brought me a delicious plate of fried eggs, buttered biscuits crusty and warm, and fresh raspberries smothered in thick cream.

They say the way to a man's heart is thru his stomach; maybe Jack thought to see if it would work the other way around. But, no, I don't think Jack thought that. He was just being the kind, thoughtful person that he was. He was also kind and thoughtful to anything, human or other animal, that needed help or could use it.

It was a cruel twist of fate that he had the misfortune to be attacked by a large grizzly bear one evening when he made the mistake of stepping thru his front gate, about 15 feet from his front door. Turning to close the gate, he was hit and knocked down, then half scalped on the left side of his head. Then the bear let his head go and grabbed his left arm and began dragging him away thru a clump of young cherry sprouts. Suddenly the bear dropped Jack's arm and departed. This was in Hagensborg, years after we moved down the valley.

Jack was taken to the Bella Coola Hospital for the night, then on to Vancouver the next day. There they repaired the damage, including a skin graft on his head. This happened October 20, 2005. In time he healed, tho the damaged head skin remained very tender and easily scratched. On November 21, 2007, cancer finished what the bear started.

I believe our daily schedule was a bit more flexible when I was growing up. Sometimes breakfast was rather late, then the other meals would also be late. The morning and evening chores were usually fairly regular. The swan feeding was done on a regular schedule so they would know when to be at the feed place, which was one big advantage to the birds in having all the grain come to Lonesome Lake.

One of the winter jobs at The Birches was harvesting the tops of birch trees for brushing the long rows of garden peas. We cut off the top-most branches when they were bare of leaves, sharpened the cut ends with an axe, then piled them all lined up neatly. All one had to do, later, was just to pick up an armload and slide it onto the wagon and then unload them at the garden. Bundles of those branches were carried in our arms to be distributed down the pea rows. Then one sharpened branch was shoved into the soft ground on one side of the peas. Then another one was shoved into the ground on the opposite side of the peas so they leaned into each other. We did that all the way down the long rows. The brush was for the peas to climb on. To pick the peas, one had to reach thru the branches to find the pods, swelled with large, sweet, delicious peas. They were worth all the trouble and time it took.

We canned 50 or 60 quarts each summer. All five of us usually worked at the pea-canning job. There were big tubs full to be shelled. That required a lot of time, too, but it was done in the shade. Well, the peas were picked in the shade, usually in the dewy, cold morning.

Then one summer someone down the valley gave us a big sack full of string off hay bales. We used the birch branches no more, on The Birches.

With small, sharpened stakes driven into the soft garden soil every three paces in pairs, the previously tied-together hay string was then tied to one end stake. As one person walked along the pea row unwinding the ball of string, another person placed the string around each stake, snugged it up, then went on to the next one and so on until we would have a six- or seven-line fence on each side of the pea row. We could do that job just about as fast as one could walk. Much better than the brush; easier to pick the peas, also. Of course Jack and I used the same system on our farm, having acquired a full roll of new baling twine for the job.

Altho we chose to mow the grass for hay in the cool of the morning, there was one thing we preferred to do in the heat of the day— swimming, in the frigid water of Lonesome Lake. Our parents made us get in that awful cold water and learn to swim. Even on a hot day, in a nice sheltered bay, the water was cold. We were told not to just creep in, but to plunge right in and paddle vigorously and we wouldn't feel the cold so much. Oh yeah. We felt it, all right. I can still feel it, about 70 years later. We did learn to dog paddle, tho, and at least to stay afloat, for a few minutes anyway. They were right, of course. One certainly should learn to swim if they were ever going to play around on the water. And over the years, we did lots of playing around on the water and loved most of it.

Jack could even swim under water. I wouldn't, tho. I hated to put my head under the water and refused to learn. The water got in my ears enough without me actually submerging my head.

My folks didn't actually schedule time to play the violin. Dad played when he felt like it. Uncle Frank had taught him how to play the instrument. When Dad learned to play *Old Dan Tucker,* Uncle Frank gave him a spare fiddle that he had.

Then in time I grew up enough that I could play, too, and he taught me to play his violin. After a lot of squeaks, squawks and many sour notes, I finally learned to get the notes right most of the time. Then he bought a fiddle for me and we could create our own concert hour, with Dad and me on the violin and Mother singing beautifully.

For music we also had a wind-up gramophone and a stack of records, which we often played. Our Aunt Isabel and Uncle Earle brought them to Lonesome Lake when they came and spent the winter with us in the early thirties. When they left, they gave us the records and gramophone. They made many a blustery, cold evening serene. We didn't necessarily wait for a wild evening to play the gramophone; we would play it any time we chose.

When I was growing up at The Birches we had several games we played, usually in the evenings. Anagrams, cribbage, checkers and chess were the only games we had. I did not play chess; just my brothers and Dad played that game. It was too difficult for me to checkmate anyone. I just watched the experts fight it out on the battlefield.

At Arbordale we played a wider variety of games. We had Monopoly, Chinese checkers, checkers, Parcheesi, Wide World, and Snakes and Ladders. Our Monopoly games sometimes went on for several evenings because we slightly changed the rules and allowed each player to go into debt. There was a limit on the debt. But we could make the game last longer that way.

One other thing we did, not exactly on schedule but more like annually, was picking poison parsnips out of wet and boggy parts of the pastures every spring as soon as they began growing. Being in semi-warm swamp water, they would begin growing before any other plants did. The cattle, being hungry for anything fresh and green, grubbed them out of the mud and ate them. The cows had no natural instinct to tell them the roots were deadly. A globular root the size of a walnut will kill a full-grown cow, in terrible agony. We wanted to save the cows that agony more than we needed to keep the cows for their products. After my parents lost two or three cows in rapid succession one spring, parsnip picking became one of the spring jobs—cold, wet and red muddy.

One of the areas to be picked was the lower end of Barn Field, where springs kept the ground nice and wet so the poison parsnips grew fast and early. That was where those cows got theirs. We picked that area for a few springs, then Dad dug long ditches to drain the field and the parsnips didn't grow there anymore.

Those ditches were three feet deep and about 18 inches wide. Two four- or five-inch square rails were laid in the bottom of the ditch, one on each side. A cover plank about a foot wide was placed carefully on top of the rails, leaving a channel for the drainage water to flow thru. This material was all split cedar. Then all the soil was shoveled back into the ditch.

One interesting thing was revealed when those ditches were being dug. The area had been covered with large balsam and aspen trees at one time in the history of Lonesome Lake many years earlier. It had to have been several feet lower then than it was when Dad was digging those ditches. He encountered logs and stumps over a foot in diameter, still completely sound from being buried in two feet of cold mud. The cold and wet will preserve wood for a very long time, even wood that would rot in a year on the surface of the ground.

We didn't need to de-parsnip the field any more, but we still had to wade knee-deep in red or black muddy, cold water in the north pasture, in the cold shade of the alders, to search every square foot of any likely, and even un-likely, looking places for those awful plants. They loved the cold and shade. Come to think about it, they loved the sunny exposure, too. They just were sneakier in the shade. They didn't grow their leaves so early, but floated their roots on the water. Only later did they send up robust leaves to attract the cows.

No, seriously, not to attract cows or any other animals. The parsnips don't want to be eaten. Native animals don't seem to eat them, except beavers. But they only trim off the small side roots and leave the round root floating on the pond.

Cows won't eat the poisonous roots when they develop a mass of long white rootlets, looking much like a mane, extending out into the water. They will, however, wade into the muddy ponds and gobble up the well-grown, less poisonous leafy top, which doesn't seem to hurt them. In a natural setting, cattle would not live where poisonous parsnips grow. We put them where they would not naturally be; therefore, we must protect them.

For a number of years my people ran the non-milking cows on the range between The Birches and Tenas Lake, about three miles south, where there were dozens of wet places, ponds and swamps, and of course poison parsnips. Each spring before turning those animals out the Edwards family spent several days sloshing thru those cold, muddy areas, dragging a big wet gunnysack into which they put the cold and muddy parsnips. We spread out to cover all the ponds, but kept within hearing with frequent shouts.

When our sacks were full and dripping, we had to go up on dry land and hunt for a big hollow stump to dump our harvest into. Or find a good rock-pile up on the mountain, in which we could bury the parsnips. We surely didn't want the cattle to find a huge stash of what we didn't want them to find only a few of.

The area with the best crops of poison parsnips was where I chose to preempt. It was the best choice for a farm for me and I was very familiar with it. And as on The Birches, my property had to be searched for those poisonous plants each spring for as long as we lived there.

Tho the name of my property was changed twice, the parsnips never changed. They grew even in dry edges of dry watercourses, and in the thin soil of the various islands in the Atnarko River.

After several years of doing that cold, wet job of cleaning several miles of parsnips, Dad decided to put the cattle at Elbow Lake, about

10 miles south of Lonesome Lake. He thought there were no parsnips in that area. He was mistaken.

Some time in the thirties he bought a beautiful shorthorn bull calf and brought him to The Birches. Two or three years later, the bull proved there were indeed parsnips in that area of lush feed, swamps and muddy places, and vast sedge meadows. That was a sad loss, and we still would have to hunt for those dreaded plants. Only two or three people could work at the picking job, as someone had to stay home to take care of the milk cow.

As Mother had fallen down over a log in the trail and injured her back when we were hiking up the valley to pick parsnips on the area that I eventually preempted, she really didn't want to make that 10 miles over the rough trail to Elbow Lake and beyond. I wasn't of much use yet. I had to do some more growing. For a few years Dad, Stanley and Johnny did the parsnip picking in the swamp where Corsair, the bull, got his. My memory is pretty hazy here and there is no one alive now that I can ask.

Some years later, I seem to recall, Dad and I were mucking around up there picking parsnips. Then, due to beavers making dams in the area, and clearing land, something changed. We didn't do so much hunting for parsnips each spring.

Then Jack came into my life. Next Susan came into our lives. The year she was born, 1959, Jack and I took the Edwards and Turner cattle to the summer range in the spring. As baby Susan would be better off at my parents' home than being carried by one of us, we left her in the tender care of Mother.

Jack and I took the cattle to the summer range, then searched the swamps for parsnips and found lots, so many that we had to pick for two days to get the worst places cleaned out. As I was nursing little Susan I had lots of milk, but there was no one to take it. I wanted desperately to return to my child. Instinct insisted she must be starving. Conscious thought told me she was not. I trusted my mother to take good care of her granddaughter. Instinct can rule one's feelings.

I knew I would have to remove the unused milk or I would start to go dry. Anyway the over-filled mammaries were getting uncomfortable. Instinct kept yelling, "Keep the milk for your hungry child. She is starving. She hasn't nursed for days!" Sometimes instinct is hard to deny. In time I gave in to common sense and milked it all out on the ground, a terrible waste. There surely would be more, certainly, by the time we got home. And of course there was.

Oh, I was an awful mother, just like a mother bear. When Susan was really young, the only people I felt comfortable being near her were her grandparents, on both sides, and my aunt Isabel and Uncle Earle. When she got older I relaxed a bit and allowed friends to look at her as I held her in my arms. Strangers I would turn away from and give a rather hard eye to, I am afraid. That old protective instinct again rearing its head. Then sometime when she got older still, or when I became more relaxed, I proudly showed her to interested people, tho I still kept a protective pair of arms around her. Even my teeth were ready to bite should anyone make a false move towards us.

I even threatened a friendly Land Rover once. Jack and I were hiking down the valley and had stopped on the relatively traffic-free tote road near the Atnarko settlement when the baby needed changing. As the roadbed was the most level area for the job, we chose it. I had just taken the dirty diaper off when around the corner came a vehicle, chugging along. It was going slowly over the rough road. I leaped to my feet, with hackles raised and teeth bared, and stepped towards the innocent Land Rover, ready to do battle. Jack picked up the baby. The vehicle stopped. Driving the vehicle was our good friend, Bill Webber. No threat at all. I was a little embarrassed and surprised by my reaction to the threat to my child. Instinct ruled again, briefly.

I was not concerned with Bill. He was our friend. He had driven the three of us from Bella Coola to Atnarko when we came home from Vancouver, where Susan was born on February 19, 1959. So we had a nice, but short, visit.

chapter 34

HORSESHOES & PICKET PINS

Horseshoes and picket pins, to some a pollution, to others a feeling of companionship and a cause for wondering and oneness with others who have tramped over the same ground as we are now exploring.

The mountain whose feet lie along the east shore of the south end of Lonesome Lake slopes gently up to form the softly rolling alpine area of 7200-foot Trumpeter Mountain, about 5000 feet above the lake. This alpine area, pond-dotted, flower-strewn and sparsely forested with alpine balsam and pines stunted and twisted by snow and wind, is where Jack, Susan, Skye and I loved to hike. Susan was still just a small child when we started making those hikes.

We had to climb up the 5400 feet carrying heavy packs to get to timberline. Even Skye had a pack. Picking our way up, stepping over windfall and forcing our packs between trees grown too close together, panting, we made our slow way up the mountain. We stopped frequently to enjoy the ever-changing view as we slowly ascended.

Arriving in the alpine, of course the walking became much easier, and suddenly even our packs seemed lighter. We were at timberline, but we could see for miles. The top of 13,177-foot Mount Waddington was visible, 40 miles to the south/southwest. Anahim Peak, about 20 miles to the north reared its black basalt head. To the west, beyond the Atnarko valley, lay the string of lakes that are Hunlen Creek, far below us, as they are at only 3600 feet in elevation. Beyond the lakes rose a range of saw-toothed mountains. The tallest is Talchako Mountain, at 9000 feet. And far to the northwest rose 10,000-foot Stupendous Mountain, which overhangs the Bella Coola Valley. We could see all those distant vistas and we were only a little above timberline. The highest point on Trumpeter Mountain was a ways back from the slope into the valley and rose to about 7200 feet on a gently rounded hump.

As we hiked along, I noticed an old rusty horseshoe lying on a piece of bare, rocky ground, as if it had just fallen off a horse's hoof. With interest and a suddenly growing feeling of connection with whoever had been here before us, I stooped and picked it up and carried it along.

As we continued on our way across the flower-strewn, ever-changing, sweet-scented land, many questions entered my mind. Who had been here with horses? Where had they come from? Certainly not from Lonesome lake. Did they come to hike, or ride, over the alpine just to see and enjoy? Did they enjoy it as we did? How many were they? Did they have a child and a dog along? Had they come alone to hunt for meat or trophy, and was the horse being ridden? Or was it to carry camp gear in and meat out? I pondered those things as we went along, accompanied by the implied presence of other hikers.

Sometimes we would find picket pins driven deep into the black, clinging, muddy soil of a small meadow—evidence of someone staking out a horse to feed on the rich alpine grass while camp would be set up for the night. Sometimes there would be two or three pins left in the meadow, suggesting that several people had overnighted there. As they had left the pins in the meadow, perhaps they would make another hike later.

All of these questions added another dimension and pleasure to an already wide horizon, and planted a little seed. That seed grew into the "Loopin" trail.

A little scouting around revealed a good route up Trumpeter Mountain, which needed very little modifying. With a trail, we could get horses up there, greatly reducing the labor involved, to visit that beautiful area. Then none of us except Skye had to carry a pack on our back, and she didn't mind. Her food was in it.

We tried to make at least one hike to the alpine of Trumpeter Mountain, or Junker Lake to the west of us, each summer for a number of years, weather and haying permitting.

One summer we chose to take three days off and spend the time on Trumpeter Mountain with two of our horses. The weather was glorious for most of the first day. We selected a dry, little, flat place for our sketchy lean-to plastic tent. Jack set up the camp while Susan and I and Skye took the horses a short way down a slope to a nice little meadow. With each of us holding a halter rope, we let them graze.

Not too long later thunderheads began crowding over our heads. Then they began fighting and were soon drenching us in a cold, hard downpour. One of us rushed back up to the camp for raincoats. Searching thru our stuff, a very unpleasant fact was revealed. There were NO raincoats. Someone had missed getting them in the packs. All we had to keep the cold rain off us were two gunnysacks, which had been holding our bedding. Those would have to do. Folded correctly, they would keep most of the rain off for a little while.

The person not holding horses also had a minor problem. As the place we had selected for the tent was flat, and very dry, none of the water that ran off the roof, would soak into the ground, or run off. Ditches had to be dug around the tent to encourage the water to run off rather than run under our beds.

When the horses were finished grazing, we were all pretty wet and cold. Even the horses were shivering a bit. They had short summer coats and were quite wet themselves. With the trees in that area being rather spindly there was no good shelter for them. Of course, soon after we went to bed the rain stopped. The big, black clouds all drifted away. The night was clear, the morning, cold, until the sun rose and another nice day had arrived to warm us all up.

It would not be too uncommon to find horseshoes lying in the trail if one travels where shod horses have walked, but who would expect to come across a meat-grinder clamped to the trunk of a small balsam tree in the alpine? We did just that. Hiking along among trees set well spaced out, we passed under a dense clump of balsam and walked right into a heap of old cans of food and the meat-grinder. Most of the cans had lost their labels. Curiosity took aver, as it always does when I find someone's old garbage dump. We had to investigate. There were empty jars there, too. A few of the cans still had labels and informed they were beets. Now who on earth would horse pack canned BEETS to a hunting camp? I can't think of any food more disgusting. Of course I wasn't being asked to eat it, but I also noticed they had been left. As we did not see any other labels, perhaps they were all beets and the pile of cans had been carried there and dropped by someone who didn't like beets and was determined to get rid of them for once and for all. Oh, but then what was the meat-grinder for? Wait a minute; the meat grinder was broken, so it can't have been for anything. Perhaps the meat-grinder had been taken there to be disposed of along with the beets? As there was very little rust on any of the stuff it will take a while, a very long while, to all rust away.

Everything takes place slowly in the alpine. Even moose and caribou tracks, sunk deep in the tough, spongy moss-clad alpine surface, remain clear for ages. Caribou antlers, almost grown over with alpine birch and willow, remain visible, bone-white and quite solid many years after being shed, and long after the last caribou left the area.

Seriously, I think the cans had been horse-packed there to supply a moose-hunting party and the meat grinder had been used to reduce a tough old bull to something a human could chew. While trying to grind the moose up, they had broken the meat mill. Disgusted, they decided to leave everything but the tough old bull and beat it for home and a good feed of tender beef.

Well so much for trying to restore history with so little evidence. There were no remaining signs of a camp. No fire-pit, no piles of horse buns, no signs of tent poles. Really nothing to indicate anyone had ever camped there except the cans and the broken meat grinder. It was a nice enough spot for a camp, altho there was no grass very near and water was even farther away. There are many places on that mountain far better set up with those essentials, including trees for tents to be fastened to and to tie horses for the night.

One summer Jack, Skye and I were on Trumpeter Mountain with Guenevere when on to our flower-strewn lunch site came a man, a woman and three beautiful buckskin mares. Their route took them right to us, where we were having lunch while Guenevere was staked on a long chain about 200 feet away, having her lunch on a patch of good grass. She danced on her chain and whinnied a greeting to the strange horses. She was alone and was ecstatic to see them.

The fellow kept hold of his three, pretty, well-mannered mares while we visited. At one point he mentioned what an empty area Trumpeter Mountain was. He remarked there was nothing there. To him, I guess, nothing was there. He was a trapper.

I don't know what anyone would expect to find on that open, rolling alpine area to catch anyway. In winter it would be covered with feet and feet of snow. Perhaps there would be lynx in the sub-alpine and varying hares. Lower, in dense forest, there might be martens and wolverine, those large, much maligned members of the Mustelid family, including mink and weasels.

In a little while he left with his mares, whose beauty was exceeded only by their manners. Guenevere whinnied anxiously and watched them until they vanished over a far-off rise on the skyline. Then, disappointed, she shook herself, stood gazing in the direction they had gone for a short time. Alone once more, she began to graze. Soon we packed up and continued our own hike over the gentle land.

Besides horseshoes and picket pins, a meat grinder and a pile of cans, we have found several ten-gallon red gas drums stacked near a rock cairn, a recently dropped arrowhead, and a nicely worked canoe paddle, far from any water. All evidence of a human presence and companionship. They made us ask many questions.

On one backpacking hike the whole family was camped in an alpine valley near Molly Lake, about 2000 feet higher than Turner Lake. It had rained earlier, but it was mostly clear with bright moonlight. Every wet grass stem and bush was a silvery-gold hump. We humans were all asleep in the tent. Skye was supposed to be sleeping just outside. In the midst of all that unseen beauty, loud barking and the sound of large galloping hooves rudely awakened us as they thundered past our tent. In a second they disappeared into the distance. We got up to try and see what the dog was chasing. We didn't see them, but the scene outside the tent was worth being waked up for. Even the small cumulus clouds were silvery-gold.

Skye returned shortly, panting and grinning. She would not tell me what she had driven away so noisily, but from the sound of the hooves, I think it was a moose, a big one.

In the morning we left on the long hike home. As we walked along over the alpine vegetation, we were further visually rewarded by yesterday's rain. Under the edge of every tree and flower plant hung, vibrating gently in the low slanting rays of sunlight, rubies, gold, emeralds, sapphires and brilliant white diamonds. As we passed they returned to just plain raindrops; but on ahead gleamed new beauties, as fine as the ones we left behind. Too soon the rising sun dried the drops of water and the show was over.

As much as we loved the expansive vistas of the alpine areas with all the beauties, different from the valley beauties, it was with a feeling of completion and security that I, at least, greeted our home on our return. No one ever told me how they felt, but from their actions I suspect they felt the same. Unless it was very late, or we were very tired, we usually at least visited the garden, as well as the cats, and of course I had the milking to do while Jack made supper.

We were glad to be back on our own place and in our own house.

chapter 35

SKYE, BORDER COLLIE

As painful as losing a beloved pet can be, with no dog after I lost Pup and Kilo we got Frog in the spring of 1958. Within two years we had lost her as well, we think from some kind of worms that our worm medicine didn't protect her from. I just had to go and get myself another dog in time. I saw an ad for border collie puppies in a newspaper and sent away for one. She came eventually.

With wagging tail and paws that fly,
Here comes border collie Skye.

Skye arrived at Lonesome Lake on CF-HEO in January 1962. She was about two months old, a fuzzy, sweet fur ball with an uncontrollable tail and laughing mouth.

When she was a little older I began training her the basics. We did this as a regular thing each evening before she had her supper. At the end of her lessons she received her food. She learned quickly and was a joy to teach. If I had known then what I have learned now, our schooling would have been even faster. I was short on knowledge and sympathy for that sensitive little creature. It took me a long time to recognize this.

I took baby Skye when I hiked the daily five miles to feed the swans when she was still quite small and fuzzy. I soon found that she had a lot of trouble with the soft snow forming huge, heavy snowballs that hung from her belly and between her relatively short puppy legs. After that I left her at home if there was much soft snow on the trail. She wanted to go, but I thought she should use some of her energy growing rather than lugging around snowballs. She never made a fuss when I didn't take her. She was a patient little thing.

As her schooling advanced, and she was firm on voice commands, I introduced hand signals as I gave her the words. She quickly picked it up. I did this in case there was ever a situation where I could not tell her what I wanted her to do because of too much noise, or she herself had gone deaf. As it turned out later, both conditions were to happen.

The first time I had to give her my hand signal to come was when a helicopter landed in our field in front of the house. Skye was very interested in the slowly rotating rotors as the pilot warmed up the engine. She wanted to leap up eight or nine feet to play with the rotors. I gave her the signal to come and she did, immediately.

Another time I used hand signals, I had to control both my dog and a truck driver on the road near the bottom of the famous hill. Jack, Skye and I were hiking down the apology of a road, known as the tote road, on our way to pick up our mail. I had carelessly allowed Skye to stay on one side of the road when Jack and I crossed to avoid a large muddy puddle. Skye continued on her side. Soon a vehicle came splashing slowly along the road, where vehicles seldom ventured. Fearing Skye might try to cross to me in front of the truck, I hand signaled her to stay there and at the same time I asked the driver to stop with my other hand. The drover stopped. I asked Skye to come, by signal. When she was across the road I released the driver and he went on his way, all neatly done. We thanked him for his cooperation. After that I kept her with us.

Skye and I practiced the hand signals often on our trips down to feed the swans or any other time when I thought we should. On those trips I could stop her on the ice, then keep going until she appeared to be only a tiny black dot. Then I signaled her to come with a wave of my arm and she come running as fast as she could on slick ice. Dog claws have very little hold on bare ice, tho they seldom fall.

Sometimes I would get her running fast towards me on the ice, then hand signal a down. On her belly, she would slide a dog-length or so, while trying to find purchase on the ice, with her claws acting as skids rather than brakes, to try to stop. There she would wait for the signal to come. I did not ask for very many difficult slick-ice stops, however. She did her best to obey me. She could not help it if she could not stop instantly in those circumstances.

Once Skye made me really proud of her. Actually she made me really proud of her many times in her long life. The incident I am going to mention here was very special. Jack, Skye and I were accompanying two or three BC Parks people to the Big Lagoon where they were to be picked up by aircraft. We all had stopped on the trail where it ran along the side of a steep slope into the river, about 15 feet below. The BC Parks people wanted to talk to Jack about something. As I was behind with the dog and there was nothing of interest going on that she could help with, she gave me a stick she had picked up from the trail. Not bothering to look too carefully, I just tossed it up the hill above the trail, almost on top of a sleeping deer. At least the deer had been sleeping before I threw the stick, or perhaps hiding. As Skye always did when we threw sticks for her, she launched herself after it, not having seen the deer either. As the deer left her bed in one neat bound I just said one word, "come." Skye was almost to the stick, but she left it and returned instantly. I praised her lavishly. I have to admit I was a bit scared for my dog for a few minutes. After all we were in the park, with park people right there. They seemed rather impressed. I had recalled her many times after throwing a toy for her, then sending her on to retrieve the object. This was the first time in her life she had been asked to leave a so-attractive live animal. To me that she returned at all was amazing. But I had schooled her many times on leaving her toy, but not with a distracting live deer right there in front of her, bounding

344

away. However, she also knew she must NOT chase deer anywhere outside our fences AND not until I told her to, anywhere. She must have learned that lesson well.

Just about any job we did, Skye wanted to help with. She always went along, whether we were weeding the garden, picking berries, hiking, or anything it was safe for her to be in, she was there. Mowing and raking the hay were out, for her own safety. She could help with the hauling, however, and any handwork on the hay. She helped on any log hauling we did. She came along near the end of the log and grabbed the bark in her teeth and tried to stop the log from moving. There used to be quite a few logs and braces that had raggedly ripped off bark and wood. Some of our buildings and fences—all gone now due to the 2004 wildfire—were also chewed.

While we were doing any garden work Skye wasn't allowed to help with, she just went to her assigned place by the fence, out of the way, where she could dig a nice hole to keep cool in while we labored in the sun.

She would walk carefully behind me when going across the hay fields on a narrow trail and not mash down the uncut grass. All I had to say was "grass" and point behind me and that was where she went. She soon found out it was all right to go all over the fields after the grass had been cut, or it was winter and there was no grass to worry about. She usually stayed close to us, anyway.

Skye made many trips with us, but if we were going out to the big world, such as to Vancouver, I had to leave her with someone to look after her.

Skye loved it any time one of us sat or lay down on the ground to rest. She could get our attention more easily than when we were walking around working. If Skye couldn't play with us because we were working, she just went somewhere near, but out of the way, and lay down until we were once again available for play; that is, when we wanted to rest. She seemed to think that if we weren't working there was no reason why we couldn't throw sticks or whatever she brought to us even if it was six feet long, covered with snow, or mud, sand and dog spit, and weighed 15 pounds.

That little dog really enjoyed our trips to Junker Lake. There is a quarter-mile-long, beautiful, soft golden sand beach there where we used to go for fun and relaxation and the longhaired dog could swim.

On one trip to that area Jack was laying on his back, enjoying the restful scenery, smell and atmosphere of the lake as the little waves gently lapped the edge of the beach nearby, when a small piece of driftwood fell on his belly. He ignored it. Soon it was picked up and dropped again. Jack opened one eye, and seeing who had dropped the stick on him, closed it again. So the stick was nudged, then picked up and carried away to be chewed, pawed and liberally coated with dog spit and sand, and then once again hopefully deposited on his belly. Susan and I were egging the dog on. Poor Jack. He had had enough. He grabbed the soggy, spit-covered object and hurled it as far as he could into the lake, little thinking about what would happen next. Susan and I had a hilarious time as retriever Skye leaped into the lake, swam out, grabbed the stick, swam back to the beach and trotted, streaming water, directly up to Jack and laid the wet thing neatly on his belly, then stood there and gave herself a really good water-flinging shake.

I seem to recall they kept up that wet game until Skye became cold and Jack was soaked. I think he then decided to stand up. It's too bad he had to spoil such a marvelous game. They really were having (soggy) fun.

Skye was never a very forceful cow dog. She was too polite. I could send her off to bring a cow and she'd go to the cow, circle around behind, then stand there politely waiting for the cow to stop grazing and head off to me. She followed close behind, believing she was driving the cow. If the cow stopped to eat on the way, she waited.

She may not have been much good as a cow dog to drive cattle, but she could at least tell me where in the pasture they were. Due to thick brush, and a relatively noisy river flowing by to confuse the sound of the bell one of them wore, and a temporary hearing problem with me, I could not tell where they were. I'd ask her where Friendship was and she'd race off in the right direction. I followed. When I arrived at the cows, Skye would be standing behind Friendship, happily waving her tail and grinning. Friendship, a three-way mix of Hereford, Holstein and Ayrshire, large, fat and longhorned, would be placidly grazing, waiting for me to sling a rope over her horns to lead her to the milking place. The others followed along, with Skye bringing up the rear.

While I milked, Skye went and lay down in her assigned place, which she would defend by the border collie "eye," making two or three longhorned cows shake their horns at her, then back off and go away.

There was one time Skye did show her "teeth." Not to the cows, but to Jack and me. Susan, Jack and I were having a moderate little argument about something that escapes my memory. Skye was lying nearby and seemingly thought we were getting too wound up and gave a tiny little growl as she looked at us worriedly. I don't know what she thought, but perhaps she detected something in us that we ourselves weren't aware of. Anyway we all called off the argument and made up. The dog's growl made us take stock and improve our relationship. I really didn't think it was all that bad.

Once on a trail clearing and cattle moving trip to the fall pasture area at Elbow Lake, we were getting the herd organized for traveling when one nasty-natured old cow tried to punish Skye for just having the temerity to walk by behind her. The dog was wearing her pack of three quarts of chainsaw gas and one quart of oil. The powerful kick from the cow sent the totally innocent little dog flying into a shallow ditch. Skye was undamaged, but one side of her saddle had a huge dent, and one gas can was flattened. Fortunately, it was not broken and no gas leaked out. When a herding dog is not intending to drive something, she is not prepared to duck or otherwise avoid a kick, and is an easy target for any irritated prey animal.

Skye's greatest conquest of a bovid was over our one-ton Hereford bull, Domino.

During the summer the bull ran with the cattle on the summer pasture, but over winter he spent his days in his own corral, the strong one where Cloud learned about cans, detailed elsewhere in these memoirs. At night he lived in his stall in the barn. Jack carried his water to him all winter, but in the spring when water rose in the creek across the field, we let Domino go across the field and get his own water, after the cows had been put in the barn.

Sometimes Domino would get distracted by some tiny anemic new grass in the field and forget to return to the barn on his own. I didn't want to drive him back, so I asked Skye to "go bring Domino." Rising from her place beside a stump near the barn, she'd race across the field, circle around behind the huge placid animal and wait. He continued to graze, once in a while turning his hornless head a bit to look at the friendly dog who just wagged her tail at the attention. Eventually, big old Domino raised his head and ambled across the field to the barn, Skye right behind him, sure the decision to move was hers alone. She thought she was in control. Perhaps I am putting thoughts in her mind, for I really have no idea what Skye thought. Tho surely she did think. She was highly intelligent and sensitive. At the barn, the little dog returned to her place as Domino tromped into the barn, down the hall and into his stall.

After she was 13 years old Skye became tired and did not want to make hard trips carrying a pack any more. She had carried an eight- or 10-pound pack on most of the trips we made until we were coming back from a trip to Junker Lake. She suddenly sank down on the trail and didn't seem to want to go any farther. We lightened her load, but she still lagged behind. Jack took all of her pack and I complainingly took her saddle. I thought she was just lazy, tho she had never acted lazy once in her entire life. It didn't occur to me that she might just be getting old. She had no trouble carrying her pack to Junker Lake. Anyway I never asked her to carry a pack again. She probably had some arthritis, too.

As Skye's age approached 15 she could no longer run free because she was getting somewhat senile, and being deaf, I could not keep her safe from the various hazards, such as falling in holes or getting tangled in branches. I kept her in a stall in the barn for a lot of the time, for her own protection. One day she was helping us with some work up on the mountain and had lagged behind a bit. Soon we heard strange barking back where we had been and went to find out what was wrong. She had rolled into a hole and could not get out, as she was partly on her back. Normally she would not have fallen in the hole to start with.

In the barn she was safe, but lonely and sad. Her health continued to sink and her joy faded. She was miserable. She sleeps in a deep grave in the garden with a sack for a blanket.

Oh, Skye, I am so sorry. You loved everyone. You never hurt anyone or anything. Your loyalty was equaled only by your patience. You never complained about cold paws or if your meals were late. You even learned to go in cold water and swim, when you really didn't like water at all when you were young. In time you came to enjoy retrieving from water. You were a wonderful and entertaining companion for all of your life, and you were part of my family, too.

I lost Skye in January 1977, then went dogless until March 1993 when I adopted a tiny female Australian shepherd, about six weeks old. She resembles a border collie so much that most people think she is one. And she acts like one also. Her name is Liesel. She is black and white with some tan trim—and smart. She is getting old now and is not too steady on her feet and she is deaf. She will be 16 years old on February 7. Being not too careful where she has dropped stuff that should be out in the yard, I have to keep her outdoors. She has the run of my barn–woodshed and can come or go as she pleases. She has a blanket-covered kennel to sleep in, in the barn. She never made a mess in the barn. The other accidents I have to excuse. I think there was something going wrong with her signaling, which would tell her to go outside. Several times she would be eating, then suddenly stop and rush out of the barn to do her business out in the grass or snow, depending on the time of year. In two years she never crapped in the barn.

It is now May 3, 2009 and Liesel is still with me, tho she is getting frail and has a very fickle appetite. She eats cooked hamburger and dog biscuits. If she lives to May seventh, she will be sixteen years and three months since birth.

She made it to June 14, 2009 and then died in her sleep. Her grave is marked with a long, volcanic stone Jack found on a rock bar in the river.

Now I am dogless again.

Liesel

Oh Liesel-gum, you are getting old now and really tired. You are 16 years and almost four months since birth. I wonder if you think back on your long life and remember how you used to go on long interesting hikes up the Salloompt with Breezie and me, and how he gobbled up the rich grass while you played in the little creeks. Do you remember carrying a pack on your back when you, Susan and several other people and horses were going along the trail and you had to travel under my horse's tail to avoid getting stepped on by Susan's horse? You never got trod on, either. Those horses must have liked you, because they never hurt you.

Do you remember all the fun you and I had finding things and you bringing them to me? Do you remember chewing, pawing and rolling rocks, and barking at them?

Do you remember how patient and gentle you were with those little goat babies and the young calves? Do you ever think back on how you used to play with snow when I shoveled out my trails, and how you got all that snow in your face?

I remember very well the time you risked your life to keep that mama bear from me and would not come back to me when I called. I was scared you would get run over, you were so busy keeping the bear away from me, and you would not come back until you felt the bear was far enough away that I was safe. Then to pay you for your selflessness, I abused you verbally and physically all the rest of the way to Susan's place. And after we got home, how you went to your house and spent the night there, too sad and sorrowful even to eat your supper, because I told you to eat it in a nasty voice. I am deeply ashamed and sorry.

Oh, Liesel, I miss you so.

chapter 36

BREEZIE CHALLENGE

Many things in our lives can be a challenge, even horse training—especially horse training.

When Jack and I left Lonesome Lake and moved farther down the valley, we brought out the four horses we had then. One of those was a black and white tobiano five-year-old mare, named Bess. I had started riding her when she was a well grown two-year-old. As a five-year-old, she went in various horse club activities. We did this for several years. Then I became bored with gymkhana and started schooling Bess in jumping and some other stuff.

Then one day I realized that I needed a new horse to teach. My limited knowledge did not allow me to teach Bess anything more, but I could start out again with a shiny new horse. And this time around, with all the new information on horse schooling I had been absorbing, I just wanted to see what a new horse could teach me, rather than the other way around. Suddenly I was facing a new challenge. I was hooked on the idea, and wanted that new horse now!

With a couple of trips to the Chilcotin country, home to many, many horses, I found my heart's desire, or rather he found me, in a snowy corral where there were five or six other horses.

When I walked into that corral, the herd milled around a bit, then stopped about 50 feet away and stood watching me, somewhat unsure about a stranger in their corral. One young horse, a palomino, left the others and walked slowly up to me, stopped, stretched out his nose and lightly touched my shirtfront, looked me straight in the eye, then turned and walked back to the herd, his message delivered. He stole my heart and kept it for the rest of his short life.

One of the first things this young gelding taught me was that it is not necessary to have a big struggle to teach a horse to let you lift his legs for hoof maintenance, shoeing or whatever. All one really needs to do is show the haltered, but not tied up, horse that you are not going to cause any harm to his very essential legs. Horses' legs and feet are very important to them and they naturally feel protective of them. Also, if you don't tie a horse he does not feel trapped. If you do not push horses past where they are comfortable with what you are doing with them, they will learn to trust you and will do what you ask, if they understand. Since you, the teacher, have the bigger brain—tho not the greater sensitivity necessarily—it's still up to you to figure out how to ask.

Oh, how I wish I had known for most of my life at Lonesome Lake what I learned from Susan and several other teachers after I moved. They taught me to let the horse tell me how he or she feels about the situation, and I am very thankful.

I started this yellow horse, Breezie Future, when he wasn't quite two, but all I was doing was just getting him used to me brushing him all over, right down to his hooves. Then I began lifting a front leg, then putting it down gently and not trying to keep hold of it. Soon he was letting me hold the leg up for a few seconds before setting it back down softly. That way it was not long until I could hold the leg between by knees and trim his hoof. I set it back down before he got tired and demanded it be set down.

Not long after that I began putting my arm over his withers. Then I added a bit of weight, just for a short time. He seemed completely unconcerned. This method of introducing a young horse to carrying a weight, even a rider, was one I used most of my life at Lonesome Lake. I don't know where I got it. Not from Dad. I never saw him start a young horse to riding. His horses were for work and packing. Even a well-trained packhorse won't necessarily accept a real live predator on his back until he learns the human predator intends no harm.

It was not long before I was standing on my mounting block, then just lying over his back and reaching down his other side and petting him. Then I just gave a little jump and was across his back, briefly, then slid down again.

One of my horsemanship teachers, Lori, had put a concept in my mind, which I had never thought of. She told me that when I began training a young horse to be ridden, I was a guest in his house. Suddenly I realized how right that concept was. Altho I had tried to act as a guest on our first rides, I had never thought of it so plainly. Perhaps that is why I never got bucked off. I never learned to ride a bucking horse. I felt that if a horse would want to buck, then I didn't ride it. No horse has ever deliberately put me off. I can say this now because I can't ride any more. Arthritic hips do not allow it.

At Lonesome Lake I had several horses who would have made excellent jumpers, but I failed to recognize the potential for pleasure, having jumped horses only from a standing start over a log in the trail. I hadn't found anything wonderful about that kind of jumping, or pleasurable.

However, in the fall of 1990 Susan took me and two of our horses to Williams Lake to play in their Cariboo Fall Fair. They had several events, one of which was indoor jumping. It was the first time I had ever seen horses jumping under a rider and I was captivated. A pair cantered around the indoor arena and went up and over, more or less together, each horse and rider over their own fence. As the space was somewhat limited, there were only four fences, or maybe six. I am afraid my attention was riveted more on the horses than it was on the number of fences, and the thought burst into my mind that, heck, my horse can do that!

After we returned home I began making small jumps for Bess. Soon she was going over them quite handily. Then we progressed to running a real pattern, jumping several jumps as we cantered thru the course and I began to see that I had really missed a lot in my life.

As I was jumping stirrup-less, to please a nasty-natured corn, it was necessary to be in pretty good balance with my horse. For a saddle, I used one I made for myself. It was light, flexible and very comfortable for me and for my horse. But it didn't have stirrups.

It was not like running down a straight line of jumps. My courses involved many turns, and turns require balance or you and your horse tend to part company readily.

What was to stop me riding horses was gradually worsening arthritic hips. That was the practical reason for getting Breezie. I had hoped a smaller, narrower horse might be better for me to ride, as Bess is quite round and wide. Breezie was more comfortable.

I set up one jump course that had 11 jumps, but only five fences. Four of them were taken both ways, which involved quite a few lead changes as we cantered around the course. And the ride was delicious, something like good music in motion. The balancing with the powerful animal, turning, going straight up and over the next jump, landing softly, then cantering on, turning, changing leads, the feeling of oneness with the power that lofts the unit of horse and rider safely into the air for two or three seconds of weightlessness—I can't really convey in words what I felt; this is the best that I can do to try to tell others what it was like on those rides—and a deep love and trust for my partner, and total concentration and oneness with her.

When I had Breezie well along in his education, Bess became surplus. I sought a good home for her where she still lives, now 25 years old. Bess had a happy girl who learned to ride better on her broad back and became an excellent rider over fences. Bess is a bit stiff in her legs now, but some days she will take some happy children for rides. I had given her away to those kind people. I do not consider my pets to be commodities, and Bess is very much a pet.

With nothing better to think about, I came up with the idea of designing a course involving walk, trot and canter, circles, straight runs, a backup, turns on haunch and forehand, and stop. The horse was to be guided over this course while I sang a song in praise of all the things horses will do for us if they understand what we want. The course takes four minutes to run. The song, listing all the things we ask horses to do for us, has 14 verses, and takes four minutes to sing as one rides the horse over the course. That was a challenge, which I never got quite right but I had a heck of a lot of fun practicing. (I'm only including a small portion here to avoid monotony.)

Oh what friends we have in horses,
They're so honest, sweet and kind.
Oh, what friends we have in horses,
Tho sometimes they're hard to find.

Anything we ask them to do,
They will do if they understand.
Oh what friends we have in horses,
They're so honest, sweet and grand.

If we ask them for a sidepass, they will neatly step across.
If we ask for a ride in darkness, they will give it and not get lost.
If we ask them for a lead change, they will give it crisp and nice.
If we ask them for a quick stop, they will stop as if on ice.

Anything we ask them to do, they will do if they understand.
Oh what friends we have in horses,
They're so honest, sweet and grand.
They're so honest, sweet and grand.

The last line was to be sung slowly as the horse partner takes seven slow steps with the front feet on a quarter circle to stop at position

"A" on a dressage arena, using the traditional letters AFBMCHEK as the guide points.

We had two public goes at it but neither one satisfied me. Breezie did his part better than I did mine, but then I had to keep my place in the song and his place in the pattern. He had learned where he should be in the pattern by where in the song I was. If I lost my way, then he also lost his. I probably would have gotten it if I'd had more years to ride and practice.

Breezie had turned three when I started him on jumping, just going over low fences, 18 inches high. He could jump that easily. By the time I had to stop riding, he was taking a 33-inch triple bar, joyously, at age six.

My highest jump was with Bess. She cleared 42 inches.

Horses seem to be capable of feeling when their human companion is hurting, and can be very gentle and quiet. When my arthritic trouble reached a certain stage I could no longer jump on my horse and ride off on whatever I had planned to do that day. I had to get on his back and walk around for 10 minutes or so, painfully, then get off and sit for a short while to let whatever was going to happen to the joints happen, then I could get back on and ride for a half hour or so. While I was sitting, Breezie would stand close to me with his head within inches and not poke at me or bother me in any way. Normally he would have been poking his head into my face, picking at me, if I let him, which I didn't. I pushed him away if he invaded my space that way. His standing quietly, close to me, was not offensive so I let him, as I felt he was expressing sympathy.

The last year I rode Breezie I had to give up jumping, tho I could still do ordinary gentle walk, trot and canter, until the middle of June 2004. The challenge to keep riding was just too much to rise to. The price was too high.

As I could still look after him for the following winter, I kept him until spring, then began looking for someone to adopt the young fellow. He had great potential as a dressage horse and he could have made a good cow pony. And he had some chance of becoming a useful school horse with the local riding facility. He could have made a therapy horse, too.

The owner of the riding school liked him and had promising grounds, very clean and neat. I gave her a month to try him out and if at the end of that time she considered Breezie suitable to teach people how to ride, she could adopt him. I was going to give him away, as I didn't consider him a commodity, either. He was a pet. But it was not to be.

Just one day before his eighth birthday, he was dead. Something out in the pasture injured him fatally. No one saw what happened.

The owner of the riding school came to my place, in great distress, and told me he was gone. I was out in my garden, transplanting cabbages on the fifth of May when she came. Down on my knees, my mind screamed "WHAT?" Feeling like a large horse had kicked me in the chest, I continued to kneel as I silently absorbed that bit of devastating news. Then I asked what had happened, expecting colic or a broken leg, but she said he had run into a stick, but she really didn't know, as she hadn't seen anything happen to him. Then I asked her if I could go see him. She would have to take me in her vehicle as mine was in the shop getting its windshield reglued.

Numb with shock, we walked out to the road where her vehicle waited. As there was another person with her it was a tight squeeze to fit us in the truck.

She stopped beside the fence where my gentle riding partner lay, just on the other side of a four-and-a-half-foot-high page wire fence, topped with a stout rail bolted to the posts. He was on his right side under a cedar tree. All four legs extended stiffly towards the fence. He obviously was very dead. All the way down there I had harbored a one-in-a-million chance she had been mistaken and he would be standing up.

In shock, I tried to see what he could have run into to damage himself so seriously, but could see nothing there except some branches he had broken on the trunk of a small spruce. He was hurt somewhere else and he seemed to have lurched into the tree as he was falling. He left a lot of his neck hair, but no blood, on the tree. He lay just beyond the little spruce.

I wanted to go over the fence and say a proper goodbye to him, but as it was not my fence I didn't want maybe to do it any damage. I just reached my arm thru the four-inch squares to touch his foot and up his leg to above the fetlock. Down on my knees that way, and with my arm thru the fence, in a little while I got tired and began a cramp in my arm. I withdrew it and remained on my knees trying to adjust to the totally unexpected loss, when the tears came. I cried his loss. When the well was dry I rose and asked the lady to take me home.

Back home, completely exhausted, I returned to my cabbage transplanting, still numb from shock. Transplanting required no thought and I had nothing else to do, tho I felt like doing something.

Three days before I lost him I had gone into his pen while he munched a bucket of fresh grass I had brought him on one of my visits to him over the past 26 days. I went all the way around his warm body, rubbing my hands along his sides and poking my nose into his fur to inhale his sweet horsy aroma, one of the most delicious smells I know. That was the only time I went into his pen. The other times I just talked to him over the fence. I went in with him because that might have been the last time I would see him while he was still mine, if the lady decided she wanted him and decided in the next week, when the month would be up.

I would have liked to bring Breezie's body home and bury him here on my own land, but as he was eight or 10 miles away, I didn't see that as a very practical idea. He is buried near where he died.

I have a tiny substitute grave containing hoof trimmings, a shed baby tooth he had spat out into my hand and some mane hair, all resting on a bed of fine hay in a one-gallon ice-cream container, covered tightly with its own lid. This is set down in a deep hole partially filled with drain rock, then covered with a large flat rock that Jack wheel-barrowed in and helped me place over the top. In one side of the hole I planted a memorial in the form of a cross with these words impressed into the wood of the cross piece, then painted and varnished.

BREEZIE FUTURE
06 05 97 to 05 05 05
Loved by All
and
Sorely Missed

Losing Breezie left me totally bereft. That was the first time in my life that I didn't have a horse at all. Even when all the horses were out on the various pastures, where they went when they weren't being used every day or so, they were out there and in a matter of time two or more of them would be brought home. I knew they were there and was satisfied with that. It was with anticipation and pleasure that I awaited each homecoming. Now suddenly I had nothing.

Susan suggested I get a miniature horse. Unlike a big horse, it would be a lot easier to care for. Caring for Breezie was getting to be too much, with carrying water, etc. with my complaining hips. A mini would require little up-keep.

Susan bugged me, and my need for a horse finally won, and as she was in Kamloops at the time I asked her to find me a mini and trailer her in here. She soon found one for sale. On July 27 she arrived here with a tiny strawberry roan pinto, about 40 inches high. At last I had a horse that I could see over. I am five feet, three inches and I towered over that little mare.

I named her Sorrow, hoping she would somehow help me live with my sorrow for Breezie Future. In time she helped, but of course there was no way any horse could change history.

For the two years I had her, she certainly gave me much pleasure and more than one laugh. She is cheeky, lively, sweet, dominant, spoiled—unspoiled by the time I gave her away. A good family adopted her and seems to be having a lot of fun with her. They have a buggy for her to pull. One of the children gave me a ride in their buggy in the Bella Coola Fall Fair Parade last fall, so I got to ride her after all, or at least with her.

While I still had Sorrow, watching her play was wonderful entertainment as she lightly raced about, mane and tail flying, and her feet barely contacting the ground. She seemed light as a feather. Her performance was breathtakingly beautiful and moving. She is poetry in motion.

With my lack of mobility, even a tiny horse was becoming a chore, a painful chore. In the winter of 2007 I finally had to quit driving because of my balky hips and feet that wanted to stay crossed. Someone has to drive me if I want to go anywhere. Susan usually does it and I can go visit Sorrow any time I want to. She is only 10 or so miles away, no distance at all really.

For the first 27 years of my life I was taught that even the word "emotion" was a taboo subject. It was something that must be kept hidden, except anger and hate. I have often wondered why this was the rule at that time. Oh, being happy and laughing was OK. One must never let on that they were sad, lonely or disappointed. Disappointment was the same as sulking and not encouraged. If you were to shed a tear or two because you had lost your pet, you were told crying about it would not bring the pet back. I don't think anyone ever believed it would.

In my enlightened worldview, tears were never intended to do anything for the departed, but for the surviving. They somehow make the loss easier to accept. For me, anyway.

Is it possible the expression of sorrow by someone is embarrassing to others because they don't know how to act around grieving people? Perhaps because they were not taught by example in childhood, again by the passé belief one would be stronger to face life if they hobbled the expression of their sorrow?

Some people seem to know what to say to a person who has recently suffered a grievous loss. I think in the simple act of saying, "We are sorry about your loss," they are taking on some of the pain you feel and thus lighten the load on you. Tho it cannot change the situation, the simple connection of their feelings with yours is a sharing. A sharing that maybe is quite as essential among us as sharing of food is.

So why are we universally so disturbed by other's tears and so ashamed of our own?

chapter 37

VIOLENCE

Soon the world will be filled with sorrow,
Pain and grief for the dead and dying.
We could have stopped it had we been trying.
All that's left will be dust and empty crying.

Many brave souls who join in battle;
Many brave souls'll hear 'chine gun's rattle;
Lured on by nations false prattle,
Will lie in heaps upon the tortured land.

And those who did not want a war, or join in battle
Will also lie in heaps, beneath the rubble
Where shattered buildings used to stand.

September 11, 2001 dawned warm and sunny with a clear blue sky in New York. In Bella Coola, British Columbia, Canada, it was raining. I had just milked my dripping wet cow and brought the milk to Jack's house for him to put in his fridge. I found him watching TV. I glanced at it. I saw a lot of people running down the street, followed by a dense cloud of dust, debris and smoke. I asked him what was going on. It looked like a lot more than a riot. It was.

He told me an airplane had hit a tall building. I asked if it was an accident. No, it was no accident. I sat down to watch his TV, thinking, "Well, here comes World War Three."

I stayed at Jack's house for a while as the TV showed the airplane driving into one of the Twin Towers, and instantly exploding in a ball of fire. Horrified, we continued to watch. I had never seen anything like this before in my life. One just doesn't fly airplanes into buildings, tall or otherwise, unless there is no possible choice. This was deliberate, pre-meditated mega-murder. It was an atrocity.

Nearly 3000 innocent people died. Four big passenger jets were destroyed. Two quarter-mile-high buildings were totally shattered to bits. Another building was wounded. The shock wave did not stop at the USA border, but raced around the world. Most of the human part of the world reacted with shock, sympathy, horror and revulsion, and mourned with the USA.

What did the perpetrators of this atrocity gain? How were their lives improved? What was their goal? I have never heard answers to any of these questions. And in addition to the 3000 dead people from that attack on civilians, the response by the injured nation has caused the deaths of many thousands more, mostly innocent people, just going about their daily lives, trying to drag a living out of a stingy, rocky land.

That atrocity set me to thinking, after enough of the shock had worn off. Some of the emotional response is still with me and I imagine it will last to the end of my life. It changed my life forever. It started me contemplating how I was relating to people and other animals, especially horses and dogs, and considering how these creatures looked at life and us, and how we respond to each other, all of us, horses, dogs, cows, and humans.

If that atrocity causes even one person to try and improve his or her relationship with others, then all those thousands who died would not have died in vain.

That atrocity makes me ask why do the animals with the biggest brain, and the smallest instincts in the world, do such horrible things to one another? Especially when we will risk our own lives to rescue a complete stranger? Why can't we live together and not resort to deadly violence to solve our social problems? Or any problems? Why do we continue to do to others what we would not want done to ourselves? After all, no number of wrongs will ever make a right.

It rained all that day. Having nothing that I had to do, I sat and watched TV, hoping some idiots would not over-react and begin loosing some nuclear devices of destruction, thus ensuring a war. I hate war. I hate violence. I hate destruction of anything useful. I can see no reason for any war between intelligent reasoning beings. My dad was in the First World War and he told us all about it. It was not fun.

When it became apparent the out-of-order partial date of that atrocity was permanent, I did a lot of thinking about it and felt it trivialized the lives of all those who died that day. Also being out of order, and not complete, in a while no one will remember what it is about. I decided to refer to that atrocity as the Twin Towers Atrocity. We do not have a date for Pearl Harbor or any other remembrance anniversary, except the fourth of July, where we at least name the month and day.

Now it might seem that as it was an attack on the USA it is really none of my business. But I think it is the business of all humans. I

Twin Towers Atrocity Memorial
"September 2001. Please everybody, stop the violence and sit down and talk, and forget about who hit whom first. Don't do to others what you wouldn't want done to you. No number of wrongs will ever make a right."

feel very strongly that the human race must seek a way to solve their problems in non-violent ways and cease this retaliation response to every little problem. We do not have to love everybody; just don't bother others we can't stand.

Are there any benefits from wars, overall, after one calculates the costs—in lives, materials, and buildings, the land, and all the unintended victims and destruction?

The only benefits I can see are improved machines and medical treatments. Why can't these improvements be achieved by nations applying the same effort, but without all the destruction?

Some might argue wars teach us a lot of geography. If one wants to learn geography, why can't they just learn it without the attendant destruction and death?

Of course we did learn a lot of political geography, with the changing boundaries. Of more use were the physical features of the globe. We had a pretty good picture of the major rivers, mountains, islands, continents, etc. I am sure we did not need war to learn this. Our natural curiosity did that.

One other "benefit" of war is to reduce the world human population a bit, but surely there are gentler, less destructive ways to achieve this, such as not making excessive numbers of humans in the first place. A good reduction of humans would go a long way towards reducing greenhouse gasses and global warming. To reduce the human population to a level that the world's resources can generously support we need to STOP reproducing for a number of years. But no one can order this to happen; we all must *want* to save the Earth from our greed and over-exploitation and over population, and we must leave all other species their share of the world's resources. I feel we have no right to everything on the face of the Earth. We need to have everything that is living on the face of the Earth continue living.

Is one reason for wars to satisfy the human love of violence? Many of our games, such as hockey and football, which seem to be filled with a certain amount of violence, entertain a vast number of fans who resort to violence themselves if their favorite game is delayed for some reason. At least if what I see on TV is to be believed, that would be true.

And rodeo. I would love to see the horses that are used for bucking being quietly tacked up in the corral. Then the rider mounts in the usual fashion, rides into the arena and signals the horse to buck as hard and furious as he can. Jumping horses are not tacked up in chutes, so why should buckers be? All the stuff we have our horses do for us should be done as partners rather than opponents, I believe.

Considering the innate friendliness of horses, it bothers me that horses actually are bred to want to fight their riders. If the buckers were trained to buck rather than being bred to buck, then bucking would no longer be a negative action, but cooperation between man and horse. Since I have never ridden a bucking horse I may not know what I am talking about, but I think even friendly bucking should give a guy a pretty good ride. This statement is based on watching some of my own horses playing in the field. They can buck, spin, sunfish and stop just as well as those nags let out of the bucking chute wearing a rider. Nothing has energized the ones in the field except joy and exuberance.

One day I watched my horse, Breezie Future, demonstrate his bucking ability. As he was a new horse I had just brought here, I had kept him separated from Susan's horses because one of hers resented my palomino and chased him around the field at breakneck speed. I was afraid at least one of them would get badly injured. The field had holes and other hazards in it. I kept him in my cow's pasture for a while and let them talk over an electric wire along the top of the fence.

In time Susan moved one of her mares and I tried letting Breezie into the big field again. He was so happy to be let out in the new field, he first had a good roll, then put on the most beautiful bucking show I had ever seen. Of course I didn't have my camcorder handy. He hadn't told me he was going to play. Anyway, out in the new field, after his roll, he started bucking, all in one place, reversing his heading 180 degrees on each landing, head lowered, back arched, he spun in the same small spot. I was glad I wasn't riding him. Tho he would have been very quiet to ride after he had finished his exercises for the week.

Breezie needed a lot of warming up before a ride unless he was with other horses. If he was running free with another horse he would not need any special exercise to get him over wanting to play. But if he had been penned up by himself I always longed him before riding. On the longe line he would buck and dash about. Then after he didn't want to play, I would ask him for walk, trot and canter, and to put some energy into those gaits, until he was well warmed up. Then I sat on him and rested while he worked.

I could tell when he was ready to do his jumping just by the ease with which his body was working, much like a fine motor that has warmed up and is humming along smoothly, all bathed in oil.

The concept that the use of violence is the only way to achieve what we want from humans and other animals has caused a lot of pain, frustration, resentment, anger and fear in those we are trying to teach. There is, however, a better way.

When Dad was training a young horse to work in a team he would hitch the young one beside the older one, then drive off. Of course the old horse starts off, but the young one does not. She does not know she is supposed to. Dad taps her on the rump, gently. Startled, she starts off, too fast, and hits the bit. The bit she recognizes and stops. She has been ridden. They both stop. Dad starts them up with the same thing happening again. In a few more starts she will learn that when her teammate starts she should also, and they can then be driven off together and they are ready to haul some light thing.

When Dad was training his horses for harness work he only used the whip to ask them to move. Our best pullers were never hit, but merely asked and they did their all. To hit them would only have confused them. Lazy horses will do more work with some use of the whip, but only a little. After that, whipping will just cause the horse to jump around, back up and fuss. They know they can't pull the load and won't try any more, but get confused and worried. Dad never beat his horses. He just tapped their rumps to get a little more speed when it was necessary.

That situation would usually crop up when mowing. Then it was necessary for both horses to walk right along or the uncut grass would clog up the cutter bar. Then one had to stop the team, back up a step and stop. The driver had to get off the mower seat, pull all the uncut grass out of the cutter bar, then remount the machine and try to get a nice crisp start, and keep on walking crisply or it would soon clog again.

A horse mustn't stop to snatch a mouthful of grass as she walks by either. She must learn to grab it and keep on going. Hard-to-catch Rocket learned this so well that she could eat continuously, and almost never stalled the mower. She was much better than lazy old Rommy. Rommy did need to be reminded frequently to walk right along, or there would be a lot of stops to clear the cutter bar.

Rommy was a good horse. He carried his packs well, even if sometimes making square-sided boxes somewhat diamond-shaped by hitting trees he should have gone farther away from along the trail. He did his work well enough if it was not too hard. It seems hard work was not his job description. What was it then? Eating. Anytime, anywhere, as often as possible and as much as possible. And he was very friendly and good to ride.

So, when I started teaching horses to work, I tried to do the same as Dad did. The first horse I trained to work in harness was Rommy, at four years of age. He was a nice, sturdy, well-built young gelding. We had no trouble getting started, as I had been riding him for a couple of years and he already knew stop and start. His first work in harness was as a single horse, hauling fence rails out of the forest. I had cut them down, limbed and cut them to length, and left them where they fell.

Rommy hauled them, one or two at a time, a short way to where I piled them so they could be loaded onto the wagon to be taken to where we would build a deer-proof fence, or mostly deer-proof fence.

The next horse I trained to work in harness was Thuja. She also took to work with no fuss at all. She had been ridden and packed before I bought her, so she knew something and was not inclined to panic if things went wrong.

The people that I bought Thuja from told me how they had her and some other horses on a trip to the alpine and had left them in a small meadow while they hiked up to some interesting stuff they wanted to investigate. Looking at the surroundings thru their binoculars, they noticed "Dusty" (Thuja) had some stuff that looked like her pack underneath her when it should have been on her back. She was grazing peacefully. She was a good and honest horse for all of her life.

In 1959—the year our daughter Susan was born, and named for Dad's mare, Susan—Jack contracted to horse-pack the winter feed for the trumpeter swans. Of course Susan and I would help him. Anyway we did the packing job that year and two more years with just the two horses, Thuja and Rommy.

By 1962 the swan flock had grown, so we had to get more feed, which meant we'd need another horse. The new horse we acquired was Rocket, a short, black, chunky animal who turned out to be a good packhorse and an excellent horse for work in harness. She was not the easiest horse to catch, but she was such a good worker she was worth a bit of trouble to get hold of. It didn't help her that she was nine years old when we bought her and was not even halter trained. She was a horse who never had to be urged in any way except by voice to get her to pull. The biggest problem with her was to keep her calm while she waited for the signal to start when the load was heavy and she knew she would have to pull as hard as she could. Head high, she was coiled and ready. If I put the lines in one hand, she would relax a bit. She knew we weren't going to move right then. But the instant I took my right line in my right hand, she was right there to do her bit. On easy jobs such as haying she just walked off, head low, and quiet.

In 1965 more swans made us acquire another horse, Lucky Debonair, branded LD, mentioned elsewhere in this story. He also learned to work in harness, tho not the best puller in the world. He was a good packhorse, tho a bit tall for me to throw 100 pounds of grain up on very easily. Of course I never threw a hundred pounds of anything easily on any horse. To get it up on the packsaddle at all, with all the strength and knack I could muster, was not easy. But I could do it. I guess I am stubborn. I wanted to do my share and since I was able to boost those bags of grain up on the horses, I didn't see any reason not to. Also with two packers putting the load on together, it is more comfortable for the horse.

The next time we had to get new horses was in 1968. Rommy having been moved on to the "Green Pastures," and another jump in the swan numbers, meant we had to obtain two new horses for the fall packing.

A pale chestnut gelding, Spud, and a bay mare, Guenevere, came to help. Both had been ridden and were gentle. Spud worked quite well in spite of a crooked foot. The mare, well she, ah…while having been named after the Queen of Camelot, acted more like the idiot of Fogswamp! At least that was how I saw it then. Now, however, I believe she was simply irritated and confused by the machine she was pulling, and maybe by me, her driver. She was very sensitive and responded to the slightest signals from her rider. She did much better at plowing, logging, hauling a sled, whether in a team or alone. Packing and riding she did well at.

Guenevere was the first of several more mares I could not get to work quietly. Frustrated, impatient and disappointed, I applied the good old whip, which, of course, achieved nothing but causing her to act worse, if possible. I feel very bad about whipping her, as she continued to give me good rides and never lost her trust in me when I was riding her or just handling her. She never showed the slightest desire to do anything to hurt me back, no matter that I might be in a perfect position to be kicked.

Then there was the time when the tree part fell on her and me, knocking me out for a bit. She stopped in mid-stride and never moved. She had to have had a reason. Normally she would have jumped away when the log fell on her rump. She did not. When I came to a few seconds later, I guess, I glanced down from her back and saw her left leg with the tip of her hoof resting on top of the small log she was stepping over when I mumbled "whoa," as the log hit us. I slid off her and set her foot on the ground, then sat for a bit on the log. Soon I remounted and continued our trip.

While we are on the subject of violence, I will take a swipe at fur trapping with leg-hold traps, even tho I engaged in it a bit. The only excuse was to make a living, a good enough reason, I suppose. With our moral values, I have to wonder why people didn't invent some more humane method of catching those innocent animals. Eventually they did, but why did it take so long? Death by wolves has to be more merciful than by leg-hold trap. Wolves want to kill and eat immediately after catching and not wait for several days, as most victims of leg-hold traps must wait in terror and agony for death to release them from their pain. And we call the wolf cruel. The wolf can only use the tools she comes equipped with to acquire her food. Wolves probably do not seek to cause pain. They want to eat.

Anyway, to my everlasting shame I didn't let it bother me too much as I skinned, stretched and cleaned the small animals' skins; how they must have suffered, struggling desperately to escape the traps holding their delicate legs and paws. Martens and foxes get wounded the worst, with shattered legs and broken toes. Even checking the traps every few days there would be plenty of time for these creatures to suffer grievous wounds to their legs. Then the animals get cold from shock and exhaustion and rain, and have no shelter or water, thus increasing their agony. My sympathy was limited. My thoughts were on sewing up the mangled injuries to the skins, to increase the dollar value.

Dad really couldn't have visited his traps any more often than he did or he wouldn't have caught anything. Man leaves a lot of scent behind and the little animals won't come to the trap bait until it smells safe, which it is not.

Once Dad had me go look at some traps for him. I have forgotten now why. As I approached a fox trap, I could see some red fur where the trap was. Moving slowly, I neared the set. The little red fox had chewed every stick and small tree within reach and dug up a thick mound of snow and frozen ground. She was lying, exhausted, on the mound, almost unable to move any more. She looked up at me with frightened, hopeless eyes, but made no effort to escape. The full impact of the agony to that poor little creature hit me hard. I couldn't turn her loose, even if I had wanted to. Her leg was mangled from paw to elbow with shattered bone stuck thru the torn akin. I quickly did what I had to for the little innocent thing. Oh God, what a way to make a living!

I have never told anyone about that fox. It was just too upsetting.

Of course I took it home, to be skinned, stretched and then sold, for a pittance.

I have never forgotten it either, and with this story I am shedding the tears that I didn't shed then. And I have had a soft spot in my heart for foxes ever since, even ones that are making trouble for me.

That was over 60 years ago.

A much more recent, and pleasant, encounter with a fox I called Persilla happened at our place at Lonesome Lake the year we left there. We had killed a beef animal the fall before and hauled the guts to the garden to bury it deep in the soft soil. The next spring when the ground thawed the little fox that had been around, and was quite tame, began making tunnels into the delicious contents of the belly pit. I didn't want her exposing that rotten smelly stuff for fear it might entice bears, who could then make trouble for anyone going to the garden for vegetables.

To try to stop her I put some woven wire over it. That usually would stop foxes, as they were scared of metal. This one was not scared, but just tunneled underneath and got her reward. We also covered the filled-in belly hole with heavy planks. She just dug under it. Eventually I tried setting a well-padded rattrap in her tunnel. I didn't want to injure her toes with the trap. I wanted only to scare her with a little nip. I needn't have worried. She never got caught. She simply dug another tunnel along side the one with the trap in it. Then I stuffed chunks of log in all her tunnels except the one with the trap. She just dug another tunnel.

She was obviously smarter than I was, or at least more persistent, for I gave up first. I never saw her at the pit all summer, but she surely was there.

She never bothered our hens, either. She tried to play with Melly, the cat, but Melly didn't want to play with Persilla. Melly stood quite still in the field as Persilla made advances towards her in a playful manner, then jumped back when the cat turned to face her and growled. Persilla went all the way around Melly that way, with the cat turning with her, always facing the fox. They kept about 15 feet apart. Finally Persilla gave up and trotted off across the field. Then Melly raced for the fence, about 40 feet away, and up the corner post like a black streak.

One day Jack noticed a pair of wolves walking along outside the fence at the top of the field our house was in. As we had a sick little calf loose in the field, he asked me what I thought he should do about the wolves. I suggested he take a shot at them, thinking only to frighten rather than kill one. He shot, but misunderstanding me, killed the female, a beautiful silvery-gray creature. I helped him drag her heavy body up the mountain a short way where we rolled her into a ravine, to remove bear bait farther from the field.

I have heard the sound of mourning in cow, horse, and dog voices enough times in my life, but when the male wolf returned to our place a day or two after he had lost his mate, he gave a single howl, and I have seldom heard a more profound feeling of sorrow and loss as was expressed in that single, lonely call. I felt both guilty and sorry for him. We should have put the calf in the barn. The wolves were, after all, outside the fence.

It was all well and good to learn about geography, even if it came from reporting in *Time Magazine,* but that did not make a complete education. The three of us kids learned a lot more from books given to the family by the schools down the valley, for several years. Then we were informed about correspondence courses provided to remote families. Our parents sent away for information. The correspondence school people in Victoria, BC responded with tests to find out what John and I knew so they could put us in the appropriate grades. Stanley had already left home to live his own life. They put Johnny in grade five and me in grade four. We were both short on some things, but long on others.

We were delighted to be going to school, right in our own home, and Mother was our Home Instructor. Now we were just like all the kids out there in the big world, only better. We could stay at home and study as much as we wanted, not be held back by others as we had heard happens in public schools. We could still ramble and learn to add to our book learning.

I was able to go thru two grades in one year, and I seem to remember my brother did also. We were short on social studies, history and art. I knew how to mix paints for different shades and tints, but not the correct names for those things. I had been drawing cows, horses and deer from as far back as I can remember. I would sit out in the corral and draw cows and horses for hours at a time.

I resented being forced to study art as I considered art to be a non-essential subject that one should not be made to do, but should be taken at their own expense later in life, if they so choose. Art, music and dance are abilities a person of any age either has or doesn't have and should be left for each individual to decide. I feel that if one has a bent for art in any form, the desire to express it will drive them to work on it and they will love it. In the five grades that I went thru there was very little in the art course that I didn't already know and was doing on my own.

Art can take many forms. One day I had a professional carpenter at my house where I live now to do some work for me. I can't do any work that requires ladder climbing, so I hire a carpenter for those jobs. I was talking to him about an easy chair I had built at Lonesome Lake and carried out on my back, 12 miles to where we met Susan with her truck. The two pieces that form the back are naturally curved birch, not quite exact copies, but close. I had looked at many trees to find them. When I chopped down the tree that I thought had one curved section, I found both pieces.

When I asked how he would have handled the bent pieces for the chair back, he replied he wouldn't even try to do what I had done to make that chair. He went on to explain. He was a carpenter not an artist. Carpenters build things straight and true and on even angles. They don't work with odd angles, curves and gingerbread. Artists do that.

As all the turning on almost every piece of this chair was done by hand and "eye-balling," the result, he said, was not the work of a carpenter, but of an artist. I had never seriously considered myself much of an artist, but perhaps I have been under-selling myself a bit, something I inherited from my un-bragging parents.

No one ever taught me any art. Mixing paints is not art. The use of the mixed paint can be art. However, anyone with any curiosity at all can quickly learn how various colors mixed together form new ones. The public school system, supported by taxes, should not have to teach this to everyone, especially when not everyone will be an artist.

chapter 38

GAME TRAILS & TALUS SLOPES

From reading the various books and articles published about the Lonesome Lake area, one would get the impression the trail from the bottom of the hill to Lonesome Lake is one long and dangerous continuous cliff-hanging obstacle course for the entire 30 or so miles. Actually that is far from true.

There are some bluffs. There are some talus slopes. There are many, many sections of trail where there are hardly any rocks, much less cliffs and talus, where the trail is. It is not all a daredevil's challenge.

For a lot of the few talus areas, the trail is worked out for horses. Some places the trail builders chose to cross the river. Often where there is rockslide and bluffs on one side of the valley, it is soft going on the other. The only problem is how to make the river leave the bridges alone. Rivers generally seem not to like bridges over them and either leave the area or remove the bridge.

I think the reason professional writers exaggerate the rougher spots on the trail is to sell books. Another reason to exaggerate might be the fact that the one rough spot is more impressive than the miles of easy going, and is remembered more easily. One remembers one cold day much longer than a solid month of pleasant weather. And so with trails. The average city dweller and reader quite possibly has never even seen a talus slope or hiked over one. In fact, most of that trail is on soft valley bottom, forested, and not much more of a challenge to walk over than a stroll thru Stanley Park would be.

One of the longest sections of talus that often had to be negotiated wasn't even between Lonesome Lake and the bottom of the hill, but 10 miles south of Lonesome Lake at the head of Elbow Lake. My people and Jack and myself were almost the only ones to use that rocky piece of trail. That was where we took our horses and cows for summer feed each year. That talus is about a quarter of a mile long, and quite rough. It is open and slides directly into the lake. There is not much of any easy way over it as the whole slide area reaches far up the mountain. It sometimes gives birth to avalanches when the conditions are right.

That short section of trail, exposed to cold strong winds sweeping into the valley thru a low pass, can build snowdrifts over the trail, hiding it. The wind falls onto the lake ice and gathers the snow in its arms as it whirls across the lake in clouds. Fortunately, the rest of the way around three-mile-long Elbow Lake is in forest and no drifting occurs. Thank God for trees.

One fall when Jack went to the Elbow Lake area to bring in the horses, the trail across the slide was badly drifted. He had a bit of trouble that time. Not trouble really, just darn hard work. The drifted snow was as deep as the horses were high; only their ears were above it, if they held their heads up. Jack could not use his snowshoes because the horses could step on the tails and either break the snowshoe or throw Jack on his face in the snow, neither desirable. Due to a "white-out" condition, it was difficult to stay on the proper snow-buried trail, except by feel. He didn't want to get down on the weak lake ice with the horses.

As the snow was so deep, the only way he could move forward was by lunging into the snow with his body and ramming it with his knees, making a ditch the calm horses followed along in as he moved slowly across the sloping snowfield. They patiently endured the snow pressing against their sides. In time—a long tiring time— they reached the end of the open area and were into the forest.

As there were no more drifted talus areas, the rest of the 10 miles home were uneventful. Jack arrived home more dead than alive from exhaustion. We tried to get the horses in earlier in the fall after that.

Any time in the winter there was risk of some hardship, from ornery cold wind causing frozen hands and feet, to deep snowdrifts and avalanches. On another trip to bring in the horses, Jack came home with his hands badly frostbitten just from having his gloves off for a very short time while he haltered a couple of the horses, the cold north wind was so strong. His feet were also frostbitten, all blistered and hurting. I think he had been wearing cotton sox that time. One can freeze in cotton, as cotton will not conduct moisture away from a person's skin, as wool will. We knew that, but could get only cotton sox that year, for some reason.

Not all the experiences Jack or I had in relation to that rocky section of the trail were painful or hard work. Once when I took the horses to the summer and fall pasture area near Elbow Lake, the lake ice was singing—yes, singing. Not the complaining shrieks, booms and ripping sounds ice makes when it is cold and it is being torn apart, or squeezed together as it tries to shove the mountains aside, but melodiously. A warm south wind was slipping between the lakeshore of big rocks and an upturned frill of ice, rising perhaps two feet above the water on a gentle curve from the level ice to almost vertical, all along the shore. It took me a while, listening carefully, before I could accept that it was the wind making the beautiful music.

That lovely ice flange along the shore also prevented me making my way onto the slick ice. I had to find a place where there was no frill, as I wasn't going to jump over that two-foot-high barrier onto slick, wet ice. The warm wind was melting the surface of the ice, tho it still was safe enough to walk on. I just had to be careful not to fall down on it.

The crystals, which had formed flat on the surface of the water in the fall, were in the process of turning into granulated loosely connected crystals on the surface. They were still strongly held together just a few inches below the surface, and hard. Later, as winter melted into spring, the sun and wind would do their work. The ice crystals would become weakly connected, get more granular, and turn on end to simply disintegrate and be swept onto the shore before the soft spring breezes.

When Dad established his home at Lonesome Lake there were already fairly good rough trails around all the lakes from Stillwater to Knot Lake. The busy travels of all the four-legged creatures hiking back and forth throughout the years had created the trails. All on the softest side of the lakes and in between lakes. Since the animals don't come equipped with axes, except for beavers, and they are more apt to fall trees across the trail than remove any that are there, the fallen trees remain. They can be jumped over, crawled under or gone around. Most of the way all we did to make suitable trails for hiking over, and for our animals, was to cut out the logs and improve the hillside grades, and improve considerably the few talus sections for cows and horses. Every year it was necessary to clear out some stuff that had been brought down by snow over the winter, ever since Dad first began hiking along the trails from the Stillwater to Knot Lake.

Much later, after Jack introduced a chainsaw into the valley, the log removal became much easier. With the use of a chainsaw and mattocks, Jack, Susan, Skye and I rerouted the trail from Tenas to Rainbow Lakes, perhaps for two miles. Also, two too-often slippery foot-logs on river crossings were bypassed. So eventually the trail from the south end of Stillwater to Knot Lake was all on the west side of the Atnarko River and the lakes.

While the traveling of the various trails in our daily lives at Lonesome Lake could be downright misery, such as deep snow, pouring rain or howling cold wind—and sometimes all three at the same time—usually it was with anticipation and curiosity that I set off. I could be just going the short five-mile round trip to feed the trumpeter swans, or we might be making a three-day hike to the summer pasture to salt the cattle.

There was always something new to see, smell or hear along the way. It could be something old that I never tired of seeing, such as grand vistas up or down one of the lakes. It could be a swollen waterfall, or a tiny up-welling spring under an upturned stump with green moss all around in a cedar forest. It could be a freshly used bear bath, all wet and muddy around the rim, and a recently rubbed spruce tree with brown bear hairs stuck in the pitch and clinging to the remains of bark the bears hadn't gotten all rubbed off yet. And sometimes the tracks of a late-roaming big old grizzly bear waddling thru the deep snow.

In 1943 we built the floating bridge across the river on The Birches. As we were feeding the swans in the river, when we had the bridge in I fed them off it when the river was not frozen over too much. But if there was too much ice I chopped it out for them. There were only about 40 or 50 birds there then, so I did not have to make a very large pool for them to be fed in. If the river froze up too much I carried their feed the mile to the north end of Big Lagoon and fed them in open holes there. Then came 1953 and we built the hangar for the Taylorcraft, and the swans wouldn't come into the river any more to be fed, so the feeding was done at the north end from then on. The swans had done a lot of flying around discussing their options, and with the growing hangar rising above the willows they decided to feed at the north end of the lagoon. I carried their feed that extra mile on my back or rode my horse, Thuja, and carried the small bag of grain across her withers.

On those walks to feed the swans there were several things of interest along the way. Once a trio of wolves had been following for some distance before I became aware of them. When I saw the three, they had stopped and were just standing about 15 to 20 feet away, calmly looking at me. Two were black, and the leader was a beautiful silvery-gray with a white collar around her neck like a collie dog. Not knowing what their intentions were, I dropped my pack and took one step towards a tree, which I thought I might be able to climb. They vanished so fast they left a hairy black hole in the air where they had been standing. If they had wanted to eat me it wouldn't have mattered whether or not I could climb that skinny little pine. In three leaps they could have had me down, and I would not have been able to take even one step towards that small tree. They must not have had any predatory intentions, as they could have launched an attack on me at any time as they followed along with me. Perhaps they were curious.

Sometime in the 1960s we built a trail from the Venturi to the south end of Big Lagoon on the west side of the river, bypassing the long loop around by my people's place and the floating bridge. The bridge could become unusable by flooding at any time during the winter. After that we went on the shorter trail to feed the swans.

Three curious timber wolves regard me quietly.

Each day on the way to feed the swans there could be interesting evidence of other beings out there in the snow: martens' little dents in the soft snow from their furry feet as they travel almost endlessly thru the forest; fox tracks lightly marking the surface of the snow as they search for a squirrel; or even a little mouse racing from one snowy mousehole to another. Or there could be tracks of wing tips as a lucky owl rises from the surface of the snow, perhaps with an unlucky mouse clutched tightly in her talons. Along the riverbank there could be a fresh muddy slide path where several otters had been perfecting their glissading down a slippery snowy slope to land in the mud at the edge of the water.

Once when I was hiking along near the Big Lagoon a gray shadow trotted across my trail maybe 50 feet ahead of me and continued up a slope to disappear among the large fir trees standing about in an open area. Soon another one trotted into view followed by 13 more trotting up the slope, one behind another. Finally no more came across my trail and I could continue going my way. I don't believe even one of them saw me where I stood quietly watching. A short time later I saw six wolves cantering across the Big Lagoon ice to the east side. They were possibly part of the group of 15 that had passed me so recently.

Whoever fed the swans usually spent a half hour or so on "duck watch." This effort was to make the little greedy mallards stay out of the swan feed. Ducks can feed in many places where there is open water under trees and brush, where no trumpeter swan would dream of going with that seven-foot wing span. As mallards can get feed easily out of small places, they do not need feeding. Also, there are millions of them. There are not millions of swans and they need the grain supplied by the people of Canada. Therefore, we made an effort to keep the ducks out.

Other beautiful and interesting sights we looked forward to on the daily swan trip during cold spells were the fancy ice forms along the river. Any time the temperature hovered around 10 degrees Fahrenheit to minus 10 degrees Fahrenheit for a few days, the river would freeze anchor ice, green and muddy, to the riverbed. The water then rose, spread into side channels and then froze over. While the freezing was going on, all sorts of fancy stuff grew on rocks sticking out of the water where spray jumped up to icy caps that had grown on the rocks and formed a curtain of icicles all around the rim. Not just plain icicles, but fancy, ridged, and looking like turned table legs. Some of them resembled rows of the front legs of horses seen from the front, with the joints and sometimes even with a hoof on the end of each icicle.

The most spectacular ice work I have ever seen was a beautiful formation that grew in Bear Bath Creek on Arbordale in the winter of 1968. The creek had been in flood, and after the high water had subsided a bit this fancy flower grew in the creek where it struggled among some driftwood and logs. It was about 20 inches tall, cone-shaped, six or eight inches wide at the base, and hollow. It looked like a tall cream-colored flower, with petals grown all over the outside of it. I carefully pried it out of the creek and carried the delicate object to the house and set it over a picket on the front yard fence. Jack took a photo of it there on the picket.

Another interesting ice formation that grows in a whirlpool when the temperature drops below zero Fahrenheit is a round pan of ice created by the circular motion of the ever-circulating whirlpool. It starts out small, but grows larger as it accumulates ice on its edges on its way around its orbit. In time it is large enough to begin scraping the edge of the surrounding ice along the shore, piling up ridges all around the ever-growing pan. Eventually it gets frozen fast to the shore ice and the entire pool freezes over. Then, in time, the warm weather comes along and destroys the whole beautiful creation. But the river can always build a new one, weather willing.

Often we got to watch otter families playing in the river where it flows along some 50 feet below where our trail winds thru the forest. Other times we got to see huge frost crystals clinging to the underside of every branch that extends over the water. Warm air from the stream rises and forms these crystals. Every cobweb becomes coated with the crystals, and with the assistance of a gentle drift of air, they glint and sparkle in the light of the rising sun.

As there are no leaves on all the deciduous trees in the winter, they make up for this lack of beauty by having twigs that turn purple or yellow when wet, especially after returning to warm days following a cold spell. They are then almost as colorful as when they shed their leaves in the fall.

On our trips to feed the swans we would often see a few hungry birds scouring food out of small open places in the river where the current had kept the water ice-free. Soon after we passed they usually flew over us, also heading for the feed place. They would usually talk to us as they flew over. As we were in forest, we only got a glimpse of the big white birds winging overhead.

The trumpeter swans were so hungry and impatient that one day when we had to horse pack a plane load of grain from an unhandy spot on the Big Lagoon to the south end, they "helped" us load the horses, then followed us across the ice. Arriving at the south end of the lagoon most of the swans lay on the ice all around us and the horses, so close we had to be careful not to step on them as we unpacked and stacked the bags of grain. Some swans even tucked their heads under their wings and went to sleep there in the warm sun. Alas, we did not have our camera. It would have made a wonderful picture: two little horses and three people surrounded by about 300 trusting wild swans. Susan and I partly corrected this the next day. This happened only once.

With the grain at the south end of the lagoon we were saved two miles of travel, but it was not a good place to feed them as they could be fed in water at the north end whenever it was open, which is always better than feeding on ice. But it was only a short time until they had it all eaten and they could go back to the north end again.

This was a long time after we built the hangar and many airplanes and helicopters had landed on the lagoon. The swans adapted remarkably well to the noisy disturbance, begun by the resident airplane, CF HEO, which I flew to Lonesome Lake in 1953.

In all the nearly 50 winters, some short, some long—six weeks to three months, depending on weather—never did I ever become bored with those beautiful big birds and their music, or the hike to feed them. I didn't exactly love them, but more appreciated them, I think, and felt very protective of them, and thoroughly enjoyed them.

Winter
Thoughts along the way

Pine trees marching row on row,
Dark heads crowned with caps of snow
Snow lies deep upon the ground,

Wind shivers branches with mournful sound.
Trees cast long shadows through their boles.
Hares race headlong for their holes.
Fox tracks dent the white perfection,
Chasing mice who seek protection.
Squirrels groom their fur in tops of trees.
Sun shines bright in fitful breeze.
Sun goes down; long night begins.
Wolves rest together, chins on shins.
Moose gather food with mobile lips.
Their food of choice is buds and tips.
Beavers live in house of logs,
A frosty cavern is home for frogs.
Swans float in groups on water mild
Thru nights so long with wind so wild
Ice balls freeze on wing and tail.
Removed they must be, or flight will fail.
This stuff's churning thru my mind.
Closing words I cannot find.
I must keep going on and on
From morn to night and dusk to dawn,
Thru sun and rain and fog and snow,
Where it ends I do not know.
Perhaps it ends on mountain high.
Perhaps it ends on clouds in sky.
Perhaps it ends on lake below
Perhaps it ends on trees in snow.

The conventional way to get up on the back of a horse is by the use of a stirrup. If none is available, there are other aids to achieve that lofty perch. A log the right height is quite obvious, or a rock, bank, hay bale, etc., but in the absence of any of those things, one who isn't a good jumper still may be able to mount a horse.

Susan and I worked out a rather simple solution. I could never jump on to a horse, not even a low one, but Susan could. Susan would leap onto her horse out in the level meadow, then I could park my horse close to Susan's and by putting one of my feet on her foot, I could then get on my horse, much as if I had a stirrup. Neither horse would have a saddle.

Another solution was to build a snow mound beside the horse, then leap up from that. Or one could mount a low horse, then transfer onto the taller one if she was going to cross a deep river. I did this once, then I changed horses in mid-stream and didn't get wet.

I think Jack used the most novel method to mount a horse. He was out in a boggy, soggy, grass-covered, snowy meadow and had to take the horses some place where he would have had to wade, but the ground was too soft for him to jump from. He lined two horses up close to each other, then placing a hand on the back of each, he could swing himself up and land firmly on one.

Of course if there are trees, you can sometimes find a bent one which would serve as a launching pad. You must be careful to land softly on the horse's back, tho, or next time she just might step away right as you leave your tree and leave you mounting a shadow.

I can remember getting up on old Ginty by waiting until he put his head down, then I could wrap my arms and legs around his neck. When he raised his head, I would swing back and forth under his neck until I swung high enough on one side that I could swing up onto his withers. Catching one heel over that high fin, I would then be able to wiggle around to get astride his back. We never went anywhere, I just liked sitting on him.

The date is the day before Christmas 2008. I have been watching the news, and seeing all the trouble those poor people were having with a few inches of snow on the streets and roads made me start comparing life at Lonesome Lake to life in cities, where snow can fall in winter.

At Lonesome Lake we never had power outages and had to freeze in the dark. We never had to cope with frozen pipes. We seldom had to shovel snow off our driveway, except for one winter when there was 52 inches of white stuff blanketing everything. That winter we had to shovel out the trail to the barn and the outhouse, much to Skye's delight. She helped by leaping up to gather up shovels full of snow in her widespread arms. Of course the soft snow engulfed her head and body, but she always jumped up for the next batch. While she waited for the next lot of snow, she could shake her head and body free of the snowy assault.

In the Salloompt where I live now I have to do more shoveling of snow, and like Skye, Liesel also loved gathering flying snow. Unlike Skye, Liesel didn't want to wait for the snow to get to her. She wanted to grab the snow right off the shovel. I had to make her wait; it was just too dangerous for her. I throw the snow quite strongly and if she had grabbed the shovel it could have broken teeth or injured her mouth. She never considered those possibilities. There were times when I had to think for her.

chapter 39

THE FREEDOM OF WHEELS

I guess most people learn to drive a vehicle while they are in their teens. Continuing my record of being unconventional, I waited until I was 65 to embark on the road to become a driver. But then I guess I came by that naturally enough too. Dad didn't learn to fly an airplane until he was in his sixties. But I suppose a lack of need, or opportunity, could have been a factor also.

I had actually driven a car for a few lessons while living with the Hatches in the Fraser Valley when I was down in the Vancouver area learning to fly. I didn't do enough driving then to get a license. My instructor thought I should. As I could not use a vehicle at Lonesome Lake, there seemed to be not much point in the expense at that time. I had learned enough to be able to make a three-point turn, not so different with a car as with a team and wagon except one needs more room with the team.

Having moved away from Lonesome Lake and living where there was a road, finally there was opportunity and need. However, I was determined not to invest in any vehicle until I had enough money that I would not have to go into debt for it.

I didn't want to take the Old Age Pension after Jack, directly, and I by inference, were slandered by one account of our lives at Lonesome Lake where we were considered welfare bums because Jack didn't have a nine-to-five job with an employer. The creator of the story apparently had never heard of self-employment. Then our federal government paid one and a half million dollars for a ghastly painting. I decided that if they were going to waste taxpayers' money that way I might as well let them waste some on me, too. So, with Susan pushing me, and my own desire for the freedom of being able to go wherever I chose, as soon as I started getting OAP checks I said to myself one morning, "OK, I'll get a truck."

I made up an ad for a light truck, standard transmission. Susan put up the ad. Within two weeks I had an answer. Someone had a little two-wheel-drive Ford Ranger. It was in Bella Coola. As I could not drive then, the owner drove it to my place in Salloompt. I looked it over and didn't find anything wrong with it. Still I wanted to think about it for a day or so. I did a bit of research on Ford Rangers in general, then had a second look at the truck. And I had Susan give it a driving test for me and she thought it was all right. So I bought it.

Then all I had to do was learn to drive. I never questioned whether or not I could learn. I darn well was going to. After all I had been driving horses on mower, rake, wagon plow, logging, for most of my life. Surely driving a vehicle couldn't be that much different. Except for other people using the road sometimes, it wasn't. Well, the seat was softer and I was out of the wind and rain and didn't have to balance on a bouncy load of hay—quite a few differences, actually. Susan was my instructor. She is a very good driver who has done a lot of driving.

With precious driver's license in hand, I set out to improve my rather sloppy driving skills, as I had just barely passed my written test and my driving test. In fact, the driving examiner advised me to get an automatic truck rather than perfect my use of brake and gas pedal to start up on hills. I thought I should get my finesse developed so I could get going on hills without stalling the engine. In time I did. Even good enough that I could stop on "the hill," on an 18 percent grade, and start up again. I also was able to get started on those steep hills on North Broadway in Williams Lake and didn't stall my motor.

With Jack and Liesel as passengers, I drove up logging roads and went exploring all over the valley. Then I felt I could tackle the famous hill. This time I would be driving up it. Years earlier Jack and I walked the 12 miles up the hill, carrying packs.

I didn't find driving up the hill nerve-wracking. I didn't have any spare thought for trivial things; I had to concentrate on my driving and other traffic. My first trip up that sloping highway was in August 1996. I had been driving for only two years and had a lot more to learn.

Driving in the easy atmosphere of the valley does not prepare one for the congested or more impatient traffic of Williams Lake and Highway 97 South, and all the huge freight trucks and log-carrying trucks. As Jack, Liesel and I were going thru Williams Lake, then on to the Okanogan country to get a young heifer, we were soon on Highway 97 South. There the speed and congestion increases considerably. I soon found myself boxed in between two huge vehicles going much faster than I was used to going.

In the valley I had driven on the slow side until I felt confident enough of my feel of the vehicle to try going faster. Out there on that proving ground I had to adapt in a hurry, and I found I could speed up to 90 kilometers per hour or get run over. With a big truck in front and one to the left, one behind and a rail or drop-off to the right, one sure better adapt to the environment in a hurry. When I returned from that trip I had learned to drive faster, anyway.

Finally arriving at the dairy farm where I was to pick up my new heifer, we found the rack about six inches too low and eight inches too short for her. For an Ayrshire, she was huge. She was only seven months old. Ayrshires I was familiar with were dainty, small cows.

By mail I had asked the farmer to leave the heifer's horns on, as I prefer my cows to have horns. They are useful to handle and tie the cow up with. Anyway, as we could not get her in my rack, I asked if he would consider selling me a younger, smaller calf. He wasn't happy about it as the calf he had left the horns on would have to be dehorned as an older animal, which is a much nastier operation than doing it when they are young.

There was no problem getting the smaller heifer in the rack and we set off to the friends we would spend the night with.

On the way to those people's place I made a bad mistake, and only by me and the other driver doing the right thing did we both avoid a serious accident. The other driver swerved and I accelerated, and we avoided a collision and didn't hurt my calf. But it sure scared me.

At our friends' place I parked near their house. As there was nothing else to tie my calf to, I tied her to a corner post of the rack. It was stout and solid enough in the truck box. The calf had never been tied up before. I had trained her to lead only enough to get her in the rack at the farmer's place. Tied outside the constraints of the rack, she had a fit. I expected that, but in the morning after she had been tied up all night and still had fits when anyone came near her, I began re-thinking my decision to buy her and re-examined the possibility of getting materials to enlarge the rack. I had taken tools with us in case any alterations had to be made. Our friends had lots of stuff we could use to enlarge the rack. I phoned the farmer and explained the situation. He was willing to change heifers, and left the one with horns where we could get her and went on with his business. He had 80 cows to milk and tend. He was a busy farmer.

Back at the farm, and with the aid of the farmer's helper, we exchanged heifers. With very little trouble we soon had the horned heifer, Dolly, loaded and were on our way.

At our friends' house we left Dolly in a shed close to the house. All was quiet until everyone was in bed, then the complaining began. Dolly was lonely and she let us know. I got out of my soft bed and went out to see what she needed and the complaining stopped, so I went back to bed. Soon the complaining began again. That would not do. People had to get some sleep. The heifer would have to move far enough from the house that she would not disturb our hosts.

Jack led Dolly, and I drove, to a place far enough away, we hoped, where I could park on more or less level ground and there was a tree to tie the heifer to. The only sound for the rest of the night was a noisy thunderstorm and hard rain beating on my roof, too close over my head, where I slept in the truck. In the morning we headed for home.

Near the top of the long Little Fort Hill, I stopped to let the motor cool off. When we decided to continue my battery was as flat as a run-over toad. Absolutely no power.

In time a freight truck stopped to check brakes before heading down the long hill. Thinking I might be having some sort of trouble, the driver crossed the road to ask me if there was a problem. I told him my battery was flat. There was no way he could give me a boost, but I thought his concern was very kind and thanked him. He went on down the hill. Soon a vehicle that could boost me came up the hill and he also advised me not to shut the engine off until I got the battery checked, which was good advice. Then we were on our way again. We had been worried there for a bit. Thank God for the kindness of strangers.

We stopped at the first place there was a service station and had the battery checked. The mechanic tightened something and said it should be all good. I guess it was, as I had no more trouble on the way back to Bella Coola.

We camped near Lone Butte. In the morning before we started off I was looking Dolly over and noticed matter oozing out of her eyes. I phoned the veterinarian in Williams Lake for an appointment to have the heifer checked. It was quite a while after we arrived in Williams Lake before the vet got to Dolly. After he examined her the vet said Dolly had pinkeye, a common disease in cattle and highly contagious. He gave me some ointment to treat her with. In time she was well. I kept her away from my other cow for a month and she did not catch the pinkeye.

I had noticed some stuff on her hair below her eye while I was halter training her, but as it just looked like clear tearing, as if she had gotten something in her eye, I let it pass.

Finally we were ready to leave Williams Lake and head for home.

I had a pretty good load on my little truck, so we had to climb Sheep Creek Hill in second gear. Fortunately there was not a lot of traffic for me to interfere with.

Long before we got to Bull Canyon my heifer was getting tired and wanted to lie down. She had been on the truck for too many hours, probably around 10. The rack was too narrow for her to lie down in. We started looking for a place where we could get far enough off the road to unload her. The first place that was available was on the way down the hill to the Bull Canyon campsites. A short way off the highway there is a nice grassy area where we could get the truck off the road, put our ramp up and back the heifer off. Just beyond was a sign saying, "No Horse-riding Beyond this Point." Well, Dolly wasn't a horse and we weren't riding her, nor had we passed the sign; I felt we were safe enough. And never mind the heifer being tired, so was the driver, which was worse.

Anyway we had Dolly safely tied to a tree, where she promptly lay down, and Liesel was tied near her. We were preparing to get some rest, too, when along came a Park Ranger. She had a bit of a meltdown about the cow until Jack explained how the heifer and the driver both needed to rest, and badly. Then she cooled down a bit and even allowed us to go down to the campsites and get some water and use the sanitary facilities there. I left the dog with the cow, however. The Ranger said no animals were allowed off Highway 20, tho humans seemed to be allowed and they certainly are animals, some of them being much less considerate of the environment than any cow, horse, dog, or any other creatures that could be there. Anyway, we were thankful that she allowed us to get some fresh water, and the tired heifer and driver to rest before driving on. After a couple of hours or so of sleep and rest we loaded up Dolly and drove on across the endless Chilcotin.

We camped near Nimpo Lake. The rest of the way home was uneventful, even coming down "the hill" with my slightly over-loaded little truck. It did well.

That trip was not the first time Jack and I had been up and down the hill. It was just the first time I drove it, and the road had been greatly improved from what it was like the first time we were driven over it, in June 1962 with Susan, on our way to Vancouver.

I made a second trip to Williams Lake with Jack and Liesel in late September 1996. I wanted to stretch my wings [wheels] and drive that long endless highway again in fall color time. I also wanted to look at the possibility of exchanging my two-wheel-drive truck for a four-wheel-drive vehicle the same size. Jack didn't want to go to start with, but in time he decided he would go. We all did go on that second drive up the hill and the fall colors were spectacular, much better than the colors usually are here in the Bella Coola area. Except for the abundance of aspen in the Chilcotin area, the colors there are no better than they are in the Lonesome Lake area. In the Bella Coola area there are not the frosty nights that seem to enhance the colors farther inland.

I did find a four-wheel-drive Ford Ranger. I liked the look of it, but when the dealer let me test drive it I soon found the transmission was messed up and the brake was on one wheel. I took it back to the dealer and they put it up on the lift and got the braked wheel working, but they had to drive it to determine what was wrong with the transmission. I went with him; Liesel stayed quiet in my truck. The dealer agreed there was something wrong. He said the truck would need a new transmission, which would take about a month to get. They had to find a used one in good condition. They would take my truck as part payment for the four-wheel drive, at a fairly good price, very little less than I had paid for it two years earlier. I told them I would take the truck if they got it fixed up by the end of October. I told them I didn't want to drive that road too late in the fall. Around mid-October the dealer informed me the truck was ready. We agreed on the price. Liesel and I were prepared to set off for Williams Lake.

I guess I was not quite enough prepared. I knew I should have chains for the hill. But as the new truck had larger wheels than my truck, I didn't want to buy a set of chains for that one trip, then get another set for the new vehicle, and I was assured I'd have no trouble getting up the hill. They were mistaken. Perhaps an experienced driver wouldn't have had any trouble.

Two or three switchbacks above where the road crosses Young Creek, the snow on the road had turned to ice from the wheels running over it. My truck suddenly stopped moving forward and began making decisions for itself, and paid no attention to brake or steering wheel. Right on the very edge of a steep slope into a ditch filled with ugly huge boulders, the front wheels grabbed a bit of traction and finally paid attention to the brakes. There I sat, afraid to move, as I had no idea how tenuous a grip the wheels had on that sloping edge of the road. I really did not like the look of those boulders right in front of me.

As I sat there I began to get cold. What could I do? I thought the slope was too steep to drive across to get back on the roadway and it might cause the truck to roll into the boulder-filled ditch. I was starting to shiver when a Highways vehicle came slowly down the hill and stopped near me. He didn't have chains on, but he did have four-wheel drive and he wasn't slipping.

The road was so slippery that he had to hold onto his vehicle as he made his way around it to talk to me. He wanted to know if I was going up or down. He told me the road was worse higher up. I had been trying to go up, but at that point I only wanted to go down. I just didn't know how I was going to get safely back on the road. He said he couldn't help me, as he would not have enough traction to do anything. He did tell me I could drive out on that slope and not roll. With that bit of knowledge, I did get out all right and drove carefully back down the hill. Several places the truck felt as if it would lose traction again, even on sections where I had no hint of slipping on the way up. Somewhere below Young Creek the snow and ice were left behind and I could breathe again.

Arriving home in the dark, I found out why I had been turned back. I was urgently needed at home. Sparks were coming from somewhere east of my house and were being blown over my house every few minutes by an east wind. When I drove past where the sparks seemed to be coming from, I had not seen anything. I went out on the road and found out what was happening. A strong wind had brought down a green aspen tree on the power line. The wind was lifting it off the wire, then letting it back down again. Each time the tree rested on the wire it burned and sent sparks flying towards my house, about 60 feet downwind. As aspen sparks live quite a while, they were a potential for disaster for my house.

My roof, being asphalt shingles, was fairly safe, but my porch wasn't. I phoned our volunteer fire department and BC Hydro and then stood on my porch for the next hour or so watching each spark that was blown towards my house. In time Hydro got the power shut off and the sparks stopped. There was an impressive amount of heat from that wire, which could cause green aspen wood to burn so quickly. The tree only had to lie on the wire a moment and it was glowing, and the sparks were flying with the wind.

A few days later and with barrowed chains—thanks to the kindness of our local garage—I again set off for Williams Lake. Partway up the hill there is a level spot where one can back out of the way of traffic. I stopped and attempted to put the chains on as I was meeting bits of snow and it was a long way up to another good spot to stop. I spread out the chains for one wheel, and try as I might, I could not get the thing to lay so all the cross links were on the same side. Thinking I must really be the stupidest person in the entire world, I returned to the valley.

The next day I phoned the garage that had loaned me the chains and explained, somewhat sheepishly, that I could not get the chains on. They seemed to be twisted. They told me to bring the chains in and they could solve my little problem. On examination they found the chains were, in fact, twisted. They fixed the problem.

On my next attempt to get up that hill, with chains on, I finally clanked my way to the top and far down the road until we were out of any snow. Then I removed them and drove on into the dark.

I stopped at Pinto Lake, a short way beyond Tatla Lake. There I ate supper and fed Liesel, who would also sleep in the truck.

Before we went to bed, we hiked a short way to the beautiful little lake that lay partly ice-covered and sparkling in the bright moonlight, in a light but cold breeze. Returning to the truck, I spread my warm wool quilt across the bench seat and went to bed, with Liesel comfortable below me on the floor. Sometime later I woke up. We went for a hike to stretch our muscles, then back to the truck for more sleep.

With two warm bodies breathing in there for several hours, my windshield became thickly covered with frost on the inside as well as on the outside, and required quite a while to melt. In time I could see to drive on thru the night. There was very little traffic, so the big log-hauling trucks—carrying stacks of tiny logs, six inches in diameter—and I had the road pretty much to ourselves.

Hours later we arrived at a turn-off to another campsite on McIntyre Lake. After offering Liesel a drink in the marshy edge of the small lake, I was once more soon asleep, undisturbed by my faithful companion sleeping on the floor.

Daylight awakened me. In a short time I was descending Sheep Creek Hill. There was a bit of frost on the road, but not enough to make me any trouble, fortunately. I drove thru the sleeping town, then up North Broadway to my dealer's place. There sat the truck I had driven all that long way to buy. When I took the truck for a test drive, she ran smoothly. I bought her. The dealer drove my old truck away behind his building and I never saw her again.

With all the stuff I had in my old truck transferred to the new one, including my little dog, I set off for home; I had a new set of chains, too. As the new truck, with four wheel drive and a larger engine, did not seem to perform on the hills any better than the old one had and seemed less cooperative, I named her Sulky. In time

I learned her own habits and began to appreciate her, but she remained Sulky.

I camped near Towdystan and it snowed during the night, but not enough to make me any trouble. I did use the chains between Green River and far down the hill until after we ran out of snow. I did not use the four-wheel drive. I was scared of messing something up until I had learned more about it. Once I became easier with it, I used it often, and really liked the extra power. Years later I sold her and missed her much as one would miss an animal.

With a truck I began hauling hay for my cows and horse, saving Susan the trouble as she had enough work hauling hay for her horse herd. Jack helped, of course. He was tall and could throw those bales up on the truck so much easier than we short people could. That first tuck could take only 20 bales, but Sulky could haul 25. We had 500 to haul, to feed my small herd thru the winter.

When we moved to Bella Coola, I thought life would be easier than it had been at Lonesome Lake. Instead, in some ways it was harder. At Lonesome Lake horses cut most of the grass with a mower. Down here I had to hand mow a lot of grass for my cows, as their pasture dried up and could not feed them all summer. On Glengarry, the place jointly owned by Tom, Susan, and me, I hand mowed the large yard and hauled it to my cows with my homemade rubber-tired wheelbarrow. With a truck, I went to other people's places and hand mowed grass and hauled it home. I could have given the cows hay, but they do better with grass when milking, so it was worth getting grass for them.

With the four-wheel-drive truck to haul it, I soon started thinking about getting a one-horse trailer so I could take Bess to the rodeo grounds without bothering Susan, and play with her there when there was no one else using the arena. Suddenly more freedom and it was more economical than hauling one horse in a big four-horse trailer.

I drove Sulky almost six years, then there was a rumor going around that the "rust police" were going to yank all the vehicles off the road that had any rust on them. By then Sulky had some rust. I was afraid I would lose the use of her on the road, so I looked around for a rust-free truck that I could afford. I could not afford to be kicked off the road. I needed to go places and haul things too much.

I soon found a less rusty four-wheel-drive standard truck with a short box and an extended cab, a Toyota. I bought it and sold my dear old Sulky to my neighbor who lived right beside my small place. The Toyota could haul a bit more hay than Sulky, but we had to extend the box. I drove it almost six years before I had to quit driving due to arthritis.

When I could drive, Jack, Liesel and I made a trip to Hagensborg once a week, and one to Bella Coola every two weeks. Going that often we could take advantage of the frequent sales in both stores and often got some good buys. Or we just waited until what we wanted came on sale if we didn't really need it immediately.

As soon as I got wheels I joined the Trail and Nature Club, I think they called it. Jack had been hiking with them for several years before I got my first vehicle. Jack had done a lot of biking around where some hikers lived and had gotten to know some of them, so they often picked him up when going on a hike. With me having a vehicle I could also join the hiking club people, or we could go on hikes up logging roads or wherever we wished without the other hikers. But sometimes we needed their larger trucks to get over the rotten roads.

Jack, Liesel and I hiked to some really lovely places with lakes and flowers galore. Those were just day hikes.

In the summer of 1997 the hiking club planned a three-day trip by vehicle to a place way off the highway near One Eye Lake, called Perkins Peak, some way beyond Miner Lake.

Driving up to the alpine on a goat trail of a road was really an adventure. I surely needed that four-wheel drive on that trip. On the lower slopes there was a poor road left by people who had done extensive logging in the area, but when we broke out in the alpine the road became a poor bear trail, full of rocks, sharp turns and steep pitches. We parked our vehicles on the narrow rocky shore of a large lake lying at the foot of Perkins Peak. The more ambitious hikers took off for the top of the peak, while Jack, Liesel and I just hiked on the easier going around the lake. I found some nice rocks, Liesel chased a fat marmot up a rockslide, and we had lunch and rested. After we had rested a bit I tried to get Liesel to swim across a small bay on the lake. She refused to go into water that was up to her belly and would not cross that bay. There were quite a few flowers around the lake in some places.

On the other side of the high ridge leading up to Perkins Peak there was an old abandoned silver mine. After getting away from the lake there was a fairly good, tho narrow, road around to where we could almost get to the mine. I looked in vain for one tiny piece of silver I hoped to find in the mine tailings. Liesel helped, but we found nothing.

The next day we all arrived at a beautiful lake quite a way off the highway, out in the lodge pole pines, incorrectly called jack pines. They called it Big Stick Lake. I do not know if the sticks are big or the lake, or if both are large.

A lovely sandy beach lies along the shore at one end. When we were there only a light wind wrinkled the surface, but I imagine, considering the size of the lake, some pretty impressive waves could pound that beach. It was warm in the sun when we had our lunch. Shortly after, we headed for home. The others would stay for a while. We had arrived ahead of them, so we left sooner, too.

We had gotten out of step with the others because we wanted to go to Big Stick the evening before the others left Miner Lake. As we had some trouble finding Big Stick, we camped short of it and got an early start the next morning, arriving at the beach at about the same time as the sun did.

In the morning before leaving our camp, Jack and I had gone

off in different directions for toilet purposes. When I returned to the truck Jack was not back yet. Then I had an idea. I asked Liesel to find Jack. Keeping her leash on, I followed her as she followed his scent. There was a drift of air and she tracked him over to a hedge of brush about 15 feet away from the trail he would have walked on. Following Jack's scent, she wandered among the pines until she could see him, then rushed the last few feet to celebrate with a loving caress from Jack and praise from both of us. It was the first time she had been asked to find any person and she knew just how to do it. I could not have done what she did. I would have had to yell to achieve the same thing. She was good at finding many things.

chapter 40

TRAVELS WITH SUSAN

I guess on the first trip we made out of the valley, travelling with Susan before she was born, I was carrying her in her snug basket with internal heating. Her birth was due in mid-February, but on January 1, 1959 something went wrong, and we got the doctor in from Bella Coola on our little Taylorcraft with Dad as pilot. It turned out there was not too much seriously wrong with me or our child, but the doctor thought we should go to Vancouver for the last of the gestation and birth.

We could not go on our own plane as there had been some damage to HEO due to a strong wind when Dad landed with the doctor. When the doctor didn't return home for a day or two, his wife got Search and Rescue to fly to Lonesome Lake to see what was wrong. With the Search and Rescue Fairchild Husky at Lonesome Lake, they were able to fly the doctor, Jack and me to Williams Lake.

Before we left Lonesome Lake, we had moved our cattle, two cats and Frog to my people's place. The cats and dog had empty mink pens to live in, while the cattle ran with my parents' stock. When we left home much earlier than we had planned, we had hoped to return home somewhat earlier than we finally did. I think the cats and Frog were glad to see us, especially poor little Frog. She had just had a 4 by 10 pen for those two and a half months. I don't remember if anyone took her for walks or not, but Mother had enough work just looking after them without very many walks, I would think. Anyway, they all looked in good enough shape on our return, and we certainly appreciated all the work my people did looking after our critters for that long a time.

From Williams Lake, in a day or so Jack and I flew on a DC3 to Vancouver airport. There they whisked us off to St. Paul's Hospital by ambulance. After various checks in the hospital we looked for someplace not too expensive to stay until the baby was born.

I seem to remember we found a place that was relatively inexpensive on Comox Street. There did not seem to be too much out of line on the gestation, so we just had to mark time and wait. We found cheaper accommodation on Nelson Street and moved. It was below street level and had no view. As we were close to the hospital and Stanley Park, it was a good location. We took hikes around the park every day there was decent weather.

In the Nelson Street house sometime in the night things started happening and Jack alerted the taxi, which usually parked near our house, and we were soon on our way to St. Paul's. The date was February 18. Our baby was not presented as well as could have been desired and was a long time coming. Eventually she came, and was soon complaining, or perhaps rejoicing, on the 19th at about 3:15 a.m.

We spent about a week visiting Jack's folks on Saltspring Island, then we three headed for home. We took the Union Steamship, *Northland Prince,* to Bella Coola where someone—I think Aunt Isabel or Uncle Earle—met us and drove us up to their place. I may not remember this correctly.

We stayed in a rental cabin in Bella Coola for a few more days before our friend Bill Webber drove us up the valley. There was a lot of ice on the road near the bottom of the hill, but Bill was careful and we made it okay.

As we did not have any kind of carrying chair for our little girl, someone found a biscuit box that I could carry on my back with a sack and some kind of straps. With several stops for feeding and changing, we arrived home on March 15, I believe.

The next carrying box we had for her was a strong, heavy wooden box she could lie flat in. It was bolted to a stout homebuilt wooden packboard. It was covered with something to protect our precious daughter from insects and any tree debris that might fall on her. And we had to keep her from falling out of the box if her "mount" should fall down.

Over the years we made quite a few trips out of our valley as Susan was growing up, usually taking two or three weeks. In June 1962 we made a three-week trip to Saltspring Island to visit Jack's parents and do some business in Vancouver. In August 1969 we flew to Vancouver on a Twin Otter. After doing business in Vancouver we visited Victoria and Parksville, where Jack's mother was living at the time. His father had passed away some years before.

When we made trips to Vancouver we usually stayed in the St. Francis Hotel, which has long since been torn down. Chinese food was a special treat for all of us, and we particularly enjoyed both the quality and price of the meals at the "Only Seafood Restaurant," also long gone now. That was where I found out how good deep fried prawns are. We also enjoyed the odd movie, with *Mary Poppins* being a favorite we ended up watching more than once. Jack and I had entertained ourselves watching movies while we were waiting for Susan to be born, and I remember enjoying the musicals *Oklahoma* and *Seven Brides for Seven Brothers.*

Still in 1969, we took in the Pacific National Exhibition Parade and PNE exhibits. Altho the parade was nice enough to watch, I would rather have been riding in it. Many years later I got several chances to ride in our own Fall Fair Parade here in Bella Coola Valley, on Bess and later on Breezie Future. While at the PNE we got to watch a beautiful performance of the RCMPs Musical Ride. I enjoyed that a whole lot.

In the fall of 1972 we flew to Williams Lake, hiked from the airport down to the city, then took a bus to Vancouver.

In Vancouver we attended to business, then went to Parksville to see Jack's mother. The three of us visited with Joan and hiked around the area, exploring Jack's old stomping grounds. He had spent a bit of time there as a child and wanted to revisit some places. Susan met a cute little reddish blond Welsh pony named Casey, nearby, and spent a lot of time with him. I think she missed our horses. Casey was a sweet little guy. We returned to Bella Coola, on the passenger and freighter ship *Northland Prince,* November 1. Once again Mother must have taken care of Skye and whatever other of our animals that needed it.

The end of September 1975 we made another trip to the Vancouver–Parksville area. This time it was just Jack and me, as Susan had basically left home in February.

As my mother was too tired to take on looking after another dog, I found someone down the valley to care for her. I told them NOT to turn her loose, as she would surely try to go home to find us. She was partially deaf by then and I did not want her hiking thru grizzly bear country alone when we would be gone for over two weeks. They did not hear me, and four days later they let her go. Of course, poor Skye trustingly headed home. She had no way of knowing we had not gone home. All she knew was we were gone and had not taken her along. She got as far as the Stillwater, where we left our boat. She always travelled up and down the Stillwater by boat, so she went no farther. She divided her time between waiting at the boat and the cabin we camped in at the north end of the lake, and all she had to eat for two weeks was some half rotten salmon the bears had left on the beach.

Away on our trip, trusting that Skye was safe, we had some dental work done in Parksville and had a nice visit with Joan. I seem to recall Susan had joined us for part of the time in Parksville, then she left to go on a camping trip with some friends before heading up to Williams Lake to meet us later in the week.

We were planning to buy another horse on the way home, so after a long, monotonous, bumpy trip across the Chilcotin by bus, we disembarked late in the evening and set up camp near the road.

In the morning we hiked into the ranch and had a look at the filly we had been considering. We decided to buy her; then it was time to head for home.

We had planned to get back to Lonesome Lake by using a route over the flank of Trumpeter Mountain, but early snowfall, lost trails and various other problems made a change in plans. Instead, we ended up coming down the Hotnarko River trail.

On reaching the Stillwater at last, Susan and I crossed the river on a high suspension bridge put in by BC Parks years earlier, to get to our boat. We had left it well up along the shore to discourage "borrowers" of unattended boats.

Someone had, indeed, stolen our boat while we were gone, but they had at least returned it to where we had left it. Of course, because they had actually cut the chain we had locked it with, now they were unable to tie it up again. Fortunately, the water had not risen, so the boat was okay. Anyway, angry about the theft, we shoved it into the water and rowed down towards where Jack and the filly waited on the other shore.

As we passed the Ratcliff cabin, a small black and white dog came trotting down to the beach. I remarked to Susan, "That looks a hell of a lot like Skye." Sure enough it was Skye and she was very glad to see us. Then I had another reason to be angry. Skye was supposed to be safe, 10 miles away with people at Atnarko. She was lucky to be alive.

On all the trips I have detailed here, we were in charge and Susan was going along. The next trip, in 1983, Susan would be in charge, driving us in her car, and Jack and I would be the ones going along.

After living in Ontario for about five years, Susan settled down in the Bella Coola Valley. She owned a car by then and had been making a living driving for a car rental company, and other jobs. She still had her car, a red Plymouth Fury, an ex-police car.

With Susan owning a car, and back in the valley, it seemed like a golden opportunity to visit some faraway places. We chose to go with her to the South Coast. As we were in charge of getting the trumpeter swans' winter feed flown in to Lonesome Lake, all three of us flew to Nimpo Lake on the Dean River Air Services' Beaver aircraft, on September 25, 1983. Susan's car was at Nimpo Lake. As Jack had a lot of mail to fix up, Susan spent the time doing maintenance work on Fury. We camped that night at Nimpo Lake.

On the 27th we were in Vancouver. September 28 saw us at Mill Bay and Nanaimo. The 29th we visited Mayne Island. We were island hopping happily from place to place. On the 30th we were back at Mill Bay after doing business in Vancouver. We stayed with friends in Vancouver on October 1st.

We did more business in Vancouver, and then we stayed with the Joneses for the night. They had a rec room down in the basement. We slept there.

On the 3rd we visited Qualicum Falls. I made a sketch for a painting I would make at home. We camped at French Creek that night. On the 4th we almost finished our business in Vancouver, and stayed once more with the Joneses.

Finally finished with city business, we spent the 5th at the Joneses' place. In the morning of the 6th we left Vancouver with them and camped at Bull Canyon. Susan stayed in Vancouver. At Bull Canyon there was a hard freeze overnight. It was clear, and cold enough to freeze a gallon container of water solid. It had been left outside to keep cool. It surely did.

On October 7 we flew from Nimpo Lake to Lonesome Lake with Dean River Air Services (DRAS), the same outfit we had flown out with on September 25. So ended a very nice little vacation.

On our arrival home we found everything in order. The cow had been milked, the calf, Spinner, had been well taken care of by our trusty "farm sitter." Spinner was a black baby bull we had flown in by DRAS earlier in the summer. It was good to return home and have things in such good shape.

Susan came home on October 10, and then went out again on

November 10. The next time she came home was in April 1984. She had a large husky-type dog, called Kaila, with her. At that time she was living at Stuie, near Bella Coola. The next time we traveled with Susan was in the late summer of 1986. She then had Guenevere and her filly, two-year-old Lightning.

Susan had taken Guenevere to Stuie in the fall of 1984, shortly before she was to foal. On October 31 the blessed event occurred. Susan got to watch the big brown foal being born. Lucky Susan. Two fillies were born on Arbordale, and even tho Jack and I both kept close watch, we missed them both. Our watch wasn't close enough. Mares are sneaky, and quick with the birthing. In the wild they can't afford to be otherwise.

When Lightning was a well-grown two year old, in 1986, Jack and I and Susan, Guenevere and Lightning, and Dana, Susan's newest dog, decided on a nice trip to the Rainbow Mountains, with a horse to carry our packs. I guess Guenevere and Lightning were not consulted; we decided for them. Susan would haul the horses and us to East Branch, at the top of the hill, jumping-off place for Rainbow Mountain trips. There was just one minor problem. Susan had a car rather than a truck, and no trailer with which to haul the horses up the hill. She hunted around, borrowed a truck from our mutual friend, Chris, and a stock rack from another friend, Norman. Jack helped her heave the rack onto the truck. She backed it up to a handy bank and led the horses on to it. Soon we were groaning up the hill.

Near the top of the hill there was another handy bank where the horses could back off the truck. Guenevere was soon packed up with a special "saddle." I had made two narrow pack boxes, one to go on each side of the horse, in a harness of straps to hold the two boxes together. This went over our carefully folded bedding acting as a saddle pad laid directly on the horse's back. Then a cinch was tightened around horse and pack. Then we were off for a few days of adventure and exploring. Oh, I forgot Dana. She wore a doggy pack containing her own food.

All went well as we hiked along a well-marked trail thru the pine forest. The horses seemingly enjoyed the trip over easy going, while Dana, long-legged and also exploring, ran everywhere with her pack. On one of her frequent returns to the slowly plodding people and horses, she didn't have it anymore. It contained almost her entire supply of food for the trip. She lost it somewhere. We didn't think we could find it, as she raced everywhere thru the woods. We went on without it. Before the trip ended, Dana was eating the horse flies we caught eating the horses. We shared some, a small some, of our food with the careless dog, but we didn't think we should have to go too hungry for someone who should have been behind the horses, on the trail. She had decided to tear thru the woods. Of course, really, the fault was her owner's for not keeping hold of the untrained dog. My memory is faulty here. Susan tells me that we had more dog food in the horse pack.

We camped near Octopus Lake. There were a few grassy meadows there we could feed the horses on and some small ponds scattered among the pines.

Sometime that evening we found a disaster in the small pack one of us had carried on our own back. We had put some spare coats, some food, and a camera and a pair of binoculars in the pack. One of the items of food was a container of a delicious mixture of chili con corn. Somehow this stuff had found its way out of its container and into the binoculars. It was a mess! Jack managed to clean the instrument well enough that one still could see through them.

During the night young Lightning had an attack of colic. Susan got up and tended her for some time. In a while she was over it and settled down. In the morning she seemed to be all right, so we continued our trip. It was August 10, 1986.

We had a map and compass, but little need for the compass as the days were sunny and the trail was plain to see. It led us to where we wanted to go until we got into true alpine, then the map was right useful. There were spots where the trail faded out entirely, but we always found it again. Alpine ground does not hold a trail very well, and just to frustrate us the ground heaves with the frost; hollows form and look much like well-worn trails. Soon they run out into lichen, moss ridges, lumps and plants. There is no trail at all. Then one must go hunting for it.

Having arrived at a grassy area, we stopped for lunch. The horses could eat and so could we. Poor Dana wandered from person to person trying to find some food, but after several unsuccessful attempts to beg food from each of us, she slunk off and fell down in a forlorn heap under a balsam bush. Of course she did not know there was only limited food for her because she had raced thru the forest, removing her pack load of kibble.

For the four days we were in the Rainbows the weather was marvelous, with early sunrises and late sunsets, unlike in the valley. At Lonesome Lake the valley runs north and south, so sunrise was late and sunset came early, leaving a long cool period at each end of the day. In the Bella Coola Valley where I now live, there is one long six-week sunset between the end of November and the middle of January, if I am lucky. This is due to the sun being hidden behind high mountains when it is at its lowest arc.

One morning in late January 2009 when I got up the sun was gilding the highest snowy ledges on the top of Schoolhouse Mountain, right across the valley from my house. Some mornings I can watch the show of light change and strengthen, but it stays on the snow-covered rocky top of the 6500-foot obstruction as I lie in my bed. Another morning as I watched, a great golden beam of light slammed into the side of my garage without a sound. The sun was shining on my yard while it still shone only on the top ledges of the mountain, with no light on the mountain between the top of it and my yard. Much later in the year it would shine on the whole north side of Schoolhouse Mountain.

One of the best places in the Rainbows to look at fancy rocks is at Crystal Lake, far above the tree line and surrounded with red slopes. Beautiful unusual rocks lay about on the gently sloping shore of the lake and all around back from the water. We had lunch there, then ambled on over the highly colored mountain vistas.

I remember camping at a place we called Causeway Lake. It is a beautiful small lake nestling in a basin with a sloping wall on the right-hand side, when looking up the basin. It is mostly clad with short, stumpy balsam trees. A gentle ridge runs across the head of the basin then turns a sharp corner to go along on the left side of the lake. This broad ridge slopes gently down to the shore and is almost entirely open sandy gravel. The outlet of the lake at the lower end of the basin was hidden with thick clumps of larger balsam. A low ridge holds the lake in place in the basin. Along that low ridge a long causeway, forested and narrow, runs out into the lake. Like the period at the end of a sentence, there is a more-or-less round island about 15 or 20 feet in diameter some 10 feet from the end of the causeway. Sedge grows in the water around it and along the causeway. Over in the right-hand corner of the lake at the outlet end is a shallow bay filled with black rocks sticking out of the water and with sedge growing among them.

At the head of the lake, grass was growing along the shore and well up the slope to the skyline. A light, but cold, breeze riffled the surface of the lake.

For supper I wanted to cook some of my homemade dehydrated soup. As shelter from the wind was sketchy near the lake, I had to go down below the thin forest along the ridge to where there was a deep creek channel where I could get out of the breeze coming down the lake. There on a sandy bar on the creek bottom I built my little fire.

My soup was composed of roasted beef put thru a meat-grinder, then carefully dried in a slow oven, cooked potatoes, carrots, turnips and onions, also dried in a slow oven. It did not take long to cook up a warm supper, accompanied with bread and butter, and some kind of cake for dessert.

Sometime in there Susan turned the two horses loose so they could graze and not have to be held on ropes. It was a mistake.

They ate for some time. I sat and tried to make a sketch of the lake and the surrounding hills. I do not remember what Jack and Susan did. I was concentrating on my sketch. In time I would make a painting from it.

After wading out in the lake to eat the nice sedge growing there, Guenevere came ashore—and started for home! Someone sounded the alarm. Guenevere could not go home alone. We needed her to carry our stuff. Susan went after her while Jack tried to get hold of Lightning. Neither horse wore her halter. Lightning had a meltdown as Jack desperately hung on to her. They waltzed around thru the balsam branches, with Lightning whinnying franticly. I took Jack a rope as soon as I could.

Susan had to hurry to catch up with the old mare, who was striding off at a very determined pace. She did catch up and dragged her back by her mane. Susan was lucky to be able to lead Guenevere by her mane. Some horses are not so amiable, and just toss one aside and go their own way. Maybe Guenevere had had enough sightseeing, tho the grass there was adequate. Or maybe she was missing home. She had been on quite a few trips to the alpine over the years. Anyway I seem to recall there was a great emotional display between Guenevere and Lightning, as if they had been separated for a month, not just a few minutes. We did not turn Guenevere loose again.

A day or two later we were back at East Branch where the truck awaited our return. I believe we had seen two caribou, far away across a shallow valley.

Our next trip with Susan would be on wheels, only little over a month later on September 25.

Having taken a peek at the colorful Rainbow Mountains by foot and horse, we planned a much longer trip on wheels to get a glimpse of the much grander Rockies. I am not belittling the Rainbows or any of our gentle mountains much closer to home. They are just different, but still interesting.

On September 25, 1986, Jack, Susan and I flew with Dean River

Air Services to Nimpo Lake. Susan had left her car, Fury, there a few hours earlier when she caught a ride to Lonesome Lake on the Beaver. As it was late when DRAS finally made it in to Lonesome Lake, we arrived at Nimpo Lake too late to get any farther than Bull Canyon.

We found a level bench just off the road down the hill to the campsites and set up camp there on soft ground, rather than use one of the graveled pads intended for campers. We would be lying on the ground and we had camping equipment with us as we did not have a camper. Our camp was under large fir trees growing widely apart on sandy, soft ground. While Jack and Susan set up our lean-to plastic roof, I found a bare piece of sand on which I could arrange my little fireplace. We just needed a bit of heat to take the chill off the air. Our camp was right above the Chilcotin River where it flows thru spectacular Bull Canyon. Before starting my campfire, I scrambled 20 or 30 feet down to the stream for a pail of water to use to control my fire. The slope down to the shore was soft soil, tho very steep. There was just a hint of a beach at the water's edge, composed of water-worn pebbles.

I seem to remember we had fried chicken that Susan had cooked at her place before she drove to Nimpo Lake from the Bella Coola valley. I also seem to remember we had apple pie, from Arbordale, made from Lonesome Lake apples.

The 26th saw us to Williams Lake, then north on Highway 97 to Prince George. We camped at Willow River that night.

On the 27th we left Willow River and headed for the Rockies on Highway 16. Fortunately there were not too many clouds hanging about and we got to see the ever-changing beauty of the tilted, layered Rockies as we neared them, then moved south along their towering presence. That night we camped five miles south of Atha-baska Falls.

The 28th saw us at Golden. We had pizza in that town and then drove on to Blaeberry River. We camped near the bridge. In the morning it was raining, so we skulked under the bridge to eat breakfast. Soon we were on the road again.

On the 29th we arrived at the home of some friends of ours. They put us up for the night and fed us. In the morning we continued our journey. On the 30th we camped north of Nicola Lake.

On October 1 we arrived at Kamloops. For that night we chose a motel. Having a TV and VCR available, we rented a movie, *Black Stallion,* in two parts. We spent most of the night sitting in chairs, watching the movie. Susan and I had already read the *Black Stallion* books by Walter Farley.

October 2. As Susan wanted to buy a truck, we stayed in town until she found what she wanted. In a short time she found one. We were on our way once more. We camped near 108 Ranch.

October 3. We had business to do in Williams Lake; then it was off again on our journey. That night we camped somewhere west of Tatla Lake. We arrived at Nimpo Lake on October 4. Susan drove off to the valley. Jack and I caught a flight to Lonesome Lake with DRAS.

That trip in the Rockies was tiring, but interesting, and we saw many new landforms and other wonders.

In the summer of 1998 Susan organized a horse trip into the Rainbows with me, Liesel, her son Brendan, two of her friends, Rob and Teresa, and a dog whose name I cannot remember. We took five horses: Bess, Disco and Teke for us; and Agadir and Sandstorm for her friends.

Susan trailered our three horses, and her friends hauled their two. We all met at East Branch parking area, improved considerably since 1986 when Susan hauled Guenevere and Lightning up there in a rack on a truck.

We planned to carry our camp gear and food on our saddle horses and not take a packhorse. No one likes to tow a pack horse while riding, even tho crowding all our stuff on our saddles was not the best solution to the problem of how to take the stuff we wanted with us, either. Still, it seemed the best choice. Little Liesel had her doggy pack, which helped.

Packed up and mounted up, we headed for the alpine. East Branch is at 5200 feet above sea level, so we would do a bit of climbing, but very slowly, as there are no really steep places and we had only about 800 feet to gain to be in the alpine.

Soon there was trouble with the two groups of horses. They did not want to get mixed up. When we started, Susan and Brendan were in the lead. Rob and Teresa came next with their horses. I came behind on Bess, trailed by Liesel, so she wouldn't get stepped on. Bess got in a "swivet" because she wasn't with her own group, and two strangers were in between. We rearranged the horses and peace was back once more.

Sometime later, for some reason, Bess found herself in the lead, with Liesel faithfully behind her. I think the horses ahead of me went off the trail and Bess and I took the lead to get us back on the trail. Anyway, with me in the lead poor little Liesel, crowded in between Bess and Disco, was continuously in danger of getting stepped on by Disco or crapped on by Bess. Everyone was careful and neither thing happened. Liesel would not come behind the whole herd, as I had trained her to follow my horse wherever she was. I had not had an opportunity to train her to come behind the whole herd. She carried her pack and did her best to stay in her place right behind her friend, Bess. She was truly a good girl.

The trail we followed had been cut out for hikers, and had some boggy places and small creeks. One had to be jumped and it was boggy on each side. There was a bridge people could cross on, but it was not suitable for horses.

One of Teresa's horses had trouble with his pack and had to be re-packed. Susan handed me her horse to hold while she helped with the re-packing. Soon a noisy motorized two-wheeled contraption came grumbling over the rocks and logs in the trail. I had to get Bess and Liesel farther away from the trail than I had already pushed them. Liesel, who was resting behind Bess, rose and stayed with my horse as I pushed her farther under a branchy balsam to leave room for Disco and the motorbike. The pack was better organized and we were on our way once more.

The trail involved several more bogs, streams and mud holes. We passed small beautiful lakes lying jewel-like amongst the forest of pine and spruce. Soon we arrived on an open area where there were only short trees, sparsely scattered over the almost level landscape. On our right the level plane fell off to a broad valley about a thousand feet below. That was where we wanted to camp for the night. It was the Tusulko Valley in the Rainbows. A creek, bordered by grassy meadows, wandered thru the valley.

We started down a gentle slope where several small creeks trickled among the green pelt of small plants and the odd short tree. One larger creek drained Bluff Lake, a fairly large lake lying on a higher level than where we started down the slope. The water in that lake is so cold that it has turned blue with the cold. It is very clear and one can see the bottom 15 or 20 feet down.

Down at last where we would camp, the horses were unpacked, unsaddled, and spread out to graze. As there were five people in the party, there were plenty of horse holders. We had to keep Teke on a picket line, as he wanted to drive Sandstorm back to Bella Coola and keep the mares for himself.

With tents set up, horses fed, and a nice fire burning down to hot coals, it was time to grill our steaks. The fire had been built on a large flat rock to keep it out of any peat that could be there, and would be difficult to put out later. Around the rock the fire was on were scattered several smaller stones people could sit on, or spread food on or whatever. The evening was calm. The sky was clear. There were few insects to bother the horses or us. And a heavenly aroma rose from the grilling steaks as they sizzled and steamed. It was a lovely evening there in the beautiful Tusulko Valley. A small stream made its way under and among a tangle of alpine willows, right beside our "kitchen," laughing as it wiggled on its way. With everyone fed and the fire going out it was time for some hard alpine snoozing.

While I had been watching our horses, Susan and Brendan had set up our tents. I think they must have found the hardest ground in the entire Tusulko Valley, and the flattest.

Sometime in the early morning I was waked up by wicked leg cramps. I groaned and flailed around trying to stretch out cramping muscles. With no solid wall to the tent, there was no way I could make the cramps stop, and they were downright mean. I finally struggled out of bed and out of the tent and stood up. Then they stopped. I walked around for a while and then went back to bed and to sleep, only too soon to be attacked again. Clearly they did not approve of me riding so much all at once.

Since I could not stop the cramps there in the tent, I decided to gather up my quilt and head off in the poor moonlight to try to find a dense balsam clump. Perhaps I could find one with sturdy young trees growing near the central trunks where I could bed down.

After stumbling about in the meager light from a quarter moon, I crawled in among the small trees circling the large ones of a good balsam clump and bedded down once more, with my feet resting against the stoutest of the young trees growing there. It was just what I needed. Fortunately there was no rain, as the big trees provided shelter only near their own bases.

When daylight trickled into the valley I was up and away with our three horses, into the feed. I took my big warm quilt, turned Teke loose and held on to Disco. Beside a large white rock, conveniently placed, I parked Bess. The rock would be my mounting block. Standing on the rock, I spread my quilt over Bess's back, then carefully stepped over her and sat down, keeping the quilt in place. Then I could haul the free side up over my back, bring the ends around in front and be protected from the frosty morning chill. We were soon out in the grass, the hungry shivering horses eating happily. And I was warm there on that heated furry mobile couch. Poor little Liesel

418

remained tied there by the tent where Susan and Brendan still slept. They had not been chased out by the cold as I had been.

After the sun found its way into the valley they awoke and joined me, and none too soon; Disco was having a problem, or rather I was with Disco. Susan had put a blanket on the shorthaired mare for the night. It was fine for all that time while she was just standing there, but when she put her head down to feed she loosened the strings holding the blanket on and it slipped back on her and she panicked.

Out there in the meadow there was nothing I could use to get back on my horse, so I was reluctant to get off to fix Disco's problem, and tried to do it from horseback. With the two mares standing close to each other, I could use both hands to loosen the strings holding the blanket on Disco. With frequent reminding to keep her head up, I kept Bess more or less near the other mare, but we did a lot of waltzing around in the long grass before I got the blanket off. That Bess was patient enough to keep her head up for the long time it took me to do the job, I think was pretty good of her. She was hungry. Soon after the sun warmed the valley up the others were out in the meadow and I could let Disco go at last. She was Susan's problem then.

In time all the horses were fed, a fire was built on the rock and water was heated for hot drinks all around.

In daylight, I studied the problem of how I could keep rain off my bed during the next night. I improved the area where I had slept so comfortably and even made a nest for my companion, near my head. It would do even if it rained. There were branches that I could use to support the plastic roof.

Getting a lazy late start, we just wandered a few miles up the Tusulko valley, feeding horses as we spent the day exploring this and that as we went along. The day was warm and the scene pleasant. There were little trout in the Tusulko River and that interested Liesel. We camped again there at our camp of the night before.

The third day saw us all back at East Branch and the trailers. We let the horses have a good feed of grass that grew there on the parking area, then loaded up and headed back down the Hill. It had been a really restful and pleasant outing for all of us.

This wandering tale of my life has reminded me of many things, some a long time back and some so recent the dust hasn't settled yet. One of those was a cloud war over Schoolhouse Mountain. It sits south of me and blocks the sun for six weeks during December and part of January each year.

Where I sleep each night, I can lie there in the morning and get a full view of that mountain and get to observe some interesting events. One of those occurred on the March 6. A cloud war was being waged over the top of the mountain. I watched with interest. Several skinny little lumpy clouds were drifting slowly westwards over the mountain. Then I noticed a larger darker cloud come barreling along over the mountain, heading east. There was going to be a collision, as neither cloud appeared to be willing to give way.

As the eastbound cloud closed in on the westbound ones, they suddenly were joined by a flock of small aggressive clouds, which were adding their mass to the skinny ones. They tried to make the large dark cloud back off. The two sets of clouds pushed back and forth there over the top of the mountain for several minutes, neither one gaining anything. Then the eastbound one puffed itself up, dug its feet into the rocky mountaintop and rammed the west-bounders eastwards, leaving tatters and shreds of themselves clinging to the ledges and cliffs on the ice scoured rocky summit.

Another picture that hangs in my memory is of a cold morning in April when the rising sun flung golden fingers of light across the frosty grass. They lay there for several minutes and then faded as Liesel came trotting along, leaving her frosty little dog tracks. It had been a moment of glory.

Due to a cool spring, my cherry trees were late blooming, but when they did get going they made up for the lateness by bursting into flower with volume. The blooms were so numerous that the whiteness resembled trees covered with snow. The light from the floral display actually glowed and shone into my house. The trees are about 30 feet away, and 20 feet tall and 30 feet wide.

They made lots of cherries, but the robins got them all except for about a dozen unripe ones I stole, in order to get any.

The birds came in masses and were fighting over my unripe fruit, all hoping to keep me from having my own fruit. Then they have the nerve to raise their babies in my buildings. If it weren't for me there would not be any cherries here.

I do like watching them. They are so tame that they will fly down almost at my feet to collect angleworms out of my garden. To pay for the cherries, the robins at least left me my raspberries—how generous of them.

Anyway with the big cherry trees right in front of my house I get to observe many birds of many species, and that is almost as rewarding as the cherries would have been. I never get to watch trumpeter swans anymore, so I have to enjoy what is available.

Now as I scrabble about in the bottom of my memory, I see it is quite empty. There seem to be no more stories lingering under the chaff of my life, so I end these memoirs with these cheerful words:

The good and the bad, the happy and the sad,
all the stuff that brings me tears,
Renews the memory of the wonderful life
I lived for all those years.

epilogue

Thru fire, flood and fortune, life at Lonesome Lake, 60 miles inland from Bella Coola, BC, went on for two generations, driven by determination and fueled by the attractions of the valley.

The remote area was home to my parents, two older brothers, and in due time, to my own family. Also for company were many wild creatures, which included a small flock of rare trumpeter swans, struggling to survive. The swans and our domestic animals were friends; and some we considered family.

My memoirs give the reader a peek into our lives as we went on with clearing land, building what we needed, with horses for power and hand tools to do what the horses could not.

One thing the horses could do—and did—was pack in the year's supplies once a year for close to 50 years. Eventually airplanes took over the main moving of freight, but horses were still called upon to carry everything the final mile and a half from Lonesome Lake to our place.

Love of the valley and appreciation and respect for nature held us there for most of a century. Life could be hard sometimes, but was seldom boring and was frequently sweet and rewarding.

Trudy Turner was born in a remote homestead at Lonesome Lake in the southwest region of British Columbia in the 1920s and raised in true pioneer fashion, without running water, electricity, or cars. In fact, Trudy learned to fly a plane in her twenties, but didn't obtain her motor vehicle driver's license until she was in her sixties.

In 1939, as a young girl of 10, Trudy's father gave her the job of feeding the near-extinct trumpeter swans that wintered in the region. Trudy's story was first told in *Fogswamp: Living with Swans in the Wilderness,* which outlined the lives of the Edwards and Turner families and their experiences with the trumpeter swans.

Now in her eighties, Trudy reflects on her unusual life and describes her experiences growing up in a world that others may view as isolated and lonely, but to her was a complete and satisfying existence. Her strong personal viewpoint is a positive reflection of her character, and countered by her deep appreciation for nature and what it has taught her.

Trudy lives in Falkland, BC, near her daughter Susan and her family, and paints and writes poetry.

More **HANCOCK HOUSE** biography and history titles

Afloat in Time
Jim Sirois
ISBN 0-88839-455-1
5.5 x 8.5 • sc • 288 pages

Crooked River Rats
Bernard McKay
ISBN 0-88839-451-9
5.5 x 8.5 • sc • 176 pages

Descent Into Madness
Vern Frolick
ISBN 0-88839-321-0
5.5 x 8.5 • sc • 361 pages

A Doctor's Notes
T.F Godwin
ISBN 978-0-88839-654-9
5.5 x 8.5 • sc • 368 pages

Fogswamp
Trudy Turner, Ruth McVeigh
ISBN 0-88839-104-8
5.5 x 8.5 • sc • 255 pages

Loggers of the BC Coast
Hans Knapp
ISBN 0-88839-588-4
5.5 x 8.5 • sc • 200 pages

Nahanni Trailhead
Joanne Ronan Moore
ISBN 0-88839-464-0
5.5 x 8.5 • sc • 256 pages

Out of the Rain
Paul Jones
ISBN 0-88839-541-8
5.5 x 8.5 • sc • 272 pages

Outposts & Bushplanes
Bruce Lamb
ISBN 0-88839-556-6
5.5 x 8.5 • sc • 208 pages

Ralph Edwards of Lonesome Lake
Ralph Edwards, Ed Gould
ISBN 978-0-88839-100-1
5.5 x 8.5 • sc • 296 pages

Raven and the Mountaineer
Monty Alford
ISBN 0-88839-542-6
5.5 x 8.5 • sc • 152 pages

Rivers of Gold
Gwen & Don Lee
ISBN 0-88839-555-8
5.5 x 8.5 • sc • 204 pages

Ruffles on my Longjohns
Isabel Edwards
ISBN 0-88839-102-1
5.5 x 8.5 • sc • 297 pages

Timeless Trails of the Yukon
Dolores Cline Brown
ISBN 0-88839-584-5
5.5 x 8.5 • sc • 184 pages

Tomekichi Homma
K.T. Homma, C.G. Isaksson
ISBN 978-0-88839-660-0
5.5 x 8.5 • sc • 72 pages

**White Water Skippers
of the North**
Nancy Warren Ferrell
ISBN 978-0-88839-616-7
5.5 x 8.5 • sc • 216 pages

Wild Roses
dutchie Rutledge-Mathison
ISBN 0-88839-625-2
8.5 x 11 • hc • 72 pages

Wild Trails, Wild Tales
Bernard McKay
ISBN 0-88839-395-4
5.5 x 8.5 • sc • 176 pages

Wild Canadian West
E. C. (Ted) Meyers
ISBN 0-88839-469-1
5.5 x 8.5 • sc • 208 pages

Wrong Highway
Stella T. Jenkins
ISBN 978-0-88839-708-9
5.5 x 8.5 • sc • 360 pages

www.hancockhouse.com